Bristol
- 1979

LIBERTY AND LANGUAGE

LIBERTY AND LANGUAGE

GEOFFREY SAMPSON

Oxford University Press

OXFORD   NEW YORK   TORONTO   MELBOURNE

1979

Oxford University Press, Walton Street, Oxford OX2 6DP

OXFORD LONDON GLASGOW
NEW YORK TORONTO MELBOURNE WELLINGTON
KUALA LUMPUR SINGAPORE JAKARTA HONG KONG TOKYO
DELHI BOMBAY CALCUTTA MADRAS KARACHI
NAIROBI DAR ES SALAAM CAPE TOWN

© *Geoffrey Sampson 1979*

British Library Cataloguing in Publication Data

Sampson, Geoffrey
    Liberty and language.
    1. Chomsky, Noam   2. Linguistics – Political
    aspects
    I. Title
    410'.92'4   P85.C47   78–40941

    ISBN 0–19–215951–8

Photoset and printed in Great Britain by
Lowe & Brydone Printers Limited, Thetford, Norfolk

TO FELICITY

May she know freedom and use it

Acknowledgements

Debts to one's academic predecessors can never be fully acknowledged; but I must pay tribute by name to Friedrich Hayek and Sir Karl Popper, whose influence permeates this book not only in the many passages where they are cited but throughout. I hope they will not be too disconcerted by the transformations which their ideas have undergone here. Closer to home, I should like to thank a number of colleagues and friends who have read and commented on drafts of the manuscript. I have profited greatly from various suggestions by Fred d'Agostino, John Clayton, Henry Hardy, and Mick Short, as well as by those of an anonymous publisher's reader. I trust it is permissible also to thank my colleagues Michael Beaken and Norman Fairclough, who by dissenting from opinions which I had supposed to be axiomatic forced me to work out the foundations of my own political beliefs. I am grateful to the University of Lancaster, which allowed me the leisure in which to write the book.

I thank Wm. Collins Sons & Co. Ltd. and Random House Inc. for permission to reprint extended passages from Noam Chomsky's books *For Reasons of State* and *Reflections on Language*.

To Felicity I owe a great debt for dispelling a new father's fears that paternity might be incompatible with authorship. She was twelve weeks old when I began writing and she is twenty-four weeks old now; she still seems to be living up to her name.* Long may she do so. For Vera, no words of thanks could possibly be adequate – but thank you, anyway.

I thank Aidan and Caroline, and Anne and Bendy, for the loan of accommodation in striking distance of London libraries,

* Inevitably, my belief that the book was finished twelve weeks after I began it has proved premature: several additions and revisions were made during the winter of 1977–8.

and I am grateful to the staff of the British Museum and S.O.A.S. libraries, as well as that of my own university, for their efficient and courteous service. Finally, I thank Greg and Mima, whose power mower licked the lawn back into shape after it was almost all over.

Ingleton, Yorks.
7 September 1976

Contents

1 Introduction *1*

2 From Linguistics to Anarchism *13*

3 Liberalism and Creativity *37*

4 Linguistics versus Liberalism *90*

5 Chomsky, Race, and Foreign Policy *130*

6 What We Know and How We Know It *178*

7 Conclusion *210*

Notes *214*

Bibliographical References *247*

Index of Names *249*

We must be free or die, who speak the tongue
That Shakespeare spake

WILLIAM WORDSWORTH

1 Introduction

The thought of every age has its characteristic strengths, and characteristic weaknesses associated with those strengths. The Greeks were outstandingly skilled at abstract philosophical speculation, but they failed to control their speculative flights by submitting them to the test of empirical observation in the many cases where this was relevant. The mediaevals developed logic, and showed great ingenuity in elaborating the logical implications of their received canon of authoritative texts, but they were deficient in that toleration for novel and heterodox opinions which is a necessary component in the advance of human understanding. The great success of modern Western thought is surely science. Our knowledge of the world has been mightily increased since the Renascence by the 'scientific method', in which hypotheses freely proposed by anyone are judged by the impersonal test of compatibility with observation, with no hypothesis regarded as too unorthodox to entertain and none too authoritative to be overturned by sufficient evidence. Corresponding to this strength, our great weakness is surely 'scientism', as it has been called: the prejudice which holds that the scientific method applies to all possible subjects of human thought, or (what amounts to much the same in practice) that matters which cannot be treated by the method of science are somehow unreal or unimportant.[1]

Prominent among the phenomena which are unamenable to analysis by the scientific method, as we shall see, are certain aspects of human nature, particularly human creativity. Accordingly, the adverse practical consequences of the scientistic fallacy tend to arise when the method of science is applied to human affairs. I do not, of course, mean to say that all applications of scientific method to social or political questions are undesirable – that would be very far from true. But, while scientists certainly have a useful role to play in the creation of human societies superior to those which now exist, the scientistic fallacy works against that goal by encouraging the notion of 'social engineering' – the idea that designing and constructing a social institution or a whole human society is nothing more than a technical problem akin to designing and constructing a bridge or an aeroplane. One who commits the scientistic fallacy will acknowledge that tasks of the former kind tend to be considerably more complex and difficult than those of the latter kind; but it will not occur to him to ask whether the former tasks simply cannot be treated as technical problems with 'correct' answers because of human phenomena which are in principle not susceptible of analysis by the scientific method. It is inconceivable for him that there might be such phenomena.

In recent years it has come to be fairly widely recognized that science has been pushed too far. Ideally, this recognition would be followed by discussion of where the limits of applicability of scientific method are properly to be placed, after which the scientists and technologists could continue to benefit humanity intellectually and materially by working within their proper domain (which is, after all, a very large one) while refraining from claims to be able to do more for us than they can.[2]

Unfortunately, this has not on the whole happened. Many individuals feel obscurely that people in the twentieth century are being manipulated in undesirable ways in the name of science, but often they are not clear that this is the fault of the scientistic fallacy, as I have described it, and that the problem would be solved by public recognition of the fact that certain important human phenomena are not susceptible of scientific analysis. Instead, they react in one of two other ways.

Probably the commoner of these reactions is simply to reject science and technology *in toto*. There are many symptoms of this attitude, particularly among the young, in the contemporary world. The very marked decline over the last decade in numbers of undergraduates reading for science degrees is one. The great growth in (often quite half-baked) interest in mysticism and in the religions of non-Western (and hence, it is supposed, non-scientific) cultures is another; the youngster who practises the use of Tarot cards or the *I Ching*, or who parades along Oxford Street with saffron robe and shaven head banging a tambourine, is essentially saying that he wants nothing to do with the kind of life that is produced by application of the scientific method.

The alternative reaction to the folly of scientism is rather subtler, and very much more dangerous. It is possible to recognize that social engineering and the attitude of mind which underlies it are wrong, and yet to be oneself so heavily imbued with that attitude that one's very denunciations of scientism and social engineering themselves embody the scientistic fallacy. Someone who reacts in this way, recognizing intellectually that there is something amiss in the practice of science but unable in his heart to appreciate that there are subjects which cannot be treated scientifically, will mistakenly suppose that what is wrong is not that scientific method is being applied where it should not be, but that it is being applied in some particular inappropriate way. He will argue, say, not that social engineering is in principle a mistake, but perhaps that current theories of social engineering are too mechanical, they lack the imaginative dimension which is essential in good engineering even of the ordinary, bridge-and-aeroplane kind.

It is clear that this reaction to the excesses of scientism is much more dangerous than straightforward rejection of science. The bonzes of Oxford Street do no harm to others, and they may do some good in stimulating the rest of us to realize that there is something wrong with the current intellectual climate and to seek out and correct our error. The man who preaches scientistically against scientism, on the other hand, helps unwittingly to ensure that the error will not be corrected. By preaching against scientism he wins the allegiance of those who recognize that science has gone too far; by preaching in terms that presuppose the validity of scientism he deflects the energies of his disciples into attacks on irrelevant targets.

This book is concerned with the ideas of the man who represents this scientistic pseudo-opposition to scientism more forcefully and influentially than anyone else in the contemporary world, and who bids fair to corner the forces opposed to scientism so completely as to render any genuine fight against scientism impossible of success. The man is Noam Chomsky, a professor of the Massachusetts Institute of Technology.

There will be few readers to whom Chomsky's name is unfamiliar. Over the last twenty years he has gradually come to be seen as one of the key thinkers of our time. Month by month he has thundered out denunciations of American policy in the pages of such journals as *Ramparts* and the *New York Review of Books*. Popular accounts of his thought have been published in the U.S.A. in the series 'World Leaders' and in Britain in the series 'Modern Masters' – John Lyons's *Chomsky* is indeed the best-seller in the latter series, scoring over such diverse rivals as Einstein, Freud, Lenin, and Lévi-Strauss. Noam Chomsky is certainly the first (and so far the only) scholar in the hitherto quite esoteric discipline of linguistics whose name has become a commonplace on the lips of student activists and in the columns of the Sunday press.

There are two broad strands to Chomsky's thought. In his professional capacity, Chomsky is a theoretical linguist who has revolutionized the way in which scholars describe individual languages and the general phenomenon of human language, and the consequences of this revolution have been felt far beyond the confines of linguistics itself: Chomsky's ideas are among the most important current focuses of discourse in pure academic psychology and philosophy. Somewhat after he had begun to make his mark in these purely professional academic fields, Chomsky came to public prominence in a rather different way in his capacity as concerned citizen of the U.S.A. and member of the human race: Chomsky has become one of the most influential spokesmen of the American 'New Left', speaking and writing against such American policies as participation in the Vietnam war and support for the Zionist occupation of Palestine, taking part in peace marches and sit-ins (and sometimes landing in gaol as a result), and at the same time preaching a more general political gospel about the inherent shortcomings of present-day societies and governments and about the nature of the ideal society towards which we ought all to be striving.

Some observers have for a long time detected a relationship between the 'professional' and 'political' sides of Chomsky's thought (as I shall call them for simplicity's sake), but in the early years Chomsky himself kept the two strands, publicly at least, fairly sharply apart. Even when he gave the first Bertrand Russell Memorial Lectures at Cambridge in 1971, while he noted that Russell had likewise combined work in language and mathematical logic with an activist participation in radical politics, Chomsky drew no connexions between his own two systems of ideas. (Echoing Marx's epitaph, Chomsky entitled his 'professional' lecture 'On interpreting the world' and his 'political' lecture 'On changing the world'.)[3] In recent years, however, Chomsky has begun to link his politics with his professional activities explicitly. At first he was rather tentative about this: in the conclusion of a lecture delivered in 1969 he asked his audience's pardon for introducing 'unprofessional' considerations into what had until that point been a discussion of purely academic linguistic and psychological issues.[4] Six years later he shows no such hesitation.[5] The extreme 'professionalism' or compartmentalization of modern intellectual life, Chomsky argues, is a sign of the bankruptcy of contemporary thought. But intellectuals should make connexions between their specialized academic research and the broader issues confronting humanity, and Chomsky himself does so. In fact, he claims, the revolutionary political ideals he advocates follow as a natural corollary of the new view of human nature suggested by his academic research on syntactic structure in human language.

This book is written in order to refute that claim, and to open a counter-attack by pointing out the strong support lent by aspects of language which Chomsky does not consider to political ideals which are something like the reverse of his. Certainly there are links between Chomsky's 'professional' theories and his politics. The two groups of ideas are very recognizably the products of one mind, bearing a common stamp – the stamp of scientism.[6] But, as a matter of biography, I find it hard to accept that Chomsky's politics followed from his linguistics. I have little doubt that Chomsky would hold much the same political opinions as he does even if he had never thought about academic linguistics. Chomsky's politics are very much those of the family and social background in which he grew up, and since he reached mature years these politics have become highly fashionable among large and vociferous groups in the U.S.A., Britain, and elsewhere, quite independently of Chomsky's advocacy of them; in a very watered-down and much less consistent form political views similar to Chomsky's have been gaining ground throughout the English-speaking world for the last hundred years, and are by now almost common currency. If anything, it seems more probable that Chomsky's political and social assumptions influenced his style of thinking about language than the other way round.[7] And, far more importantly for anyone who accepts that the truth or falsity of a proposition is independent of the influences which have led people to believe it true or false, Chomsky's politics do not logically follow from his linguistics. Chomsky is entitled to argue for his political views on their own merits, and he deserves a hearing for his arguments. But he is emphatically not entitled to claim that these views, which have a long pedigree and had been considered and rejected by many before Chomsky espoused them, must now be re-evaluated in the light of fresh support derived from novel theories of language and psychology which the average citizen is not equipped to follow and must take on trust. The aspects of Chomsky's academic work which have even a prima facie relevance for political questions can without distortion be stated quite simply, in a form in which they can be readily understood by the layman; and Chomsky's argument from these academic premises to political conclusions can be seen to be fatally flawed.

The chief flaw in the argument has to do with the notion of human creativity. 'Creativity' is a key term in the liberal, anti-scientistic political philosophy on which the mighty achievements of the English-speaking world in recent centuries were founded. It is a key term also in Chomsky's professional work, and in the arguments against liberalism which Chomsky derives from that work. But the word 'creativity' as used by Chomsky bears a very different sense from that which is intended when it appears in the works of the philosophers of liberalism; furthermore (though this point is relevant mainly for expository purposes), the liberals' use of 'creativity' is much closer than Chomsky's to the sense borne by the word in everyday speech. Chomsky's notion of 'creativity' is a severely impoverished notion by comparison with the layman's sense of the word, or with the sense in which creativity is relevant for the liberal approach to life. Chomsky claims in his professional work to be showing us that Man is a creature of much greater potential than traditional views suggest, and his arguments to this effect turn on his concept of 'creativity'. But, if Chomsky really believes that his view of human nature contrasts optimistically with the received view, this can only be because he has failed to understand the much more richly 'creative' idea of Man which has long been taken for granted both by the articulate liberal thinker and by the man in the British or American street. Despite the attractive terminology in which it is couched, what Chomsky's account of human nature actually says would, if it were the whole story, make Man something much less than we usually hold ourselves to be.

But Chomsky's account is not the whole story. Chomsky's professional discoveries give us no serious reason to believe that Man is a 'creative' animal only in Chomsky's impoverished sense of the term 'creative', and it follows that his work provides no novel ammunition against the liberal position.

Indeed, the true situation is quite different. In his professional work Chomsky considers only one narrow aspect of human language (namely, syntax) – a strategy of research which, from the academic point of view, is perfectly proper and sensible. However, the rest of us are at liberty to consider other aspects of language ignored by Chomsky. Some of these, while not lending themselves in the same way as syntax to Chomsky's rigorous, quasi-mathematical style of analysis, have in fact been discussed in the non-scientific manner appropriate to them much more widely and over a longer period than Chomsky and his followers have discussed syntax. A consideration of the semantic side of language, in particular – of the ways in which utterances convey meaning – leads to a view of human nature which is sharply at variance with Chomsky's, and which suggests that political ideals very different from Chomsky's are the appropriate ones. Chomsky claims that syntax refutes liberalism, but the claim fails; Chomsky ignores semantics, and semantics strongly supports liberalism.

My professional colleagues have not, on the whole, taken issue with Chomsky on his argument from linguistics to politics, preferring to restrict their disagreements with him exclusively to the professional arena. This is not, I know full well, because they all agree with his politics, but is perhaps partly because they feel that political theorizing is none of their business. That seems to me a mistake. I wholeheartedly agree with Chomsky that for the linguistic scholar, as for scholars in other disciplines, it should be a duty (as well, surely, as a pleasure) to spend part of one's time considering the wider human implications of one's specialized professional work. As things stand, only the professional linguist is in a position to evaluate the premises of Chomsky's argument from language to politics; not so much because those premises are too technical for the layman to understand, as because in the writings of Chomsky and other linguists they are buried amid a mass of related material which is not strictly relevant for the political argument (and much of which *is* of a quite technical nature). So, if the linguistic professionals allow Chomsky's argument to go unchallenged, he will win it by default – which is no way for political questions to be decided. It is Chomsky's linguistic colleagues who, by their reactions to his academic writings, first invested Chomsky with intellectual authority; they should accordingly be prepared to intervene if this authority is used to support a misleading argument on a subject which deeply affects every man's interests.[8]

A second reason for the reluctance of linguists to address themselves to the argument from language to politics may be that many of the linguists whom one suspects of being most sharply opposed to Chomsky in their personal political beliefs are also scholars who are more or less squarely in disagreement with Chomsky on professional questions of linguistic theory. I have suggested that Chomsky's linguistic and political views are 'all of a piece', not in the sense that (as Chomsky alleges) there is a logical connexion between the two groups of theses, but in the sense that they are all views which tend to appeal to a particular type of mind; and by the same token we may expect that people who disagree with Chomsky on his political views will on the whole be people with an opposite cast of mind, who will accordingly (if they are students of language) tend to disagree with Chomsky's approach to that subject as well. A linguist in this category will be unlikely to want to treat Chomsky's argument from language to politics: it is difficult to summon much enthusiasm for the task of demolishing an argument purporting to show that q follows from p, if one believes not only that q is false but that p is no truer.[9]

In my own case this problem does not arise, however, since although I disagree with Chomsky's political conclusions I agree with his linguistic premisses. It would be convenient if all the beliefs that appealed to one cast of mind were true and all those that appealed to another cast of mind false – one would know where one was, although life would presumably be exceedingly frustrating for people with the second type of mentality. But truth, as Wilde tells us, is rarely simple, and I do not believe that we are faced with one of the rare cases. Even among Chomsky's purely professional theses I would distinguish some which are false from others which are true; in particular, I believe that Chomsky is quite wrong in what he says concerning the methods by which one ought to go about the study of language, but largely right in what he says concerning the properties which one discovers language to possess when one studies it by whatever the correct methods are. And with respect to the very specific, limited linguistic theses which are all that are relevant as premisses for the argument to politics, I might be claimed to be more of a Chomskyan than Chomsky himself. I have in previous work defended these theses uncompromisingly against various objections which have been, or can be, levelled against them;[10] and I have pointed out that, in at least one relevant respect, Chomsky quite unnecessarily yields ground to his opponents.[11]

As a final item in my apologia for authorship, I might make the point that it would be unreasonable to criticize me for writing about politics while lacking professional expertise in that field, since it is a cardinal tenet of the liberal political philosophy which I aim to defend against Chomsky's attack that politics is one area of human affairs in which there is (or, at least, should be) no role for the professional expert. The principles of liberalism are very general philosophical ideas which can readily be grasped by any man of moderate wit, and, since those principles assert that governments have no business making decisions on more specific issues, for a liberal the concept of a prescriptive science of politics is largely out of place. It is Chomsky's principles, as we shall see, that lead to the conclusion that political decisions can be made correctly only by people who have prepared themselves via a lengthy course of study which has to take into account a complex web of interconnected factors.

I should stress that, although I shall have to define liberalism and sketch the principal arguments for and against it in order to clarify the nature of the issue between Chomsky and myself, it is no part of the aim of this book to give a general defence of liberalism against its enemies. Liberalism is a venerable tradition, which has been and is being defended by abler pens than mine. My book has the much more limited aim of warding off one particular novel form of attack that has been directed against the ancient structure, and of showing that, insofar as the study of language has any special contributions to make to the debate, they are contributions which tend in the opposite direction to that suggested by the arch-linguist Noam Chomsky. Any more general discussion of political issues will be subordinate to that goal.

Some readers may feel that my book constitutes an excessive

reaction to a rather unimportant element of Chomsky's work. Chomsky has written a good deal on linguistic theory and on politics, but the passages in which he explicitly infers political conclusions from linguistic premises probably amount so far to less than two dozen pages. Furthermore, while there is a well-known tendency for scholars in abstruse, mathematical or quasi-mathematical disciplines to hold quixotic, unrealistic political views, no common-sensical man – it may be suggested – is likely for a moment to take Chomsky's political ideals seriously, so there is no need to waste one's effort in pointing out his errors.

But the influence of an idea is not determined by the number of pages used to express it. And to argue that Chomsky's political ideals could never attract enough support to be influential is to convict oneself of being out of touch with the current climate of opinion. Common sense is only a name for the beliefs which most people hold, and one generation's 'common sense' is quite different from another's. Twenty years ago – even ten years ago – Chomsky's political theories might have been laughed out of court. Contemporary undergraduates, and not merely the witless troublemakers but the serious, thoughtful students from among whom the society of tomorrow must draw its leaders, take these political theories very seriously indeed. If liberal societies are to survive into the future, it will not be adequate to ignore attacks on liberalism such as the one with which this book is concerned; they must be explicitly and forcefully refuted as soon as they are made.

To conclude this introduction, let me say that the issues with which I shall be dealing are, in my view, ones that deserve to be pondered by anybody who has a vote. I hope the book will be read by laymen as well as academics; and I have accordingly kept to a minimum the technical jargon and the heavy burden of scholarly apparatus which are commonly found (and are sometimes necessary) in works addressed to fellow specialists. Thus, when I quote Chomsky's opinions I have usually limited myself to citing one passage rather than seeking out all the places in his writings where Chomsky makes the same point. But I have striven to avoid misrepresenting my opponent by quoting out of context. Some of Chomsky's views may seem self-evidently unreasonable; but they are the result of pushing to their logical conclusions beliefs which many take for granted without considering them analytically. If what Chomsky has done with them can be used to convince people of the falsity of these common beliefs, then Chomsky will have performed a great, though unintended, service to mankind.

2 From Linguistics to Anarchism

The foundation on which Chomsky bases his iconoclastic account of human nature is easy to state: it is the observation that the languages of the world are not nearly as diverse as they might be. In Chomsky's terms, there exist 'universals of human language': particular characteristics which the communication-systems we call 'languages' – English, German, Chinese, and so forth – all share, but which they are in no way logically required to share.

The latter qualification is important. Chomsky's discussion of 'linguistic universals' is widely misunderstood as a philosophical analysis of the concept 'language': people take Chomsky to be pointing out properties which a system must have if we are willing to recognize it as a language.[1] Rather, what Chomsky is drawing attention to are hitherto-unremarked common features among entities which we recognize as 'languages' by reference to quite different considerations. It is as if, say, a botanist had noticed that the number of thorns on a rose-bush is always a multiple of seventeen. Clearly no one would suggest that having thorns in a multiple of seventeen is any part of what we mean by calling something a rose-bush. Rose-bushes are not logically required to have any particular number of thorns; if they do all turn out to have thorns in multiples of some fixed number, this will be a purely empirical finding calling for a scientific explanation.

Chomsky's linguistic universals have to do with syntax, that is, with the principles by which sounds or words are put together to form sentences in a language. In order to forestall misunderstanding, let me briefly discuss the notion that living, spoken languages are governed by syntactic principles. If we consider, say, modern English, we will all agree that certain sequences of English words constitute meaningful English sentences, while other sequences of English words are just meaningless jumbles – 'word-salad' as linguists call them, e.g. *The in go elephant whether*, or *Of of the of*. (There are certain intermediate cases which we shall need to discuss in due course, but ignore them for the moment.) It seems a reasonable and perhaps interesting task to seek some set of explicit principles which distinguish the 'good' sequences of a given language from the word-salad, and this is what linguists do. It is important to stress at the outset that the syntactic principles which linguists establish for a given language do not necessarily correspond in any direct way to anything in the minds or brains of speakers of that language. We observe that Englishmen commonly utter word-sequences of certain kinds and refrain from uttering other kinds of sequence; we know very little about the psychological machinery involved, but we can to a close approximation describe the class of word-sequences which Englishmen are apt to utter, and distinguish it from the word-salad.

This point is worth making since linguists commonly use the term 'rules' for the principles defining the class of sentences of a language, which sounds as if these principles are more or less explicitly laid down and consciously learned, like the rules of chess or good manners. Now of course there are a number of grammatical rules of this kind in English and other languages. The rule forbidding split infinitives is one such; no one obeys it until he has been taught it. But the great majority of syntactic principles in any language are not like this; they can only be inferred from usage, rather than being consciously imposed on usage. Probably not one Englishman in a thousand could quote an explicit principle governing the circumstances in which a relative clause may lack a relative pronoun, and yet we all utter word-sequences like *The bulbs I bought are on the table* or *This isn't the book I asked for*, while refraining from uttering sequences like *I met the man broke the bank at Monte Carlo* or *Those are matters over we have no control*.[2] I have no wish to denigrate rules of 'good usage' such as the split-infinitive rule, as some linguists do (and as many more are erroneously thought to do); but the fact is that the explicit precepts by which schoolteachers strive to convert the racy speech of the playground into the polished prose of a *Times* leader are rather different in kind from the principles which distinguish sentences in *any* style of English from 'word-salad' – and it is these latter principles with which Chomsky is concerned.

The syntactic universals that Chomsky has pointed out have to do with the hierarchical organization of sentences. A sentence in English and other languages consists of a 'main clause' within which will typically be included subordinate clauses of various types. A clause has a verb at its core, from which depend a number of phrases of given categories – nominal phrases, prepositional phrases, and others. A phrase will have a 'head' and modifiers, realized as individual words belonging to different 'parts of speech'; thus a nominal phrase usually has a noun as its head, which may be modified by an article, and, in some cases, by adjectives. In other words, any sentence includes a hierarchy of elements of different sizes, groups of which are nested within elements at the next higher level of the hierarchy and each of which is decomposable into a group of elements at the next lower level. This hierarchical organization can conveniently be represented by bracketing; thus the sentence *The men John wanted to see are in the kitchen*, for instance, could be diagrammed as:

$$\left[\text{[the men]}_{\text{NP}} \left[\text{[John]}_{\text{NP}} \text{ wanted [to see]}_{\text{Comp}} \right] \text{Rel} \right] \text{NP}$$

$$\text{are} \left[\text{in [the kitchen]}_{\text{NP}} \right] \text{PrepP}$$

The highest-level constituents are the nominal phrase ('NP') *the men John wanted to see*, the verb *are*, and the prepositional phrase *in the kitchen*. Of these the first is composed of a shorter nominal phrase *the men* modified by a relative clause. The sentence as a whole is grammatical because the individual hierarchical relationships it exemplifies are grammatical: English allows 'NP + *be* + PrepP' as one of its patterns for sentences, it allows 'NP + Relative Clause' as one of its patterns for nominal phrases and

'Article + Noun' (e. g. *the men*) as another pattern for nominal phrases, and so on. All the rules of English syntax depend on relationships of this sort.

An exact statement of the formal theory of linguistic universals that Chomsky has developed on the basis of these notions (which are in themselves traditional enough) would be too technical to give here.[3] But it is easy to illustrate the claim that human languages are 'all of a kind' syntactically by contrasting them with fictitious 'languages' that do not involve hierarchical structure in the same way.

Thus we might consider, first, an individual syntactic principle of English, say the principle governing the relationship between statements and the questions corresponding to them. A question is formed from a statement by moving a certain word to the beginning. *The men John wanted to see are in the kitchen* becomes *Are the men John wanted to see in the kitchen?*[4] The word to be moved (in this case, *are*) is chosen by reference to its position in the hierarchical structure; it is always the main verb of the main clause of the sentence (in terms of the 'dependency tree' notation sometimes used by linguists to diagram sentential structure, the word corresponding to the topmost node of the tree – this corresponds to the fact that, in the bracketing shown above, *are* is outside all the brackets). Now it would be perfectly possible to imagine languages whose questions were formed according to some principle having nothing to do with hierarchical structure. In Language A, let us say, questions might be formed by moving the third word of a statement to the beginning, whatever that third word might be (so that, if Language A were otherwise similar to English, the question corresponding to the statement already quoted would run *John the men wanted to see are in the kitchen?*). In Language B, questions might be formed simply by reversing the order of words in statements – so that our statement would give the question *Kitchen the in are see to wanted John men the?* But, although the languages of the world form their questions in a number of different ways, none of them use principles at all like this; counting the numerical position of words in a sentence, or reversing the order of words in a sentence, are not the *sort* of operations that ever seem to be relevant to the syntax of real human languages.

We may take this discussion of artificial, 'unnatural' languages a little further. Languages A and B were posited as resembling English in most ways, and were unnatural in just one respect, namely question-formation. But we can invent 'languages' having nothing at all in common syntactically with the languages actually spoken by humans. Remember that I said that the observable facts which linguistic science sets out to describe are that members of a given speech-community produce certain word-sequences and refrain from producing others. To describe a language, at the syntactic level, is to state some body of principles which pick out the class of 'grammatical' word-sequences for that language. Now it is easy to describe 'languages', in this sense, which are wholly alien. Let us say that Language C is defined by the following principle:

Any word that occurs in a given sentence must occur an odd number of times in that sentence.

This is to be understood as a complete syntactic description of Language C: any sequence of words from the Language C vocabulary is a good sentence of Language C if it obeys this constraint. Thus (using English words to stand for words of Language C) word-sequences such as *Whether in of old* or *Of of the of walked* would be good Language C sentences, whereas *Of of the of of* or *They walked home hand in hand* would be the Language C equivalent of word-salad (since they contain respectively four *of*s and two *hand*s).

At this point the reader may be inclined to react roughly as follows. 'Language C' is *so* different from the familiar languages that it is unreasonable to use the term 'language' in connexion with it. Chomsky has not made any empirical discovery (this objection would run) in demonstrating that the human languages share syntactic characteristics not possessed by Language C; what we *mean* by the term 'language', while perhaps difficult to pin down, is something very different from 'Language C'.

But, if this objection seems attractive, the following thought-experiment should show it to be mistaken. Suppose that we voyage to Mars and encounter a race of little green men who emit sequences of wordlike sounds at each other, and attend to those emitted towards them by others; they scan newspaper- and book-like objects bearing rows of marks having a regular relationship with the sounds they emit; and, when we try to classify the sound-sequences which we observe the little green men to emit and the mark-sequences which we see in their documents, we find that the class of occurring sequences is very accurately described by the syntactic principle quoted above for Language C. Would we, in such circumstances, refuse to say that the Martians have a 'language'? Plainly we would not; we would say that they have a language, but a language radically different from the languages spoken by humans. Now, while the phenomena reported by this traveller's tale might be unexpected, there is nothing logically absurd about them; and, once we recognize the logical possibility that there could be a language like Language C somewhere, we must admit that Chomsky is making a substantive claim when he says that the actual human languages are less diverse than they might be. (Of course Chomsky has not examined *every* language spoken on this planet, but he and his followers have examined a wide variety, and all those examined seem to conform rather well to his hypothesis about syntactic universals.)

It gets us nowhere to ask, rhetorically, 'What could the Martians possibly use such a peculiar language as Language C for?' – because Chomsky can immediately retort, 'What is it about the tasks for which we humans use language that makes hierarchical structure particularly appropriate?' A few of Chomsky's opponents have tried to construct answers to the latter question, but their proposals seem wholly inadequate; it is difficult (I believe impossible) to resist Chomsky's conclusion that there is no answer.[5]

It is true that a hypothesis which claims phenomena like those of Languages A, B, and C to be 'unnatural' for humans is not a hypothesis whose truth will seem surprising to many people. In this respect my analogy with a discovery about numbers of thorns on rose-bushes was not quite fair – that discovery would be more startling, because we observe rose-bushes 'from the outside' and thus anything we find out about them is novel in every sense. Languages, on the other hand, are phenomena that we grow up with, and Chomsky's hypothesis about 'linguistic universals' is only an explicit formulation of properties with which we are in a sense already familiar. As Chomsky (quoting Wolfgang Köhler) rightly says, a special difficulty in the study of human 'cognitive faculties' or intellectual phenomena lies in the need to establish 'psychic distance' from the facts to be explained;[6] thus, what is surprising about the linguistic universals is not the observation that they apply to all human languages but the realization that, logically, nothing requires them to apply. But this difference between the fictitious observation about rose-bushes and the actual observation about languages has no real importance. What matters is that in each case we are confronted by a shared trait whose incidence cannot be explained on *a priori* principles and which therefore calls for some scientific explanation. It may seem intuitively 'obvious' that no human language will resemble Language C; but then, to an untravelled Englishman it might seem equally 'obvious' that no bar opens in the afternoon – in neither case does the familiarity of the phenomenon remove the need for an explanation of it.

Notice, in particular, that what is wrong with Language C is not that its syntax is too 'complex', in any obvious sense of that term; in fact, stateable as it is in just one sentence, the syntax of Language C is strikingly simple. Linguists habitually exaggerate the syntactic complexity of human languages,[7] but, even allowing for such exaggerations, it is clear that no familiar human language has syntactic principles which can be stated anywhere near as concisely as I have stated the syntax of Language C. What is 'wrong' with Language C has nothing to do with degrees of complexity. Rather, what seems to be going on is that the messages humans need to transmit to one another through the medium of language are messages that come in certain fixed forms, and these forms to a large extent dictate the syntactic patterning of human languages, leaving only certain relatively superficial details of syntax to vary from one language to another. Philosophers speak of the propositions which humans express through the medium of language as characterized by various 'logical forms': a given logical form may be realized by different syntactic devices in different languages (as when Latin uses case inflexions to represent the different relations between nouns and verb that English expresses by means of word-order or prepositions). In these terms, Language C is 'bad' because, although intrinsically very simple, its syntactic patterning bears no relation to the fixed logical forms of human messages.[8] As a result, although it is not particularly difficult to imagine that there might be creatures on another planet using such a language, it seems virtually impossible to imagine what it would be like to understand them, or what it would be like to speak the language oneself. To think oneself into the mind of a speaker of Language C seems as outrageous a task as imagining what it feels like to be a beetle.

Of course, people's powers of imagining strange situations vary. What we are really concerned with is to provide an explanation for the linguistic universals. Why should the messages that humans need or want to express come in a fixed range of logical forms – why should people not exchange messages of unlimited diversity?

Since a language is *par excellence* an instrument of social interaction, one answer to this question is that unless a speaker's utterances conformed to *some* recognized principles then his hearers could never understand him. To invoke an analogy that has long been popular with linguists: the possibility of playing chess exists only by virtue of the acceptance of rules such as 'bishops move diagonally' (and many others). Take away the rules, and, though a couple of people could still pass their time pushing pieces of wood around the board, they would no longer be playing a game. But this consideration shows us only that any particular language must have some particular syntactic principles – an assertion which nobody would be inclined to question. It does nothing to show why the syntactic principles of all languages should be cut to a common pattern, as Chomsky has showed us they are. In the case of games, after all, it is quite otherwise. Human ingenuity has over the ages evolved a vast range of rule-governed pastimes, and the rules which define them are of the most diverse kinds – compare the rules of chess, lawn tennis, and wrestling, for instance. Human languages have presumably been in existence at least as long as human pastimes: why have the grammars of languages not come to manifest as rich a diversity as do the 'grammars' of games?

Chomsky's answer is that the invariant syntactic properties of human languages are determined by the mechanisms of genetic inheritance. Our use of language is largely an innate rather than a learned ability. Human languages all resemble one another in their basic syntactic pattern for the same reason that human faces all resemble one another in the basic arrangement of features. Over aeons of time such matters may evolve. But over periods of a few centuries (which are quite long enough for wholly novel phenomena to come forward in purely cultural domains such as that of games), we will not see groups of people developing faces with e.g. eyes at the bottom and mouths at the top. By the same token, the period of time during which mankind has possessed the ability to speak (although this period is longer than a few centuries, and is no doubt considerably longer even than the few millennia for which we have records of language) has not been long enough to throw up substantial variation in human linguistic ability.

The significance of Chomsky's explanation for the linguistic universals is that it appears to constitute a direct challenge to a view of human nature which has very deep roots in the English-speaking world: namely, the view associated with the term 'empiricism'. Stemming ultimately from the writings of the seventeenth-century philosopher John Locke and his successors Berkeley and Hume, the empiricist view of Man has become so widespread in Britain and the U.S.A. that it commonly passes for a mere truism which cannot reasonably be questioned. The essence of empiricism is the claim that human knowledge is derived exclusively from experience (construing 'experience' broadly so as to include exposure to the words of parents, teachers, and others as well as 'first-hand experience'). No aspect of human understanding is inborn.

the argument for innate ideas

To see how this notion might be worth questioning, let us spell out its implications a little more fully. According to empiricism, the properties which characterize a given individual must be divided into two groups, which differ sharply in their origins. On the one hand there are the individual's bodily characteristics – his anatomy, the chemistry of his metabolism, his abilities to perform various physical actions; everyone has always acknowledged that these are largely determined by genetic inheritance. Environment has some part to play, certainly: whether a man's skin is tanned or pallid, whether his muscles are well-toned or flabby, will have more to do with the kind of life he has led than with the genetic blueprint with which he began life. But such matters seem almost trivial by comparison to the great wealth of physical properties which are essentially fixed by inheritance – the complex mechanisms of circulation, digestive tract, sense organs, and many others. On the other hand, however, we have the individual's mental characteristics – his beliefs, his patterns of thought, his values, and so forth. According to the empiricist, these contrast with physical characteristics in being derived wholly or almost wholly from the individual's interaction with his environment, and in being independent of genetic inheritance. A man may 'inherit', say, the prejudices of his parents; but only in the sense that, growing up surrounded by his parents' influence, he comes to believe the opinions he hears them express – not in the sense that the genetic blueprint he acquires from his parents at conception predisposes him to any particular opinions. Mentally, we begin life as a *tabula rasa*, a blank sheet, on which experience writes what it may. Physically, a human develops to maturity along lines laid down before him at conception, unless he meets with an accident along the way; but mentally he is 'a bus, not a tram'.

Against this notion, Chomsky objects, first, that it seems

intrinsically implausible. If we accept without question that a man's physical attributes, which lie relatively open to scientific enquiry and which in many cases are fairly well understood, are largely the product of inheritance, then why suppose that his mental organization, about which we know much less, differs radically in its origin? And Chomsky objects, further, that as contemporary science begins to make concrete discoveries about Man's mental structure, so it is throwing up findings which are inconsistent with the view of mind as infinitely adaptable. In particular, the existence of linguistic universals cannot be reconciled with the *tabula rasa* account of mind. Language, although manifested through the physical activity of speech, is one of the clearest cases of a mental phenomenon. The sounds we use to make our words audible are determined largely by the anatomy of the human mouth, but the syntactic principles by which we arrange words into sentences are in no way restricted by physiology, they are purely a matter of habits of thought. Therefore, if minds are infinitely adaptable, there should be no particular limits to the diversity of syntactic patterns found among different human cultures. But observation shows that, while human languages do differ syntactically, there are strict limits to their diversity. Therefore human minds are not infinitely adaptable: we inherit particular patterns of thought, and hence of language, just as we inherit a particular arrangement of facial features, or the disposition to jerk our leg when our knee is tapped.

Even given the premiss that there exist linguistic universals, this argument is obviously not watertight. If it were possible to supply a plausible alternative explanation for the linguistic universals, then the explanation in terms of genetic inheritance would lose its force. Many writers have attempted to supply such alternative explanations, suggesting for instance that there might be something about the tasks which human languages are used for that imposes a certain kind of structuring on those languages. But I would not wish to attack Chomsky along these lines. To my mind, none of the concrete alternative explanations that have been proposed for the linguistic universals is in the least plausible (cf. note 5 above). In the case just mentioned, for instance, one would need to be explicit about what particular tasks carried out by the use of languages impose on those languages the specific structuring that Chomsky has identified; and no one has come near to doing this. One of the most obvious uses of language is to describe the world around us; and although some things in our world possess intrinsic hierarchical structure, many do not. And merely to point out the logical possibility that there *might* be an alternative, as yet unthought-of explanation for the linguistic universals has no force as an objection to Chomsky. By the same token, it is logically possible (and a good scientist will be well aware of this) that some new explanation may come to be accepted for any natural phenomenon that we currently think we understand – say, the Northern Lights. Scientific theories are always open to revision and even, occasionally, radical change. But, until someone offers a concrete and demonstrably preferable alternative, we will do well to believe the standard explanation for the Northern Lights; and, similarly, I believe that Chomsky has quite adequately made his case for genetic inheritance as an important factor in the determination of human mental characteristics. For the purposes of this book I shall take it for granted that Chomsky's nativist explanation for the linguistic universals is the correct one.

Although the empiricist view of mind is the view traditional in the English-speaking world, the nativist or 'rationalist' view, to which it is opposed, has a much longer philosophical history. We may sum up this other view by saying that it treats 'experience' – interaction with the world – as only the midwife, rather than the source, of knowledge. The contents of a man's mind are in some sense there from the beginning, even though it may take external stimulation to bring them out into conscious awareness.

The classic statement of this view is a passage in Plato's *Meno*, in which an ignorant slave is led, by answering a series of questions about a diagram, to enunciate the geometrical truth that the square on the diagonal of a square has twice the area of the smaller square. Since the slave was *told* nothing, only questioned, Plato takes this to imply that the slave, though wholly untutored in geometry, knew this truth tacitly all along: 'there are, in a man who does not know, true opinions concerning that which he does not know'.[9]

The first philosopher of modern times, René Descartes (1596–1650), held a view of knowledge very much in this tradition. According to Descartes, men are born with a stock of 'innate ideas'. Certain things are known not by experience – which may be deceptive – but by direct 'intuition', which, Descartes argues, cannot deceive. This is not to say that everyone knows these things – unreflective people will often not know them – but rather that for the philosopher, who does know them, they constitute knowledge more reliable than any that can be derived from experience. While British and American thought has been largely moulded by Locke's opposition to the doctrine of 'innate ideas', the tradition stemming from Descartes has remained relatively influential in Continental Europe.

It will be clear that Chomsky's explanation for the linguistic universals is in spirit sympathetic to the non-empiricist, rationalist approach to mind, and Chomsky has linked his work with the ideas of the rationalist philosophers quite explicitly. Echoing Plato, Chomsky answers the question as to how human beings are able to know as much as they do by saying 'we can know so much because in a sense we already knew it, though the data of sense were necessary to evoke and elicit this knowledge.'[10] Chomsky has written a book (entitled *Cartesian Linguistics*) in which he argues that his technical linguistic theories are closely related to the accounts of language given by Descartes and by certain other thinkers influenced by Descartes in seventeenth-century France.[11] In due course we shall examine more specific aspects of the relationship between Chomsky's account of language and rationalist philosophy.

It is important at this point to stress that 'empiricism' and 'rationalism', if construed quite simply and crudely, are both obviously false. If we understand the empiricist as saying that a

man's beliefs are determined exclusively by the stimuli impinging on him, and not at all by his intrinsic nature, then we can
refute the empiricist by pointing out that, no matter what
stimuli it is exposed to, a stone will never form any beliefs at all.
Plainly human knowledge is possible only because men inherit
mental faculties which distinguish them from inanimate objects
and from other living species. And on the other hand if we
interpret the rationalist as claiming that experience is *only* a
midwife to the birth of knowledge, we can reply that it is
ludicrous to ascribe to ourselves any innate, tacit knowledge
e. g. of the identity of next year's Derby winner; any knowledge
about particular individuals or events must obviously derive
from some direct or indirect experience of those individuals or
events. *Both* experience *and* innate faculties are necessary to
account for human knowledge as a whole, and disputes between
rationalists and empiricists not infrequently reduce to differences of emphasis rather than of substance. Both Descartes
and Locke wrote a great deal, and modified their opinions from
time to time, as serious thinkers will; by stressing some passages
of Descartes at the expense of others, it is possible to interpret
him in such a way that he does not conflict with Locke and his
successors.

When Descartes and other rationalists do clearly conflict with
empiricism, however, they are clearly wrong. Although no
serious rationalist, as far as I know, has suggested that we can
'intuit' the identity of future Derby winners or the like, all
rationalists have claimed that there are some factual truths –
usually, particularly 'general' or 'important' truths – which we
know or can know independently of experience; and all the
evidence contradicts this.

Consider again the passage already referred to from the *Meno*.
It is significant that the proposition which Plato's slave was led
to state was a proposition about geometry, since geometrical
statements occupy an ambiguous middle ground between
matters of fact and mere logical truths. On the one hand we can
think of 'squares' as things we construct using very accurate
instruments on very flat and smooth pieces of paper; in which

case it is purely a question of fact whether the area of one square is double that of another, and one could answer the question experimentally (e.g. by cutting the two squares out of the sheet of paper and comparing their weights). It would be a powerful confirmation of rationalism if an ignorant slave could know in advance what the outcome of such an experiment would be simply by introspection. However, we can alternatively think of 'squares' not as actual objects but as mathematical abstractions, defined in terms of elementary geometrical notions such as 'line' and 'angle' which are postulated as obeying certain basic axioms not as a matter of fact but by definition. Now, in *this* sense, the statement about the areas of the two squares is not a claim about the outcome of a possible experiment; rather, the statement is an abbreviation for a rather more complex proposition about lines and angles which, if inspected carefully, turn out to be a mere logical tautology – it differs only in degree of complexity, not in kind, from a truism like 'Red things are red'.

An empiricist would have no objection to the claim than an untutored man could come by introspection to know the truth of the geometrical proposition interpreted in this latter way; empiricists do not claim that *logic* is learned by experience.[12] (How could they? What sort of experiences could possibly be relevant for evaluating the truth or falsity of 'Red things are red', for instance?) However, the rationalist will object that the proposition is also, and more obviously, a claim of the former, factual kind; so apparently some factual truths can be derived purely from introspection? Here the modern empiricist can play his trump card: interpreted factually, the statement that 'the square on the diagonal of a square is twice the area of the smaller square' is false. Einstein has shown us that the world we live in is not a Euclidean world; the real entities which seem to be good candidates to represent Euclid's 'lines' (light rays, taut strings) do not obey Euclid's axioms. The square on the diagonal of a square is in fact slightly more than twice the area of the smaller square (though with squares that are tiny relative to the size of the universe, the discrepancy will also be tiny). The oldest example of 'innate knowledge', in other words, turns out to refer either to an innate disposition to accept the validity of logical argument, which is uncontentious, or to an innate disposition to accept a certain false belief, which is not the sort of thing that rationalists have wanted to ascribe to Man.

If we come forward to Descartes, we find that his 'innate ideas' have likewise been treated harshly by the subsequent advance of knowledge. An 'idea' can be either the concept represented by an individual word – 'bread', 'love', 'democracy' – or a proposition, represented by a sentence rather than a single word. Descartes' innate ideas included some of each kind. A certain few propositions could be known intuitively to be true: 'I exist', 'God exists'. Some passages in Descartes suggest that he believed *all* word-concepts to be innate,[13] but elsewhere his claims about word-concepts are more limited: astronomers have a very different idea of the sun from laymen, and this shows that neither the astronomer's nor the layman's idea of the sun can be innate. Many word-concepts are innate, however:

such as the idea of God, Mind, Body, triangle, and in general all those which represent true, immutable, and eternal essences.[14]

An infant in its mother's womb

has in itself the ideas of God, itself, and all truths which are said to be self-evident; it has these ideas no less than adults have when they are not paying attention to them, and it does not acquire them afterwards when it grows up.[15]

None of these claims stands up to examination. The sentence 'I exist' sounds as if it expresses a matter of fact, but it is better described as a truism, since the act of uttering it demonstrates its truth. 'God exists' is more promising. But, although Descartes perceived the existence of God in the 'clear and distinct' fashion which he regarded as guaranteeing the truth of his intuitions, there is much less consensus among modern thinkers than there was in Descartes' day about the existence of God; and many of those who would nowadays assent to the words 'God exists' would at the same time ascribe such a novel interpretation to those words that they can hardly be said to share Descartes' intuitive belief.[16] Furthermore, there are sophisticated cultures which do not even have a word for 'God' in Descartes' sense. When the Jesuits took Christianity to the Chinese in the seventeenth century, a serious controversy developed between the Jesuit mission and the Vatican authorities over how to translate the word 'God' – the Jesuits preferring to render their teaching more acceptable by using Chinese terms which, in their native context, had very different connotations, the Vatican eventually insisting on a neologism.[17] Indeed, of Descartes' four examples, 'God', 'Mind', 'Body', and 'triangle', only 'body' has a relatively direct equivalent in classical Chinese. Descartes' 'true, immutable, and eternal essences' are in reality merely words for ideas which happened to be common intellectual currency in the Europe of his day. Since Europe at that time was only beginning to emerge from long centuries of mental stagnation, it was very natural for Descartes to mistake conventional wisdom for unchallengeable truth. His example of the sun was one of the few cases where scientific discovery had already overthrown received opinion. After three intellectually hectic centuries, during which even our notions of space and time have been recast by the advances of physics, it seems improbable that a modern Descartes would feel confident in assigning any idea at all to the innate list.

As an academic philosophical theory of human knowledge, then, Descartes' system has been shown to be false, and probably no one would now seek to defend it in detail. But a philosophy exerts its widest influence not through its detailed arguments but through the presuppositions it makes at a relatively general level. A rationalist tends to suppose that we can know important truths by aprioristic reflection, and that such knowledge can be certain; an empiricist tends to suppose that we can discover truth only by trial and error, and that all our beliefs are provisional. At this fairly vague level rationalism has comfortably survived its refutation in the form Descartes gave it. Subsequent Continental philosophy and Continental – particularly French – social patterns have been heavily influenced by the rationalist outlook, while many aspects of British and American thought and society reflect the empiricist approach to life.

political
implications
of
rationalism

We shall consider various general consequences of the rationalist and empiricist approaches to society in subsequent chapters. In the remainder of this chapter, let us examine the specific political inferences Chomsky draws from his own linguistic version of rationalism.

If human minds were the 'blank sheets' of the empiricists, so that our patterns of thought and hence of behaviour were determined wholly by the environment in which we find ourselves, then, Chomsky suggests, it might be appropriate for governments to institute powerful systems of rewards and punishments designed to mould people into good rather than bad citizens: 'If in fact man is an indefinitely malleable, completely plastic being, with no innate structures of mind and no intrinsic needs of a cultural or social character, then he is a fit subject for the "shaping of behaviour" by the state authority, the corporate manager, the technocrat, or the central committee.'[18] On this view, the things that humans need for a good life are physical things – they are happy if they are well fed, luxuriously housed, and so forth; and they are made unhappy by physical experiences such as being 'mugged'. Good citizens are people who live in such a way as to enable the needs of their fellow men to be satisfied – they work diligently to produce consumer goods, refrain from robbery, and the like. An individual does not *choose* to be a bad citizen – whether we are good or bad citizens depends entirely on how our environment has moulded us; so it is appropriate, indeed imperative, for a government to arrange the moulding process in such a way that it promotes good citizenship rather than bad, and thus gives its subjects the best life possible. In Chomsky's eyes American government (among others) relies on just such manipulative devices: high salaries and every known creature comfort for those who conform and prop up the established economic and political structure, as against tear-gas, prison or the bullets of the National Guard for those who rebel.

But for Chomsky, as a rationalist, our minds are not 'malle-able'; Chomsky sees control from without as, at best, irrele-vant to human life. An infant, Chomsky argues in his pro-fessional role, is pre-programmed to speak a language of the particular kind that humans find natural; he needs the stimula-tion of his parents' speech only as a relatively unimportant 'trigger' to release the ability already latent within him. More generally, Chomsky suggests in his political role, a man's mind, and hence his behaviour, will develop of its own accord in the way that is right for him. We all accept that this is true of a person's body: it is possible to influence bodily development by external control, as for instance in the Chinese practice of foot-binding, but no one would nowadays regard such practices as other than barbarous. For Chomsky, what is true of body is equally true of mind. Rewards and punishments can at best be irrelevant to mental development, and in practice are likely to warp natural growth. Chomsky quotes Bertrand Russell, who

wrote that 'the humanistic conception regards a child as a gardener regards a young tree, i.e. as something with a certain intrinsic nature, which will develop into an admirable form given proper soil and air and light'. I think it is fair to say that it is the humanistic conception of man that is advanced and given substance as we discover the rich systems of invariant structures and principles that underlie the most ordinary and humble of human accomplishments.[19]

The principal human needs are intellectual and emotional, and the kinds of manipulation of the environment of which govern-ments are capable can do little to help fulfil these needs (al-though governments can *hinder* their fulfilment, e.g. by limiting individuals' interactions with one another by regimenting them in armies or prisons).[20] The only physical things that humans need in order to fulfil themselves are a few basic essentials (metaphorically, 'soil and air and light'), and powerful govern-ments are not necessary in order to provide these. Chomsky writes approvingly that thinkers such as Wilhelm von Hum-boldt and Bertrand Russell 'opposed the intervention in every-day life of external authority, such as the state, which tends to "make men an instrument to serve its arbitrary ends, overlooking his individual purposes"'.[21] Rather, 'the laws of our nature will achieve their fullest expression in a society of free and creative producers, linked by social bonds in a system of voluntary association.'[22] Therefore the best government is no government – anarchism.[23]

However, the notion of reducing the power of government is by no means a complete answer to the question of how society should ideally be organized. Chomsky suggests that Humboldt, writing at the end of the eighteenth century, may have seen the state as the only threat to individual self-fulfilment;[24] 'But, going beyond the libertarian thought of the pre-industrial period, Russell knew that the state is by no means the sole enemy of liberty. . . . Industrial civilization leads to concentration of power and the decline of individual liberty.'[25] Under *laissez-faire* capitalism, Chomsky argues, some individuals will accumulate wealth which enables them to exploit their less fortunate fellow men, e.g. by forcing them to work long hours at mindless jobs that hinder their self-fulfilment as effectively as a life sentence in prison. Capitalist society encourages such exploitation, and is therefore fully as objectionable as the tyranny of a despotic state. Accordingly our political ideal should be a form of socialism. However,

the consistent anarchist . . . should be a socialist, but a socialist of a particular sort. He will not only oppose alienated and specialized labour and look forward to the appropriation of capital by the whole body of workers, but he will also insist that this appropriation be direct, not exercised by some elite force acting in the name of the proletariat.[26]

To call modern Russia a 'socialist' nation is a 'cruel joke';[27] Chomsky frequently quotes the nineteenth-century Russian anarchist Mikhail Bakunin's prophetic remark that 'The people will feel no better if the stick with which they are being beaten is labelled "the people's stick"'.[28] We must hope that 'The . . . course of social evolution may lead the working man to understand that he can take control of the institutions of modern society, and can become "dependent only upon the community of fellow-workers, not upon the arbitrary will of [*either*] a special set of privileged beings, the capitalists," *or* the "official caste" of a state socialist bureaucracy.'[29]

What this means in practice is that we should aim at a régime of 'democratic socialism', in which the production and distribution of goods are controlled by small self-governing groups of workers linked in a loose federation – 'a society of free producers, who organize production and distribution without external authority'.[30] Quoting Fernand Pelloutier, Chomsky suggests that society should ideally be 'a free organization limited exclusively by the needs of production and consumption, all political institutions having disappeared'.[31] The centralized power of the state should be 'overcome by smaller self-governing units, in part territorial, in part industrial, along with other forms of association'.[32] Chomsky quotes with approval Bertrand Russell's view that

Anarchism is 'the ultimate ideal to which society should approximate' [but that] For the present . . . some variant of guild socialism [is] a reasonable prospect for the advanced industrial societies, with workers' control of industry, a democratic parliament representing the community, some restricted forms of state management, a guarantee to all of the material necessities of a decent existence, and 'the organization of citizens with special interests into groups, determined to preserve autonomy as regards their internal affairs. . . .'[33]

In political theory, such an ideal is known as 'syndicalism' or 'anarcho-syndicalism', and derives from the thought of P. J. Proudhon and Mikhail Bakunin.[34] Chomsky illustrates his political ideal by means of an extended discussion of the anarcho-syndicalist social structure which existed in parts of Spain for a short while in the Civil War;[35] and he suggests (writing in 1969) that life in N.L.F.-controlled areas of South Vietnam, and possibly in Communist China, may also represent hopeful approximations towards his ideal.[36] (In the latter connexion one must remember that in 1969 very much less was known in the West than is known now about what life was like in China; Chomsky admits that 'The scale of the Chinese Revolution is so great and reports in depth are so fragmentary that it would no doubt be foolhardy to attempt a general evaluation.')

Particularly objectionable activities of the contemporary governments which Chomsky attacks include their use of superior power to influence the way of life of weaker nations; the outstanding example, during most of the period in which Chomsky has been politically active, was American participation in the war in Vietnam. Of course many people with political ideals very different from Chomsky's felt that what the Americans did in Vietnam was a mistake, e.g. because of the great cost in human misery of prolonging the war, and the little apparent likelihood that it could ever be won. But Chomsky had more philosophical objections to the war. Chomsky saw the struggle in South Vietnam in terms of an insurgent movement springing from among the indigenous population pitted against a government which, while manned by natives, was maintained by American power and was quite alien to the traditions of Vietnamese society. An attempt by one nation to induce another nation to adopt an alien social system may be compared to the kind of psychological experiment in which the experimenter 'shapes' the behaviour patterns of, say, a pigeon by applying a schedule of positive and negative 'reinforcements'.[37] By supplying food pellets for desired movements and electric shocks for undesired movements, it is possible as a *tour de force* to induce a pair of pigeons to play ping-pong, for instance. But, since humans are not 'infinitely malleable' mentally, such experiments cannot normally be expected to succeed with them. In the linguistic case, for instance, an infant needs only a minimum of external stimulation to acquire a first language, provided that language belongs to the restricted class of natural human languages; but on the other hand *no* pattern of external stimulation, Chomsky suggests, could ever cause an infant to grow up speaking an 'unnatural' language, such as Language C discussed above. Similarly we have no reason to assume that a nation could be induced by rewards and punishments imposed from outside to adopt some particular social system which had been selected as 'desirable', if that social system had no natural roots in the life of the nation.

Furthermore, whereas the empiricist tends to downgrade the importance of human minds (they begin as 'blank sheets', and later are merely repositories for links established between external stimuli and overt behaviour evoked by those stimuli), the rationalist recognizes that minds are highly complex entities in their own right, with their own organizational principles which are reflected only indirectly, if at all, in observable behaviour. This means that, even if one succeeded by means of a sufficiently strong schedule of rewards and punishments in imposing some 'desired' social pattern on a nation to which it was alien, the resulting situation would be very different from that obtaining if the nation had spontaneously adopted such a form of society. If the South Vietnamese had been induced by fear of American arms and Con Son Island tiger cages to abandon insurrection and obey the Thieu/Ky government, an empiricist who approved of that government would see no problems remaining; the rationalist appreciates that obedient behaviour may mask a rebellious and frustrated heart. 'To determine whether the fundamental human rights are being honored, we must consider, not just what a person does, but the conditions under which he does it – whether it is done under external control or spontaneously, to fulfill an inner need.'[38] Earlier Vietnamese history offers a striking exemplification of this principle in the way in which the Vietnamese seized independence as soon as China became internally weak in the tenth century, despite having been administered for a millennium as to all intents and purposes an integral part of China.

The argument by which Chomsky derives prescriptions for the organization of society from observations about the syntax of human languages is, clearly, a fairly loose one. Chomsky recognizes this looseness: 'It is, to be sure, a great intellectual leap from observations on the basis for cognitive development to particular conclusions on the laws of our nature and the conditions for their fulfillment'.[39] Chomsky's professional colleagues in particular are apt to take this looseness as grounds for dismissing Chomsky's argument out of hand, since linguistics and psychology themselves are highly formal, quasi-mathematical disciplines within which arguments are expected to display a logical watertightness approaching that of proofs in geometry or physics. But it would be a mistake to reject Chomsky's argument for this reason. The fact is that all theoretical discourse on political and social questions is logically somewhat loose, if judged by the exacting standards of physics, geometry, or formal linguistics, and this looseness reflects the intrinsic nature of the subject rather than poor scholarship. There seems to be a rough trade-off among intellectual disciplines, whereby the greater the 'human interest' of a subject the less that subject lends itself to formal axiomatic treatment. Political theory ranks relatively low on the scale of logical exactitude, but it ranks very high on the scale of human interest. Men are political animals; unless we are content simply to abdicate responsibility for our political destiny, we must think about political questions as logically as we can while accepting that the fabric of our political discourse is likely always to be of a coarser logical mesh than the products of the physicist or the geometer.

Accordingly, I shall try not to attack Chomsky's argument from language to politics by making mere debating points about trivial non sequiturs in his reasoning – which would be easy to do but pointless. I aim to show that Chomsky's argument is, not just somewhat leaky, but fundamentally, radically wrong. The facts of language do strongly suggest (while not logically imposing) a certain concept of human mind, and this in turn suggests a certain kind of political ideal; but the concept of mind, and the political ideal, are both very different from those advocated by Chomsky. Chomsky's rejection of liberalism in favour of his own brand of socialism is based on a misunderstanding of what his own – and others' – linguistic discoveries tell us about human nature.

3 Liberalism and Creativity

One of the difficulties in discussing Chomsky's political philosophy is that it is not altogether clearly defined, and this is not Chomsky's fault alone: the anarchism of Proudhon and Bakunin was never the most lucid of political ideals. Proudhon has been described as a writer who 'assembled an immense number of contradictory propositions leaving his readers to reconcile them as best they could';[1] Bertrand Russell, no foe in general of radical political views, described Bakunin's anarchism as 'a form of madness'.[2] In order to sharpen up the debate between Chomsky and myself, let me now introduce the liberal political philosophy which I aim to defend against Chomsky's attack. Liberalism is a rather clearly defined and consistent philosophy, and, whatever unclarities there may be in Chomsky's positive political statements, it is certain that Chomsky opposes liberalism. Just as Chomsky claims to derive his version of socialism from more general philosophical and psychological considerations, so liberalism springs both historically and logically from a particular philosophy of human knowledge: empiricism. The founder of the empiricist philosophy of knowledge, Locke, at the same time provided the liberal political theory which inspired the Glorious Revolution of 1688 and became the philosophical foundation on which British, and hence also American, public life was subsequently based. In our own time liberal thought is represented most notably by writers such as Friedrich Hayek and Sir Karl Popper; Popper is also the outstanding contemporary philosopher of knowledge, and the two sides of his thought are explicitly and very closely interwoven.

As I have already said, it is not the aim of this book to present a full-scale account of the liberal political ideal together with a defence against all possible objections. It would be presumptuous of me to try to do again what Hayek's *Constitution of Liberty* has already done admirably. At the same time, however, I cannot – as, at an earlier period, I might – simply take the general nature and justification of liberalism for granted and plunge immediately into discussion of the specific issues raised by Chomsky's work, since nowadays these ideas are not at all widely understood. For a century now, liberal ideas have become steadily less fashionable. Anti-liberal views have decade by decade diffused from academic intellectuals to politicians and have eventually begun to spread among the many people who are not actively interested in theoretical issues. Even if this trend continues, it still has a long way to go before it will be complete. Many ordinary Britons and Americans still take the liberal ideal very much for granted; British and American institutions have moved only a certain distance – British much further than American – away from the pattern prescribed by liberalism.[3] But, among people whose business is ideas – academics, journalists, and the like – the decline of liberalism has proceeded so far that there are now many who hold illiberal views not because they disagree with liberalism but because they are simply unacquainted with it. Accordingly it will be necessary in this chapter to digress away from language and (until the last pages of the chapter) away from Chomsky's views, and I must ask readers who are well acquainted with liberal thought to bear with me until I return to the proper subject of this book.

One symptom of the decline in understanding of liberalism is that the term 'liberal' has come to be used in ways rather different from its original sense, which is the sense relevant for this book. Both in the U.S.A. and in Britain, a 'liberal' is nowadays seen as a middle-of-the-road man. Americans often speak of 'woolly liberals' or 'wishy-washy liberals', suggesting that a liberal is a sentimental compromiser who cannot bring himself to adopt a rigorously consistent political stance.[4] In Britain, 'Liberal' is the name of a small political party whose policies, while nowadays rather nebulous, are felt to fall somewhere between the Socialist Left and the Conservative Right.

This modern sense of 'liberal', though not very well defined, is now so deeply entrenched that it might be desirable to adopt an alternative term for 'liberal' in the sense I have in mind, if an alternative term were available (but none is).[5] Liberalism properly understood is very far from being a middle-of-the-road philosophy. If liberalism can justifiably be criticized, it is more likely to be for harsh inhumanity than for sentimental ambivalence. If liberalism, conservatism, and socialism are to be arranged on a single scale, then, philosophically speaking, it makes more sense to think of liberalism and socialism as the two extremes and conservatism as occupying a middle ground (although it might be yet more accurate to treat the conservatism/socialism dimension as lying at right-angles to that which distinguishes liberalism from both of them). The terms 'right' and 'left' in politics referred originally to the seating plan of the French National Assembly; since liberalism never made much impression on French political thought and behaviour,[6] to insist on analysing political opinions in terms of left v. right is to prejudge the issue against liberalism. In contemporary British politics, liberals are certainly not found exclusively in the Liberal party. At present it is obviously the Conservative party which comes closest to standing for liberalism, though the principled liberalism of Margaret Thatcher and Sir Keith Joseph has by no means always characterized their party in recent years. Bryan Magee, the popularizer of Popper and member for Waltham Forest, reconciles belief in a kind of liberalism with acceptance of the Labour whip. One of the leading parliamentary spokesmen for liberalism in matters purely economic, Enoch Powell, was last elected as a United Ulster Unionist. And on the other hand members of the Liberal party sometimes make remarkably illiberal statements.[7]

Like any other political philosophy, liberalism is largely a thesis about how goods should be produced and distributed. (The term 'goods' is not intended in a narrowly materialistic sense here; a good is anything that some people want and that is not in unlimited supply like the air we breathe, so that attendance at a concert or a university education are 'goods' as much as is a pound of steak or a car. Liberalism does also have implications for purely non-economic aspects of social life, such as the conventions regulating sexual behaviour; since this aspect of liberalism is not central to the dispute between Chomsky and myself, I shall not emphasize it in what follows.[8]) According to the liberal, the production and distribution of goods should as far as possible be controlled exclusively by the impersonal mechanism of free competition between individuals in an open market. It should be open to any individual to produce goods by any method he wishes using whatever resources he owns or can buy or hire, and to sell the goods he produces, or his labour, for whatever price he can get. The proper task of government is to maintain the free market in being and to protect individuals in their enjoyment of the rewards they derive from participation in the market, and it should take on as few other tasks as possible.[9]

This task is itself by no means trivial. Thus, a government will be responsible for defence of the state against external threats and maintenance of law and order internally. It will enforce whatever contracts its citizens freely enter into with one another; and it will intervene to break up monopolies and prohibit conspiracies in restraint of free trade. (Such conspiracies include cartels, which keep the price of given types of goods higher than they would be in a competitive situation, and trade unions, which elevate the price of given categories of labour by collective wage-bargaining, and which interfere with employers' freedom to hire and fire by enforcing closed-shop agreements and security of tenure.[10]) If government monopolizes the issue of currency, then it must ensure that its currency retains its value. Government may also need to make itself responsible for providing certain kinds of goods which cannot be supplied competitively, such as roads. But government should definitely not seek to decide economic issues which can be settled by the free play of competition. Government should not, for instance, interfere with the market by legislating for price controls, rent controls, or minimum-wage laws. It should not take on the responsibility for supplying a given product through public ownership of the industry which manufactures that product, or determine the availability of such services as medical care or higher education by paying for these services from taxation (and still less by public ownership of hospitals or universities). Nor should government use taxation to redistribute wealth or interfere with patterns of industry. For the liberal it is desirable that those individuals whose enterprise or labour commands relatively high prices should be rewarded proportionately (irrespective of the individual's moral worth, or the like); human beliefs as to what is just or appropriate should play no part in determining the distribution of goods.

What makes this style of government ideal is not that a free market economy in practice gives rise automatically to a distribution of goods which might consciously be chosen as 'fair' or 'morally just', for it does not. Opinions about what is fair or morally right differ, but many people will feel – as I do myself – that a society in which an honest, likeable, diligent, though unintelligent labourer may be living in penury while a selfish, ruthless businessman enjoys a luxurious existence is not *eo ipso* particularly admirable. However, penury is a relative term: the life of a modern English unskilled labourer would in some ways have looked luxurious to, say, King Henry II. What justifies the inequalities of wealth which will exist at any given time in a liberal society is that the total of wealth increases most rapidly in such a society, and that this increase in total wealth benefits those on the lower as well as those on the higher rungs of the economic ladder.[11] The poor man of today has a standard of living as high as he has only because economic activity in the past was regulated by free competition; if we hope, as responsible men must, that the poor men of the twenty-first century will enjoy a standard of living that to us would not seem poor at all, then we must prevent our governments from interfering with the free play of market forces (as they are tending more and more to do). For a liberal, to encourage government to intervene in the economy is, among other things, to rob our descendants of their birthright. Our standard of life is as high as it is on average only because our forefathers played the risky game of economic competition over many generations; if we now change the rules of the game in an attempt to give ourselves equality and security *as well as* prosperity, then future generations, like previous generations, will be poorer than we. And it may be added, since people commonly find it difficult to spare much consideration for the inhabitants of the remote future, that the ill effects of abandoning the free market system arise quite quickly enough to be noticeable after years rather than decades.

Why should a free, unplanned economy produce more wealth than an economy in which available resources are allocated to the production of various kinds of goods by conscious, rational decisions on the part of government planners briefed to maximize total wealth? *A priori* one might expect (and many influential people have expected) just the reverse to be the case.

The answer to this question, which is the essence of the case for liberalism, turns on the notions of human creativity and human ignorance – two sides, as we shall see, of a single coin.

Creativity is the distinctively human capacity of inventing things – of producing things which are novel, not merely in the sense that they did not previously exist, but in the sense that they were not previously conceived of. The word 'things' here is deliberately vague, since human inventions fall into very diverse categories – a crucial aspect of the notion of creativity is that one cannot predict beforehand the nature of its products.

Perhaps the clearest examples of creativity are the invention of new movements in the arts and novel theories in the sciences. Not all products of the arts and sciences, of course, are 'creative' in the relevant sense. When a portraitist paints the retirement picture of a headmaster in a recognized style, the picture he produces is novel in the limited sense that that particular arrangement of paint on canvas had not previously existed; but in a deeper sense it may not be novel at all, since it may be merely one more example of a *type* of picture that is already quite familiar (even if we may find it difficult to say in words what properties an arrangement of brush-strokes has to have in order to count as an example of the type). On the other hand the emergence of impressionism, for instance, was something

[margin note: the case for liberalism — creativity & ignorance]

genuinely novel. The paintings of a van Gogh or a Cézanne were not just objects that had not previously existed (although they were this, obviously): they were arrangements of paint which fell outside previous conceptions of what counted as a picture. A common reaction in the early days of impressionism was inability to see that what the impressionists were doing was 'art' at all; the eventual acceptance of impressionism implied not simply the addition of a further group of canvases to the world's stock of paintings, but a change in the concept attached to the term 'work of art'.

Similarly in the sciences. To determine the mass of some celestial body may be to produce a new piece of knowledge, in the sense that no one knew the mass of that body before. But it is not 'creative' in the relevant sense, since the hypothesis one has confirmed – say, 'The mass of body X is 56 million tonnes' – belongs to a class of possible hypotheses which was perfectly familiar in advance; one merely did not know which particular number belonged in the slot occupied by '56 million'. On the other hand, when an Einstein reacted to certain surprising experimental data by producing a physical theory which implied, among other things, that the mass of a body is not absolute but depends in part on the speed of movement of the observer, he did something truly creative. The Special Theory of Relativity is not just a particular one among an antecedently familiar range of possible physical theories. No one before Einstein had dreamt of linking mass and velocity in this way, and Einstein's principal achievement lay not in demonstrating that his theory was the correct one but in conceiving it in the first place.

The mathematically minded reader might object here that the range of possible future physical theories, or paintings, in a sense *is* definable in advance. Any scientific theory is statable as a long sequence of words, and we can define the set of all possible sequences of words, which must include all possible future theories; similarly we could presumably define the set of all possible arrangements of pigment on canvas or paper and know that it included all possible future paintings. But what we

week

are interested in is the dividing line between the word-sequences that do count as potential future physical theories and those which do not, or the line dividing pigment-arrangements which might one day be regarded as examples of an artistic tradition as yet unborn and those which will never be anything but daubs; it is intrinsic to the notion of creativity that these lines cannot be plotted in advance. The problem is not that the lines would be fuzzy, but that we have no idea even roughly where they should run. To a scientist of 1700, the Special Theory of Relativity would have read not as an implausible theory of physics but as a senseless jumble of words (not 'word-salad' in the sense of chapter 2, since Einstein's sentences have subjects, verbs, and objects in the usual places, but rather the sort of nonsense, like Lewis Carroll's *Jabberwocky*, whose *only* virtue is grammaticality). Similarly, a cultured European who for the first time faces a piece of calligraphy regarded by the Chinese as one of the pinnacles of achievement in the graphic arts has no way of knowing that it is not the shopping-list of some very ordinary Mrs. Wong or the meaningless doodle of her three-year-old son.[12]

Although I have chosen to explain the notion of creativity by reference to the arts and pure sciences, the next point to be made is that the same notion is equally applicable in areas of life with more direct relevance to politics and economics. Indeed, while cases of creativity drawn from the arts and sciences tend to make the most successful illustrations of the notion (since they tend to be of relatively general interest), I have little doubt that if it were possible to count the sum total of creative acts performed by humanity in the course of a given year, those appertaining to the arts and pure sciences would form a small minority. (Of course, I do not intend this suggestion that creative acts might be counted to be taken very seriously, since we would not know how to individuate the items to be counted; would the invention of a complex theory, say, count as one big creative act or a lot of lesser ones?) Creativity is displayed in the invention of new machines, and, much more frequently, in novel modifications of pre-existing machines. New social institutions, new services, new types of organization, and novel modifications to existing institutions, etc., all these are examples of creative innovation. The man who first thought of making envelopes with transparent windows and thereby saved redundant labour by future generations of typists did not win the glory of an Einstein or a Cézanne – what he did was not such a *big* imaginative leap as they made; but it was nevertheless 'creative' in precisely the same *sense* as what they did. As one moves down the scale from the great creative acts of famous artists and scientists to the relatively humble innovations which are more common in technology and business (as well as in many aspects of life lacking economic implications), one eventually ceases to be able to give examples not because examples are lacking – quite the contrary – but because the many examples that do occur are too tied to particular circumstances to be easily explainable to the outsider. Does anyone doubt that the professional life of an engineer or a small business proprietor (or of a housewife) will consist in part of inventing at least very slightly novel solutions to a succession of at least very slightly novel problems posed by the engineering task, business situation, or family life? A small proportion of these creative acts are on a larger scale – a new machine, a new filing system, a new recipe – and these, if successful, may come to the outsider's notice; the endless small decisions about (in the businessman's case) modifications to the range of products, cheaper ways of organizing the supply of materials, more efficient organization of production, and so forth, also require innovative thinking even though they may be of no interest other than to the man who makes them.[13]

The corollary of the statement that humans are creative is that humans are ignorant. One could not, as a matter of logic, have known of the usefulness of envelopes with transparent windows before such envelopes were invented, since to know about them would be to have invented them. If humans are constantly conceiving novel things, then at any given time the possibilities of which we are aware must be trivially few by comparison with the possibilities waiting to be thought of. This is why the notion of describing the faculty of creativity by means

*Prediction +
creativity
incompatible.*

of the scientific method is an instance of the fallacy of scientism. The essence of science is prediction; but it is intrinsic to the notion of creativity that the nature of creative acts cannot be predicted, they can only be described after the event.[14]

Furthermore, when a new idea is conceived we cannot tell immediately whether it is a good or bad one. Even a new scientific theory will normally have to run a gauntlet of criticism and modification by other scientists before being accepted as part of established knowledge; inconsistencies or unclarities overlooked by the author of the theory will be brought to light, new experiments will be carried out to test the predictions of the theory, and so on. Similar processes are even more salient with the kind of innovations that are more directly relevant to economic life. A new industrial product must work on paper, but it must fulfil many other conditions if it is to contribute anything to the total of human happiness. It must be practical to manufacture, and must be superior in actual use to whatever it replaces. Manufacture of the product will invariably throw up a host of problems that could not have been foreseen by the original designer, and its use will commonly involve a range of benefits and of drawbacks from the user's point of view which again could not be predicted in all their detail; ultimately, the only way to discover whether the new product deserves to be translated from conception into reality is to try it and see what happens. Precisely similar considerations apply to innovations in non-economic aspects of life. As families in recent decades became smaller and more isolated from one another a problem arose in that children of pre-school age led unduly solitary lives; someone somewhere hit on the idea of the 'playgroup' as a solution. To organize a playgroup is not a trivial matter; and plainly one could not know in advance all the manifold consequences for real children (and for adults involved) of running such an institution – one could only make the attempt and see whether it worked successfully.

Of course, the well-known examples of creativity in any aspect of life will be cases which were in the end successful; that is why they are well-known. Because of this, one may be deluded into underestimating the probability of a novel idea turning out not to work in practice. But this probability is quite high; for any successful innovation in any walk of life there will be several whose 'teething troubles' develop fatal complications.[15]

Because of our capacity to create and the ignorance which goes with it, human progress will occur only if novel ideas can find backers who will stake something of value to them on the success of the novelty (where the stake may be financial capital in the case of an innovation in the economic domain, reputation or time in the arts and pure sciences, or happiness in the case of a novel social institution). People – the person who actually thinks up the new idea, and others who are in a position to try it out – must stand to gain if the idea is successful; which means that they must stand to lose, if it is not. In the economic sphere, progress can come about only from risk-taking free enterprise. Salaried civil servants cannot advance us economically, since they have nothing to gain and everything to lose by innovating; one cannot require someone to invent, or to adopt potentially-successful inventions, as a condition of his employment in a given domain of human affairs (since until something has been invented one will have no way of knowing that there was actually something waiting to be invented in that domain, and before an invention is tested we cannot know whether it will be successful), but one can certainly penalize an employee for unsuccessful innovation when there were tried and true, if less than ideal, methods available to him.

missing premises here!

Progress, then, requires that there be winners and losers; but at the same time progress advances the interests of the losers as well as those of the winners. In a liberal society, a man who becomes a railwayman at a time when road hauliers are beginning to offer in a more convenient and cheaper form most of the services previously performed by railways will earn less, until he changes his job, than a contemporary who becomes a lorry-driver, since within the railway company wages will fall and promotion opportunities decrease. From the point of view of society as a whole this is a good thing, because that individual is now less useful to society working for a railway company than he would be working for a road haulage firm, and his lower income gives him an incentive to undergo the inconvenience entailed in changing jobs. But it is the previous progress of humanity that has created the great diversity of transportation needs that now exist, and of this wide range there will be some tasks that even now are best performed by railways; so the railwayman may still be able to make a living if he is unwilling or unable to become a lorry-driver. In the Middle Ages, there were relatively few ways of life open to the unskilled man other than the ceaseless, back-breaking labour and miserable living conditions that were the lot of the peasant of those days. Thanks to subsequent centuries of progress, the unskilled man now has a choice between a much wider range of jobs, all of which provide him with a standard of living that would have seemed luxurious to the mediaeval peasant, and which, while they might not appear attractive to the scholar, are considerably more attractive to those who do them (if only because of shorter hours) than the life of the peasant. To quote two writers who will scarcely be accused of slavish adulation of the 'bourgeoisie', i.e. of those people who make their livelihood by providing the capital for business enterprise:

The bourgeoisie, during its rule of scarce one hundred years, has created more massive and more colossal productive forces than have all preceding generations together. Subjection of Nature's forces to man, machinery, application of chemistry to industry and agriculture, steam navigation, railways, electric telegraphs, clearing of whole continents for cultivation, canalization of rivers, whole populations conjured out of the ground – what earlier century had even a presentiment that such productive forces slumbered in the lap of social labour?[16]

A liberal society, then, is one in which patterns of production and distribution of goods are determined by the impersonal mechanism of open competition between individuals acting as free and independent economic agents. The alternative is for production and distribution patterns to be settled by decisions on the part of those who govern, who will determine the pattern of production according to their beliefs about what products are most needed and how available resources can best be exploited, and will determine the pattern of distribution according to some explicit scheme laying down who is entitled to what, which may be of very diverse kinds depending on the attitudes of the governors. We need a name for this alternative type of society. I shall use the term *authoritarian,* since in such a society certain individuals' opinions are taken as authoritative for deciding economic issues; compare the way in which intellectual questions in the Middle Ages were settled by appeal to the authority of certain canonical writings, while the scientific revolution of the Renascence replaced 'arguments from authority' by competition to explain data between hypotheses which any man was free to propose and defend.[17] The distinction between liberal and authoritarian governments and societies is a continuous gradient rather than a yes-or-no question; no society is, or perhaps could be, at either logical extreme. But the liberal, while recognizing that government must inevitably decide some economic issues, will aim for it to decide as few as possible, whereas the authoritarian of one brand or another will aim for government to do all it can to ensure that the economy conforms to his particular beliefs as to what is desirable. Even if no society occupies either of the extreme positions on the liberal v. authoritarian continuum, societies certainly differ very markedly in their relative positions on that scale.

The authoritarian may be motivated by very laudable moral ideals. The socialist, in particular, will believe, as does Chomsky, that the disparities in income inevitable in a liberal society are unjust, and should be replaced by an equalitarian system of distribution.[18] This means that no individual will have an economic incentive to maximize production; but that does not worry the socialist, since he envisages government using its authority to organize the economy in such a way that total production is maximized.[19] But this makes sense only if a government and its servants can know how an economy should be organized so as to make best use of available resources; and no finite body of humans at any given point in time can ever know this. At any particular moment there will always be endless inventions (in the widest sense) not yet made which, when they are made, will enable more value to be derived from the same physical resources. If humanity is ever to have the benefit of this extra value, people must be free to try to enrich themselves by applying their powers of invention. The authoritarian ideal is scientistic; it fails to allow for the ignorance which is unavoidably entailed by our creative capacity.

It is important to realize that the problem is not only that we will never at any given time have made all the inventions that are waiting to be made, but, perhaps even more importantly, that under an authoritarian system when an invention is made there is no means of discovering whether on balance it will benefit humanity to proceed with it. Consider the case of a novel machine; its manufacture will use materials and labour that could have been used for other purposes, and in a liberal economy the importance to humanity of these other purposes will be reflected in the cost of manufacture of the machine, while the total of advantages (balanced, perhaps, by some disadvantages) conferred by possession of the machine will be reflected in what people are willing to pay for it. If the latter figure is greater than the former, then the total wealth of society will on balance be greater if the machine is made; and, since this will be reflected in the fact that the manufacturer stands to make a profit, the machine *will* be made. In an authoritarian economy, wages and prices must be consciously decided by the governors rather than emerging from the free play of market forces, and therefore these quantities cannot act as they do in a liberal economy to allocate labour and resources to the places where they really will produce most value, as opposed to where someone thinks they will produce most value.[20]

The ignorance entailed by human creativity is not the only kind of ignorance that is relevant to the case for liberalism. Liberals often argue that, even if all the facts which are relevant for deciding how best to allocate the resources of a society are known to members of the society, that knowledge is scattered over the entire population. In order to formulate consciously a pattern of production as successful as that which will emerge if the economy is unplanned, it would be necessary to assemble knowledge drawn from the whole population in the minds of one or a few planners, which is impossible; therefore the only sensible way of rationing resources for production is to stand back and let free competition impose its own rationing system. The authoritarian may, however, reply that this argument has become less forceful in view of modern data-processing technology; perhaps we *can* assemble all the relevant facts in a large computer. I find such a reply unimpressive; many of the relevant data, such as individuals' preferences among various consumer goods, are facts which people would have great difficulty in stating explicitly, accurately, and fully to an enquirer. But the liberal has no need to found his case on the ignorance resulting from the dispersal of information, since the ignorance associated with creativity provides a basis quite adequate for his argument. If we agree that humans regularly invent ideas which are genuinely novel and many of which have economic implications, then we must accept that no techniques of information processing could at any given time assemble all the information relevant for planning the ideal economy.[21]

The point being made here is one that ought to have some appeal for intellectuals. We commonly think of the products of an economy as 'things' – tangible goods or, at the most abstract, tangible services; but in fact one of the most important products of any economy, and one of its most important needs, is knowledge: knowledge about how to organize production so as to satisfy the wants of consumers most efficiently. Employees produce things; enterprisers produce economic knowledge by testing alternative ideas about how best to produce what things. The nature of authoritarian government is to hinder the process of economic knowledge-generation, and society needs such knowledge so much that this cannot be a wise thing to do.

The socialist may be correct in holding that replacement of a liberal government by an authoritarian government whose distribution scheme approximates to equalitarianism will raise the standard of living of many members of society (although the rise will at best not be great, since incomes are distributed pyramidally). But this rise will be a once-for-all affair. Under liberalism the average standard of living of members of a society rises constantly, although at any given time some individuals will be ahead of others, and a minority may be moving downwards; under authoritarianism everybody may be at the same level, but this level will not rise, and in fact will fall (since there is no incentive for people to do their jobs – including the training of their successors – well, and since creativity is needed not only to increase the wealth of a society but to maintain the progress already made in the face of unpredictably changing natural conditions).[22]

The incompatibility of authoritarianism and progress is obscured by several factors. One is the gradient nature of the authoritarian/liberal distinction, which means that a society that one tends to think of as 'authoritarian' may yet include enough freedom to permit some progress. More importantly, a highly authoritarian society can progress quite well if it remains in contact with a more liberal society, because it can use the economic knowledge generated by the liberal society to make up for its own failure in this respect. Since the contemporary world includes one large nation (the U.S.A.) and several smaller ones which are highly liberal, as well as a number of highly authoritarian nations (and many in between), this parasitic kind of progress is rather common. Englishmen have grown familiar since the Second World War with the sequence of events in which a new device of some kind is invented in Britain but fails to find backers here for the expensive and risky process needed to translate it from an idea on paper into a series of experimental prototypes and finally into an efficient model that can be mass-produced cheaply enough to find a market; this process is carried out in America, where there are more enterprisers able to back their hunches with cash, but (if the invention turns out to be successful) consumers in Britain as well as everywhere else finally reap the benefits which accrue from the availability of the new device. Britain, while more authoritarian than the U.S.A., is still of course very liberal compared to many other nations; for instance, our prices are largely determined by market forces. The authoritarian economies of Eastern Europe do not permit prices to be determined in this way, a fact which could result in a disastrous misallocation of resources; the problem is solved, at least with respect to trade between the member nations of the Soviet bloc, simply by using the prices reigning in the open market of the West.[23]

A further factor which leads people to question whether authoritarianism and progress are really incompatible is that the particular kind of freedom which is most obviously necessary for progress is purely intellectual, and this is the last category of freedom to be affected by the growth of authoritarianism. Socialists often argue that though in an ideal society production and distribution of goods must be controlled by conscious plans, intellectual life will remain free.[24] But this escape-route from the adverse consequences of socialism is only apparent rather than real.

In the first place, few if any economic advances depend exclusively on intellectual freedom. Even the inventor of the transparent-windowed envelope could not know in advance that there were no hidden snags to his invention – perhaps the edges of the window might have tended to rip on the franking machines, for instance; so the profit eventually to be made by marketing such envelopes involved risking a certain amount of capital in testing out the practicality of the invention. Clearly the development of an idea with greater potential for economic benefit – say, a notably more efficient power-source for cars – is likely to involve the risk of much larger quantities of capital. In a liberal society there will be many individuals with capital to risk, and those who prove to be good judges of such risks will increase their capital and hence their ability to back further enterprises. An authoritarian society may establish a department of state devoted to research and development; but nothing can guarantee that its salaried employees will be good judges of commercial risk, and they will have no incentive to judge well (since they could not justly be penalized for backing ideas that turned out to be failures).

Furthermore, it is naïve to suppose that intellectual freedom could survive indefinitely in an economically authoritarian society. Thought itself may be free, but an individual human mind will never come up with anything worthwhile in isolation from a wider community of minds. Thinkers need access to journals and books in order to discover the current state of play in their discipline, they need to find publishers for their own articles and books so that their ideas can be criticized and improved on by the scholarly community, and they need time to think when they could be working in more obviously productive ways. All these things require a considerable diversion of resources away from alternative uses, and since creative thought is by definition unpredictable (to predict that so-and-so will invent a specified idea next year would be to invent that idea this year) there can be no guarantee that the resources are being well spent. Therefore it is inevitable that in an authoritarian society, in which the allocation of resources is planned to yield maximum production (as opposed to a liberal society in which many people will own private fortunes which they can spend as they please, for instance by endowing or engaging in scholarship for its own sake), original thought will eventually fade away as universities and related institutions are starved of money or required to shift the balance of their activities away from pure research and towards the teaching of (supposedly) useful established knowledge.[25] Intellectual freedom will disappear in an authoritarian society without there necessarily being any plan to suppress non-canonical ideas, as there is in the Soviet Union.

Chomsky, clearly, will claim that the term 'authoritarian' is not properly applicable to his anarcho-syndicalist version of socialism (while agreeing that it does apply to the Russian kind of socialism). But the distinction between a 'free' and an 'unfree' sort of socialism is plausible only so long as we ignore the nature of the interactions that would have to occur between Chomsky's

[margin handwritten note:] this is hard to take seriously given the history of state-supported institutions

'self-governing economic units'. Any enterprise (irrespective of the political complexion of the society in which it exists) must have a stock of capital (certain fixed assets, e.g. land, buildings, tools, of which it has the use), and must receive a continuing supply of certain goods of various categories, in order to make its products. (In some cases the 'capital' and 'supplies' may be very abstract in nature. For instance, the most important component of an author's capital is the knowledge and ability contained in his mind – what is often called 'human capital' – although he will also need to use a library of books and a typewriter; his 'supplies' may include visits to his subjects, as well as paper and typewriter ribbons.) The supplies input to one enterprise will be the output of other enterprises (even in the case of an enterprise which processes raw materials the raw materials have to be mined or otherwise collected; a mining enterprise requires supplies of pit-props and electrical power – and many other things of which I am ignorant – which are produced by enterprises of other kinds). In a complex society, almost any given good which is not a consumer good might be used by any of a large number of diverse enterprises – either as part of its continuing supplies, or as a capital asset, depending on the nature of the good. (In principle this is true of human capital too – we may think of different enterprises as 'using', in a not necessarily pejorative sense, the abilities of their employees; but discussion is likely to be clearer if we concentrate on the case of material goods.) This means that a complex society must somehow make virtually innumerable decisions about which enterprises to assign given goods to. In a Chomskyan syndicalist society, it will constantly happen that syndicate A and syndicate B would both like to use good X, and X can by its nature only go to one of the two. Now, if decisions of this sort are made by the federation which links the syndicates together, then that federation will in fact determine almost every detail of the nature of the society. The members of the syndicates would still be left to decide how to organize their work between themselves, but almost any re-organization is likely to require some modification in the nature of the supplies or capital assets of the syndicate, and whenever that is so the federal government will effectively make the decision as to whether or not to carry out the re-organization. (The same would seem to apply to consumption, in the sense that there will be consumers belonging to different syndicates who would each enjoy any given consumer good; again, it seems that only the federal government could adjudicate between them, if the free-market price system is ruled out as a method of rationing.)

This means that it is of no avail for Chomsky to *say* that the federal organization linking his 'self-governing' enterprises will be 'loose' or 'restricted'; it will in fact have to be enormously powerful. Its members may be democratically elected, but since it will have an immense quantity of work of its own to carry out (and work which will clearly require great expertise) its members will necessarily be quite remote from the people who are actually doing productive work. Chomsky's so-called 'anarchist' society in fact collapses into the centralized state capitalism of the Soviet Union, when one thinks out, more fully than Chomsky has done in print, how it could actually work in practice. (The fact that the members of the federal government might be democratically elected would be a point differentiating such a society from that of the Soviet Union; I would predict, however, that such a society would be so unpleasant to inhabit that it would not be allowed to last long if democracy were retained.)[26] Chomsky quotes the anarcho-syndicalist Diego Abad de Santillan, writing shortly before syndicalism was given its chance in Spain, as saying:

. . . we find no need for the hypothesis of a superior power to organized labour, in order to establish a new order of things. We would thank anyone to point out to us what function, if any, the State can have in an economic organization, where private property has been abolished. . . .

Our federal council of economy is not [sic, for 'will not be', presumably] a political power but an economic and administrative regulating power. It receives its orientation from below and operates in accordance with the resolutions of the regional and national assemblies. It is a liaison corps and nothing else.[27]

The answer to the question in the second sentence quoted is that the state will need to reconcile the inputs and the outputs of the various syndicates, and that this function becomes necessary *precisely when private property has been abolished* (property-owners can be counted on to do the job themselves, as they will seek to maximize returns on their investments in competition with one another); any organ which carries out that function will be much more than a liaison office, and no 'resolutions of regional and national assemblies' could possibly suffice to determine how it is to make its endless detailed decisions.

Chomsky might argue against me that I am gratuitously presupposing that the representatives of the syndicates will be unable to reach an amicable agreement between themselves when several of them would all like to have the use of a given good; only if such agreements are impossible will it be necessary for the federal government to impose a decision. Certainly I do believe that the amicable-agreement system would be a complete non-starter; if humans were all sufficiently unselfish to be able regularly to resolve such conflicts amicably, no governments would have arisen on Earth in the first place.[28] (Chomsky surely would not suggest that the mere fact of grouping people into syndicates implies that they will be less selfish in defending their collective interests than people commonly are in defending their individual interests; it is usually said that committees behave much *more* selfishly than any of their members in isolation.) In practice, each side in such a debate between syndicates whose interests conflict will be familiar with hugely complex reasons why it ought to be allowed to use the good in question and will be unable to master fully the countervailing reasons favouring the other side or sides, so that in many cases no side will give in (and if such negotiations did succeed they would surely be so time-consuming as to leave very few man-hours over for productive work). But even if, *per impossibile*, the amicable-agreement system succeeded, this would not affect the 'authoritarian' nature of the resulting society, in my sense of that term. A society is 'authoritarian' if economic decisions are made by treating certain human opinions as authoritative, and that will be as true in a society in which such decisions are taken by different people in thousands of bargaining-rooms scattered about the country as in a society where they are all taken by one group of individuals in a central committee-room. In a liberal society, by contrast, human opinions, although of course they play various important roles, never act as the ultimate arbiter in economic conflicts (i.e. competitions for scarce goods). In a liberal society, if A wants X and B wants X and A is willing to pay £100 for it while B can only pay £99, then A gets X. Given that X is only one of many inputs to the respective enterprises, it will be a matter of opinion whether A can really afford £100 or not for this particular item; but if A consistently overestimates how high he can go, then he will soon be put out of business by competitors who undercut his prices. Since the amount that A can afford for his inputs depends on what people are willing to pay A for his products, prices in a liberal economy function to assign goods to those uses where they will produce most value; and a price system, under liberalism, is sensitive to all the innumerable variables in a complex economy, while any human decision-maker can take into account only a tiny subset of the whole class of relevant factors. So, even if people were selfless enough to make a Chomskyan, syndicalist system work without appealing to the federal government to resolve disputes, the result would be the same overall economic inefficiency and poverty which result from centrally planned socialism. Fortunately, people are not so unselfish as that.

The only circumstance in which a syndicalist economy might function adequately for a while would be where syndicalism had just been adopted as a political system in a society whose economic structure had until then been determined by market forces. In that case, the syndicates could simply decide (explicitly or tacitly) to continue with the pattern of capital distribution and product exchange between syndicates that had obtained before the switch to syndicalism. But such a political system could not last more than very briefly, because Nature would soon begin to pose new problems that would have to be settled by authority if they were not settled by market forces.

Syndicate A needs to replace worn-out equipment; syndicate B uses raw materials from an exhausted supply; two experienced members of syndicate C have retired or died; three young men have left school and need to be assigned to some particular work. Events of this kind create problems with respect to which the interests of different syndicates will diverge sharply, and the decision to 'carry on as before' does nothing to solve them; if they are not settled naturally by market forces they will have to be settled arbitrarily by central government fiat, and as this process continues syndicalism will soon turn into the state socialism which Chomsky opposes. In Spain, Chomsky points out that it took only a few months for anarcho-syndicalism to be replaced by orthodox Communism, but Chomsky wholly fails to grasp the argument that this was inevitable. He quotes a writer who ascribes the downfall of the anarchists to 'the unsuspected complexity of modern society', but he dismisses this explanation, without discussion, in favour of blaming a middle-class Communist counter-revolution.[29]

If syndicalist society can work only by 'carrying on as before', then it would clearly be wholly incapable of exploiting innovative thought, the one factor which has allowed life in the modern West to be so much pleasanter than it was in previous ages (and which could do the same for the inhabitants of less fortunate parts of the world, if it were allowed to). We have seen that Chomsky, following Pelloutier, advocates an economic order which is 'limited exclusively by the needs of production and consumption'; but for a creative, innovative species like Man the 'needs of production and consumption' are not fixed – we can only discover them through an unending process of competition to serve consumers better than they have been served before. An oak-tree needs just 'soil and air and light', and the needs of future oak-trees will be the same as the needs of past oak-trees (short of biological mutation). The needs of men are not fixed in anything like the same way. For instance, I need (and have) a typewriter. This is not a mere self-indulgence – I really need one, if I am to function as a writer; yet such machines did not exist until a hundred years ago, so before then no one

could have been said to 'need' one. Thus it is strictly meaningless to talk of giving 'a guarantee to all of the material necessities
of a decent existence' (cf. p. 33 above) – any specification of
those necessities would be entirely arbitrary.

There is, of course, another sense of 'need' in which no one
does need typewriters or any other products of human inventiveness: if they all disappeared, humans could survive without
them after a fashion. Humans lived, though not as long as they
live now and in far smaller numbers, in the Stone Age.[30] But no
one, and certainly not Chomsky, suggests that we should
voluntarily re-adopt the way of life of that period. And between
the miserable life of the Stone Age and the luxurious life of the
middle-class American of today there is no sharp divide, only a
long continuum of progress. There is no particular standard of
living which represents the 'decent way of life', so that those who
live better than that standard can reasonably be condemned as
plutocrats who are morally bound to hand over their excess to
relieve the poverty of individuals below the magic line; any
standard of living may look impoverished or luxurious, depending on the standard that one happens to use as a reference.

A socialist may be inclined to object to my presentation of the
contrast between 'liberal' and 'authoritarian' societies on the
ground that it ignores the question of justice. Freedom from
coercion is desirable in its own right, and I have argued that a
society which minimizes coercion will also make most rapid
progress. But I have not argued that the distribution of rewards
in such a society will be just – indeed, I seem to have admitted
that it will not be. Freedom and progress are good, but justice is
good also; according to John Rawls, 'Justice is the first virtue of
social institutions, as truth is of systems of thought.'[31] By what
right do I simply let freedom and progress count for everything
and justice for nothing in arguing for liberalism as against
socialism?

There is a certain hypocrisy about this question as it is put by
socialists in practice, since they commonly claim to offer not
justice *instead of* progress but justice *as well as* progress; in the
parasitic situation referred to above this offer need not necessa-

rily be self-contradictory. There is a real sense in which progress, or indeed even the maintenance of current standards, within a modern authoritarian society is achieved at the expense of those Americans whose economic gambles have failed – a factor which rarely enters the socialist's calculus of justice. But, ignoring this point, which arises from the accidental fact that those who advocate political reform in a world of nation-states are normally arguing for reform in a particular country, the general question remains.

An answer to the question begins by pointing out that the intuitive notion of 'justice' is ambiguous as between two rather different concepts which cannot both be realized in the same society. The first concept is that all particular transactions between individual agents should be 'just' in the sense that each agent receives, in exchange for any goods he hands over or services he performs, the actual value which those goods or services happen to have in the society he inhabits; the second concept of 'justice' is that the total of goods received by any individual in his lifetime should be proportional to his moral worthiness in some sense. The liberal claims that the former concept of justice is realized in a liberal society, and that, apart from its intrinsic attraction, this concept of justice has the virtues of being compatible with individual freedom and of conducing to economic progress and thus raising, as rapidly as possible, the values of whatever goods and services individuals have to offer. The liberal argues further that the second concept of justice is intrinsically unrealizable, and furthermore than any attempt to approximate to it is incompatible with individual freedom and with economic progress; for all these reasons this second concept does not deserve to be one of our goals.

To see that the second concept of justice is in principle unrealizable, consider the simple case where our moral principles declare everyone to be equally morally worthy and hence entitled to an equal total of rewards. The trouble is that the policies which have to be applied in order to equalize rewards are policies which destroy the measure by which we can tell whether rewards are equal. In a liberal society, prices act as an accurate yardstick of the relative value in that society of different goods, so we can compare individuals' total rewards from society by comparing their total expenditure. (Let me stress that of course I appreciate that there are many 'goods' whose value cannot be stated in money terms, such as the love of a virtuous woman, whose price is far above rubies. But, unlike the categories of goods which can come into existence only through the division of labour, 'goods' of this kind are in no sense the product of organized societies, and even the most interventionist of governments, one hopes, cannot influence their distribution; so it is both proper and inevitable that they be left out of account.) If government intervenes to equalize individuals' rewards, then prices automatically cease to correspond to any real property of goods. Thus, if the possessor of some rare and very valuable skill finds himself taxed at a disproportionately high marginal rate, it will be sensible for him to exchange some of his (effectively) badly paid working time for more leisure. As a result his output becomes artificially scarce and therefore artificially dear, while the goods he would have used as inputs to his work become artificially cheap. In practice, governments which embark on this sort of intervention find it necessary to compensate for the effects of one act of interference in the economy by another act of interference, and so on, so that more and more economic decisions are made by government rather than by market forces; the logical conclusion of this process (already reached in the internal economies of the people's democracies)[32] is that the quantities of various goods produced, and their prices, represent more or less wholly arbitrary decisions. (Often, rationing systems have to be used to supplement pricing as a means of determining distribution, and rationing clearly involves even more governmental guesswork.) In such a situation an individual whose tastes run to things which happen to be in shorter supply, or priced higher, than they would be in a free market gets fewer rewards from society than an individual with opposite tastes, even if their aggregate expenditure is equal. In Russia, for instance, I guess that people who enjoy sport or study and are relatively indifferent to the quality of their housing get a far better deal from society than individuals with the reverse tastes (who are surely quite numerous). But I can only guess that (or at least, I could only guess it were it not for the accidental fact that Russia coexists with some relatively liberal economies whose prices can be used to make the comparison); it is characteristic of an authoritarian economy that one cannot know how different individuals' aggregate rewards compare, because one has no objective measure. So in practice the choice lies not between an unequal distribution of rewards in a free market and an equal distribution in an authoritarian system; rather, it lies between an unequal distribution in a free market and an unknowable (and therefore certainly unequal) distribution under authoritarianism.

The case for authoritarianism becomes even worse if we say that the morally proper scheme of distribution would be, not equal shares for all, but some subtler arrangement. Almost anybody, surely, would want to say this; if Chomsky means his equalitarianism literally, few will agree with his concept of justice. Would Chomsky really feel that the plausible slacker who skimps his work when he does it, and claims illness as an excuse for absence whenever he can get away with it, is morally entitled to the same rewards as the dedicated toiler who throws heart and soul into his work and thinks more about the tasks that need to be finished than about the hour when he is free to leave? However, we have no windows into men's minds that would enable us to measure their true moral worth – we cannot reliably distinguish between the slacker and the genuinely incompetent. So a distributive principle which tried to be more sophisticated than equalitarianism would involve yet more governmental guesswork in addition to what we have discussed already.

A further important problem is that it would be very odd to apply a scheme of distributive justice as between only those individuals alive at the same time, since what we do now has important effects on individuals not yet born. (If we were entitled to leave the unborn out of our calculus of justice, then it would be sensible not to waste resources e.g. on planning and building schools which will only begin to take pupils five years or more from now; nobody would agree with this.) But unforeseeable changes in natural conditions and human inventiveness together imply that we have no way of ensuring that the rewards accruing to our descendants will be *equal* to ours, and furthermore it does not seem very natural to want them to be so; many people hope that their children and grandchildren will have *better* lives than they have had, and my own moral intuitions suggest that it is right that people should aim for this. (Chomsky, no doubt correctly, holds that the monotony of production-line working conditions is one of the worst aspects of contemporary Western economies. If he were convinced that it is impractical to abolish these conditions within the working lives of those now suffering them, would he conclude that there is no reason to strive for their future abolition? Of course he would not.) Yet individuals cannot be more morally worthy simply by virtue of being born later, so this moral intuition is incompatible with the idea that rewards should be proportional to moral worth. If equality of rewards as between individuals across time is not a proper goal, what makes it appropriate as between individuals at a given point in time? If one accepts the liberal argument that in order to raise future individuals' rewards we must allow free play to market forces now, with the inevitable result that present individuals' rewards will be unequal, then we will do well to agree that equality of rewards as between present individuals is *not* a desirable political aim. The idea that this kind of equality is a proper aim of politics is very new as a widespread, fashionable view, in Britain at least; we must hope that it is a temporary aberration which will soon be abandoned as its implications come to be understood.

The fact that one of these implications is the abolition of individual liberty is easy to understand; any exercise of freedom involves the use of some goods, and in an authoritarian society no subject has the ultimate right to dispose of any goods. Even free speech requires for its exercise standing-room within earshot of listeners, and standing-room is certainly a good which can be controlled either by the market or by authority (in the people's democracies it is frequently denied by authority to dissidents). Furthermore, if 'free speech' is to mean more than the right to indulge in uninformed, empty saloon-bar rhetoric it requires the use of goods (such as newspapers) which are much costlier than an hour's rental of a soap-box. Other freedoms much more clearly require the use of goods for their exercise. A liberal society depends on the concept of private property; the great majority of goods are at the disposal of some particular individual or another, and no individual or institution is entitled to the use of another's good unless he can provide the owner with some good of equal value in exchange. This applies no less to the government; governments are special in that they alone can coerce people to part with their goods (if they could not they would not be governments), but taxes in a liberal society *taxes* resemble other economic transactions in being fair exchanges; a liberal government maintains the free market against external aggressors and internal criminals, subversives, and would-be monopolists, and in exchange its subjects pay tax in proportion to their gains from membership of the market – ideally, through a flat percentage tax on personal expenditure which returns an aggregate revenue just covering the necessary costs of government. For practical reasons a tax system may have to be less than ideal in a liberal society; but for a liberal it is indefensible to tax progressively (as in modern Britain, where income tax is levied at a rate rising from a 'standard' 34 per cent to a maximum marginal rate of 98 per cent on levels of income which are by no means rare), or to tax capital (either during life or by way of death duties), or indeed to apply any taxes which produce more revenue overall than is needed to maintain the free market in being; taxes of these kinds are not imperfect approximations to a liberal scheme but rather systematic violations of it. Such forms of taxation, where goods are taken from an individual without any pretence that he is receiving a fair return for them, are straightforward theft (though they are not called theft in law for the obvious reason that in this case the thief, unfortunately, controls the legislature). Illiberal taxation is commonly justified as a means of improving the lot of the poor, but this is no justification; individuals do not need government as an (inefficient) intermediary if they wish to make charitable donations, and no one has the right to give away goods to which he himself has no title (a principle that is widely accepted except when the middle party is government).

If one does not accept the morality of private property, clearly, these arguments cease to be valid; and socialists commonly reject the notion of private property as a desirable institution.[33] But notice that there is no rational halfway position; either individuals have the ultimate right to dispose of all their goods except those they relinquish in exchange for others of equal value, or they have no ultimate right over any of them. If an individual is taxed at a rate equivalent to, say, 60 per cent of his personal expenditure in a society where the total costs of market maintenance are only, say, 15 per cent of total personal expenditures, then what right does he have to lay out the remaining 40 per cent of his outgoings in ways that he chooses? (If the reader feels that I am prejudicing the case by choosing a figure as high as 60 per cent, he must be forgetting all the taxes we pay in addition to income tax.) Clearly, if the 60 per cent taxation is legitimate, the answer must be that he is entitled to spend the rest of his money on himself only because government happens to have decided to let him do so. In other words, on this view government is vested with the *ultimate* right to dispose of *all* goods, and an individual subject's 'property' is 'his' only in the sense that a slave's chattels are his, because his owner happens to permit him to keep them. If it is true that any exercise of freedom requires the use of some economic goods, then to ascribe legitimacy to a government which practises blatantly illiberal taxation is effectively to say that the government has (not merely the power, but) the right to permit or to forbid any particular exercise of freedom; and freedom on government sufferance is no freedom at all. A society of free men must be a society which, among other things, refuses to acknowledge the legitimacy of a government unless it proportions the taxes it levies on individuals to the individuals' debts to the government for services rendered. Late twentieth-century Britain is a society of slaves.

Opponents of liberalism sometimes object that liberal societies provide 'freedom' only in a peculiar sense, because a poor man in such a society is not 'free' to drive an expensive car or to send his son to Eton. Obviously, if a society is called 'free' only provided that anybody can dispose of any scarce good he wants, then no society can ever be free. But a liberal society, through the institution of private property and through the phenomenon of economic growth, functions so as to maximize the area of freedom available to an arbitrarily chosen individual. An authoritarian society, in which the right to dispose of all goods is vested in the governors, allows no freedom to any of the governed.

In a liberal society, competition functions to ensure that no one receives less in the market-place than the value of what he has to offer. Competition for customers guarantees that goods will not be priced higher than they are worth, so the selfish and ruthless businessman will make a large profit or receive a high salary only if the products of his business are very valuable to fellow-members of his society – thus a liberal government harnesses selfishness to the service of society. (Of course, if ruthlessness implies breaking the law the situation is different; a liberal government must strictly enforce laws governing fair trade and penalize those who break them.) Competition between employers for labour guarantees that no one need work for less than his work is worth. The socialist notion of 'exploitation' to which Chomsky appeals rests on the assumption that an employer *chooses* how much to pay an employee, while the employee is forced to take what he can get. But this asymmetry represents a superficial, false view of the situation (and one held only by relatively naïve socialists – Marx himself believed no such thing).[34] In a competitive open market, once an enterpriser has used his capital to create a job he has scarcely any more real choice about the rate of pay than has the employee who takes the job. If the employer sets the wage too low, he will fail to attract the calibre of employee he needs; if he sets it too high, he will eventually go out of business because rival enterprises will undercut the price of his products. In a liberal economy, the price of a given category of labour is determined, like all other prices, not by human decision but by the impersonal interaction of demand and supply. If a society contains phenomena which seem incompatible with the notion that everyone is getting the market value of what he has to offer society, the liberal predicts that this will turn out to be caused by governmental interference in the economy.

The obvious example is unemployment; any able-bodied adult's labour must be worth something, so if such people are unable to find work the liberal economy cannot be operating as the recipe provides. In modern Britain, of course, the range of interventionist government measures tending to promote unemployment are too numerous to list. Various Rent Acts have dried up the supply of rented housing, thus freezing the geographical distribution of labour while the geographical distribution of work-opportunities changes. Employment Security laws have made it difficult for employers to get rid of employees, so that they are unnaturally reluctant to take the risk of creating new jobs. A bizarre special tax on self-employment (called a 'Class 4 National Insurance contribution', but differing from any other national or private insurance contribution known to man in that it yields no benefits whatever) encourages individuals to be employees rather than employers. And so on, and so on, and so on. The classical view is that full employment is automatic in a fully liberal society, and there is no good reason to doubt this.[35]

It is sometimes argued that one kind of governmental intervention in an economy that should be approved by liberals themselves is intervention designed to compensate individuals for the results of illiberal policies of the past. (This seems to be the principle, if there is one, motivating the so-called 'reverse discrimination' in favour of women and certain racial minorities which is currently being encouraged by legislation in the U.S.A.) I find this notion quite unpersuasive. In contemporary Britain such a policy would require government to hand over large sums to members of the middle classes who have suffered as a result of the progressive taxation of income that has occurred during most of the twentieth century, and the resources for this would have to be extracted by special extra taxation levied on people, and on the descendants of people, whose welfare benefits have been large in relation to their tax payments in the past. Such a policy would be quite impractical as well as, to my mind at least, utterly distasteful, even if there were any means of discovering how much particular individuals owed or were owed; but obviously it is impossible to know this. It is crucial to the case for liberalism that human knowledge is too limited to allow us to predict the distribution of rewards that will emerge from the free operation of market forces in the future, and a corollary is that we cannot know what distribution would have resulted today from the abolition of specified illiberal policies at some arbitrarily chosen date in the past. The cure for authoritarianism is not more authoritarianism with opposite biases, but liberalism; since a liberal society is a fluid society with much social mobility in either direction, the injustices of the past will iron themselves out automatically in the long run (though, admittedly, not overnight).[36]

If justice is a characteristic of particular transactions, rather than of the total rewards accruing to a person, then it can have no relevance to the question of how much capital (of all categories) a person possesses. In a liberal society, parents will decide for themselves (as until a century or so ago they always did) what education to buy for their children, to what extent to help them financially when they become independent economic agents at their majority, and so forth.[37] For government to tax holdings of capital (whether saved or inherited), or transfers of capital (whether as gifts *inter vivos* or bequests), in addition to taxing the consumption financed by income from that capital, is to take something for nothing; it is thus morally unjustifiable, but furthermore from the liberal point of view it is thoroughly undesirable on practical grounds. Wealth must be inheritable in order to give the relatively wealthy a motive to invest rather than using all their income for consumption; but in any case it is good that as many different individuals as possible should control accumulations of capital, since capital fuels the process of experimentation through which creativity leads to progress. As Hayek says,[38] if there were no such institution as inheritance of wealth it would be desirable, as a means of promoting progress, for the government to make randomly chosen individuals independently wealthy; but inheritance is much more satisfactory, for one thing because the genetic heritability of intelligence (of which more in Ch. 5) leads to a better-than-random chance that the heir to an independency will use his capital productively.[39]

To sum up, then, we can say this about the pattern of distribution produced by liberal government: no specific guarantees are offered to any specific individuals, but the initial (human and financial) capital of an arbitrarily selected future individual will be as great, and the investment opportunities open to present and future individuals will be as diverse and as lucrative, as society can make them. (Here I am assimilating employees and enterprisers by treating an employee as 'investing' his human capital in a particular job which gives him a return in the form of wages.) A society of which this can be said strikes me as having an excellent claim to be called just. (I note for instance that the principles of justice put forward in John Rawls's influential *Theory of Justice* agree with the principles just mentioned surprisingly well,[40] considering that Rawls almost entirely neglects the problems of creativity and ignorance.)

One obvious reaction to liberalism is to point out that any society will contain some individuals who, because they have not made – perhaps have not been able to make – adequate provision against eventualities such as temporary inability to find work, illness, accident, or old age, have literally no means of livelihood, or only enough means for a standard of life lower than seems decent for any human being. (This latter standard is a matter of opinion rather than of objective reality, of course, and it will presumably rise as the average standard of life of a society rises.) People in this situation will be receiving from society no less than they are contributing, i.e. nothing, but our feelings of compassion do not permit us to stand back and let them starve. Compassion is a virtuous impulse, and in a liberal society it will find its outlet in private charities (as opposed to welfare services paid for out of coerced taxation). Thus liberalism offers justice tempered with mercy. If the reader replies by predicting that people will not give enough voluntarily, I can only say that I do not understand (and I do not believe that he understands) what he means by 'enough' in this context.

Here I feel that I may be misunderstood as advocating a harshly inhumane and selfish doctrine which arbitrarily refuses to use governmental power to abolish the evils that afflict the poor. On the contrary, I am a liberal precisely because I wish to see poverty abolished. Thus, for instance, as a liberal I hold that there should be no laws forbidding the employment of young children in coal-mines, and I have no doubt that there have been situations, when society had progressed less far than it has now – possibly in backward parts of the world there may still be situations – in which it is in a child's own interests to be so employed; but I should certainly be horrified if anyone wished to take advantage of abolition of this law in Britain under present-day conditions. Should the reader doubt whether *any* circumstances could justify children working in mines, let him reflect that only long ages of progress separate contemporary man from a naked savage squatting in a cave, eating when he could catch wild game and starving when he could not, and reckoning himself an old man if he lived to twenty-five. Can one doubt that the eight-year-old son of such a one would deem a job in a warm mine, with a weekly wage coming in regularly and shops to spend it in, to be the height of luxury?[41] I advocate liberalism and oppose authoritarianism, because liberalism leads to progress and authoritarianism obstructs progress, and it is progress that abolishes poverty, in the sense of raising the standard of life of the poorer members of a society. The abolition of poverty in this absolute sense entails the retention of relative poverty – there must always be richer and poorer, if the poorer of tomorrow are to live like the richer of yesterday. (The gap between richer and poorer will not necessarily be extremely great, however: the U.S.A. is a more liberal and a wealthier nation than Great Britain, but also one in which the distribution of wealth is more equal than here.)[42]

Progress is a journey with no terminus; accordingly, it is surely always better to travel hopefully than to alight at any particular way-station. Some may disagree. It might be argued that, since there will always be ways of life superior to that which any given person enjoys, therefore there is no point in striving to better our lot – like a mouse on a wheel, we think we are moving forward but our progress is really an illusion. One who holds this view is entitled to try persuading a poor African or Asian – or even a poor Englishman or American – that he is foolish to wish himself richer because all standards of living, properly understood, are equivalent. I could not bring myself to do so.[43]

This, then, in outline, is the nature of and the case for liberalism. I do not claim that the principles I have sketched provide an answer to every possible question about the proper functions of government; there are certainly many political issues over which liberals can reasonably disagree among themselves. (Indeed, it would be inconsistent to suggest that we have a complete, detailed blueprint of the ideal liberal government. The justification of liberalism is in terms of human ignorance, and we are ignorant about how best to organize free markets and reduce the role of government as we are ignorant about other subjects. Liberal-minded economic theorists continue to increase our understanding of how societies can be made more liberal, and there is no reason to suppose that this process need ever end.[44] Notice in particular that the arguments for liberalism do not presuppose the possibility of what is technically called 'perfect competition'; they merely assert that we shall progress more rapidly the closer we succeed in conforming our societies to this unattainable ideal.) Nor do I suggest that a society with numerous authoritarian traits, such as that of contemporary Britain, ought to become wholly liberal overnight – much misery would be caused if this were to happen. But I do claim that as a description of the ideal type of society the foregoing is both consistent and a practical possibility. The questions my account leaves open do not conceal difficulties which undermine the basic principles of liberalism; societies relatively close to the liberal ideal have existed, for instance in Britain during the eighteenth and nineteenth centuries, in the U.S.A. before the New Deal, and nothing in our present material situation forces us to abandon liberalism now.[45] If the will to do so could be found, in the long run it would be to everyone's advantage to reverse the trend of recent decades and embark on an orderly process of dismantling the apparatus of unnecessary governmental control to which we have grown increasingly addicted.

As I have presented the liberal case, it falls into two rather distinct parts: on one hand the moral issue (I have argued that a liberal society is a just society on one concept of justice, whereas an authoritarian society must be unjust on any concept of justice) and on the other hand the more practical issue (I have argued that liberalism raises, and authoritarianism depresses, individuals' living standards). The two issues cannot be separated; the moral case for liberalism depends largely on the validity of the practical case (if the practical consequences of the two kinds of government were reversed, then the ethic of freedom and private property would lose much or all of its cogency). In the preceding pages I have spent some time on the moral issue, as part of a process of clearing the decks before I confront the main subject of this book, namely Chomsky's novel linguistic/philosophical argument against liberalism. Chomsky's argument has to do with the practical economic consequences of liberal policies, and it bears on the moral issue only indirectly via its implications for the practical issue. Therefore it is with the practical question that we shall be mainly concerned in the body of this book. As we shall see, Chomsky believes that there is a fatal flaw in the argument that liberal government is more conducive than authoritarian government to economic progress: that argument depends on empiricist assumptions about human nature which Chomsky believes he can refute. I defer a detailed consideration of Chomsky's novel refutation of empiricism until the next chapter; in the remainder

[margin handwritten note: moral & practical case.]

of this chapter I continue to explore the relationship between contrasting styles of government and the contrast between empiricist and rationalist views of human nature.

The close relationship between the liberal philosophy of politics and the empiricist philosophy of knowledge will by now be apparent. The empiricist holds that the path towards knowledge consists of individuals proposing diverse hypotheses as rival attempts to account for observed phenomena; a theory which survives the process of criticism and attempted refutation is then available to others who need not themselves recapitulate the process of trial and error by which the theory was perfected (and thus society as a whole steadily increases its level of knowledge), but at the same time all knowledge is provisional – the good scientist will bear in mind that even the oldest-established and most certain-seeming of his beliefs may be overturned by a better theory tomorrow.[46] Similarly, the liberal holds that the route to wealth involves leaving individuals free to secure for themselves the best lives they can by competing to discover the most valuable ways of exploiting natural resources and their own abilities. Once an enterpriser has pressed the risky process of developing a novel means of wealth-creation to a successful conclusion, others can reap the benefits accruing from it without taking the same risks (so that the average standard of living of a society rises steadily); but even a very old-established means of livelihood may become unprofitable tomorrow if someone discovers a more efficient way of achieving the same ends, so that a wise citizen (whether enterpriser or employee) will retain maximum flexibility in his approach to earning a living.

For the liberal it is a contradiction in terms to speak of a man being free from *any* constraints imposed by nature and fellow men, and silly to suggest, as Chomsky does, that external influences have an inherent tendency to 'warp' a man's development. One might with equal appropriateness suggest that observation of the phenomena or exposure to standard views are inherently likely to 'warp' whatever theory a man might develop by unaided ratiocination to account e.g. for the Northern Lights. Human life, both economic and intellectual, is always determined by *both* environmental influences and spontaneous mental development, never by one or the other alone. One of the problems in Chomsky's academic linguistics lies in the rather unsophisticated contrast he draws between 'innate' and 'learned' behaviour; it just does not mean very much to speak of an aspect of human behaviour, such as language, as being largely innate rather than learned – if 'innate' means 'independent of external influences', then no properties of human beings are innate.[47] Chomsky's linguistic nativism can be spelled out in such a way as to escape the charge of vacuity, but Chomsky himself seems not to be sufficiently aware of this logical difficulty in his ideas. And Chomsky commits the same fallacy very much more crudely and obviously in his discussions of politics. Thus, he quotes with approval, as a statement of the 'single leading idea within the anarchist tradition', a passage of Bakunin's which begins, promisingly, 'I am a fanatic lover of liberty, considering it as the unique condition under which intelligence, dignity and human happiness can develop and grow' – but which goes on to explain carefully that by 'liberty' Bakunin means, not any of the kinds of liberty which can be realized in our imperfect world, but rather 'liberty that recognizes *no* restrictions other than those determined by the laws of our own individual nature' (my italics).[48] Such liberty is incompatible, clearly, not merely with the liberty of other people but with simple physical reality. Thus, suppose I formulate a wish to spend the next half-hour swimming in a lake (as I well might); then, for Bakunin and for Chomsky, I am unfree unless a lake materializes in the dry corner of Yorkshire in which I write. If Bakunin and Chomsky do not mean this, they mean nothing; and liberty of this kind is possible only in the world of daydreams. To attack liberal society on the grounds that the liberty it provides is inferior to the kind of liberty Bakunin and Chomsky describe (which is perfectly true) is in the highest degree irresponsible. Since a liberal society is the freest society possible in the real world, the only possible practical effect of a successful attack on liberalism is to bring about some less free, authoritarian society.

The ideal political system is not one in which people are subject to no external pressures, which is a meaningless idea, but rather one in which the pattern of external pressures is such as to promote rather than hinder men's realization of their intrinsic potential. Since we cannot know in advance what new ideas are waiting to be thought of, and since we cannot know, of a new and untried idea, whether or not it is one whose application will be beneficial to mankind, any pressure deriving from human beliefs about what overall pattern of production is most efficient and what overall pattern of distribution is fairest must inevitably lead to total wealth being held below what it could be, and to distortion in the pattern of incentives graded according to individuals' different contributions to the wealth of society. Because of men's ignorance, the only external pressures on people which promote the realization of their potential are the impersonal pressures of free competition; intervention by human governors should be limited to preventing interference with the mechanisms of the open market or with individuals' enjoyment of the benefits they win therein.

Even the empiricist can recognize possible drawbacks in the liberal ideal. Liberalism provides freedom and progress at the expense of security; since security is widely felt to be desirable, it might be sensible to sacrifice some measure of freedom and progress in return for some measure of increased security. The British National Health Service, for instance, involves coercing each taxpayer to pay for services which he may never use, but he receives in return the assurance that if he or his dependants ever need to use these services heavily they will not be denied him because of lack of money. Within a liberal society a similar effect can of course be achieved through private insurance; but it is a characteristic of commercial insurance that the benefits it provides are defined in advance, it lacks the 'open-ended' commitment which the N.H.S. appears to offer. This open-endedness, however, is more apparent than real. The N.H.S., like any other institution, operates on limited resources; as very costly methods of treatment are developed for previously incurable diseases, the fact that the N.H.S. cannot really guarantee that a sick man will receive all known potentially-beneficial methods of treatment, which was always true, is becoming obvious.[49] Where an institution like the N.H.S. really does differ from private insurance is that, under the N.H.S., decisions about what can and cannot be done for an individual are made by a high authority outside that individual's control. The kind of 'security' that can be provided by governments is the lack of responsibility for one's own fate which is said to be one of the compensations in the life of a slave.

The rationalist, however, tends to reject liberalism for more fundamental reasons. A rationalist may be largely in agreement with liberals as to the values which society ought to promote; but the rationalist rejects the empiricist premises from which a liberal infers that an unplanned society will best promote those values. The case for liberalism depends on the belief that humans are incurably ignorant, and the rationalist does not accept this. No doubt most people in practice are very ignorant, the rationalist will tend to argue, but that is because they are not intellectuals. The important truths are already buried in our minds waiting to be born into conscious awareness. By taking thought, it ought to be possible to work out what the ideal organization for a society is; and, if so, then it would clearly be irresponsibility on the part of the intellectual to leave social arrangements to be determined by the hazards of competition between ideas thrown up by every eccentric up and down the country.

Insofar as it is based on philosophical rationalism in the Platonic and Cartesian tradition, this attitude just cannot be taken seriously. We have seen that where Plato and Descartes claimed that we had innate, certain knowledge other than of truths of logic, they have been decisively refuted; and the kind of knowledge which is relevant for deciding how best to allocate a nation's resources for the efficient production of wealth is obviously much more particular, much further removed from logical generality than were the 'innate ideas' identified by Plato and Descartes. But, as already suggested, rationalism has had its greatest influence as a general attitude of mind rather than as an explicit philosophy. No philosopher, I believe, has ever argued that it is possible by *a priori* reasoning to determine, say, whether the diverse benefits to be gained by designing, manufacturing, and operating supersonic airliners outweigh the diverse costs entailed; but, if one is brought up on a background of rationalist rather than empiricist thought, one may be inclined to overlook the fact that any such question is sure to involve many hidden factors that will only emerge when one begins the experiment. Classical rationalism does not, perhaps, entail the scientistic fallacy, but it certainly encourages it strongly.

The obvious contemporary examples of societies organized in accordance with rationalist premises are the socialist people's democracies of the East. But there are societies which we tend to think of as closer to our own which possess noticeably rationalist institutions in areas of life which, because of their tangential relevance to economics, have scarcely yet been touched by the trend away from empiricism in modern Britain and America. France offers many examples.[50]

Consider, for instance, the (originally French) metric system of weights, measures, and the like, as contrasted with the system still in use in Britain and, with slight variations, in the U.S.A. (although fated soon to disappear in both countries, I believe). The British/American system is highly complex and irregular, and can be seen to have grown up over a long period of time during which new units have been introduced as the need for them arose, while other units dropped out as they ceased to play a useful role. Although parsimony in the number of units played a part in moulding the system, so that e.g. the ell and the furlong became obsolete, parsimony was never an overriding factor; feet and yards remain alongside each other, presumably because the force of gravity makes it convenient to measure vertical distances in smaller units than horizontal distances. Indeed, in recent decades the range of units used in Britain and America has included the units of the French system for certain special purposes: namely those of the sciences, where ease of computation tends to be much more important than absolute size of units. Clearly, no one man or committee charged with producing a system of measurements would ever have come up with anything like the British/American system as it has evolved; but that fact is a virtue of our system, not a vice. There is no virtue in complexity for its own sake; but the complexity in question is a by-product of evolution by trial and error, and that process is virtuous because it produces an end-result superior in practice to anything that can be created by the fallible and limited reasoning power of a single individual. To sell eggs by the dozen seems, *a priori*, a delightfully quaint custom; it looks more sensible when one tries to design a carton to hold ten eggs.[51]

I do not suggest that the French and other nations with long experience of metric measurement are struggling to cope with a neat but impractical system; while the metric system may quite likely be somewhat less convenient in practice than the British/American system, any such difference is clearly not overwhelming. But then the system of measurements actually employed on the continent of Europe and elsewhere is somewhat different from the neat, rational system promulgated by the French Academy of Sciences in 1790. The decimal calendar and the metric unit of arc, for instance, were abandoned after a few years; the system as now used contains numerous quirks (e.g. a simple term, *livre*, for a half-kilogramme) which makes it less neat but, presumably, more practical. Rationalism dies hard, however, and the new Système International of units constitutes a valiant attempt to make the metric system neater than ever; thus there is now officially no unit of length between the millimetre and the metre, despite the imperfect eyesight of many of the ordinary mortals who will be asked to operate the system.[52]

Examples of rationalist French institutions corresponding to empiricist British ones can be multiplied indefinitely. Let me briefly cite two more. In Britain, headmasters even of state-owned schools have complete freedom over syllabus with the sole exception of a (very variously interpreted) requirement that religious education be included; in France it has been said with only slight exaggeration that the minister of education can look at his watch and tell you what book is open at which page on the desk of each twelve-year-old in the country.[53] (Recently, however, French schools have adopted more flexible syllabuses; as in the case of the metric system, even rationalists are forced by experience to revise their plans.) In Britain, local government is administered by elected councillors working within a broad constitutional framework; in France the national government appoints prefects to administer the departments in accordance with its detailed wishes. In both cases the philosophical justification of the rival systems is clear. If successful institutions are achieved only by trial and error, then Whitehall does well to leave schools or county councils free to experiment and to imitate the successful experiments of others. But if the ideal method of organizing human affairs is available to the introspection of a Platonic philosopher-king, then the sensible thing is to assemble the available philosopher-kings in Paris and provide them with the means of imposing their plans throughout the country.[54]

While rationalists will naturally incline towards an authoritarian political philosophy which demands that governments should actively organize production and distribution, nothing in rationalism implies any particular productive or distributive principles. Rationalists can and do disagree about the principles which governments should follow. There tends to be little dispute about production (people feel that the principle should be 'produce as much as possible', without realizing that in the absence of a competition-based price system we have no way of knowing whether a light-bulb is a more or less valuable product than a bottle of ink) but a great deal of disagreement about distribution.[55] It is perfectly possible to be a rationalist and claim that the 'right' distributive principle is quite different from anything that might count as a formulation of socialism. Thus one might hold that certain specified individuals or groups are entitled to particularly large slices of the national cake – say, a hereditary aristrocracy,[56] the members of influential trade unions,[57] or the governors themselves.[58, 59] However, few explicit authoritarian distributive principles other than those which can roughly be called 'socialist' are likely to appeal to many people's moral sensibilities.

One principle that has historically exerted considerable appeal is the principle which we may call 'conservatism'.[60] This principle ordains that the particular patterns of production and distribution which have emerged at any given time, perhaps from a liberal process of free competition, should remain as the productive and distributive patterns of the future. One sees the attractions of conservatism. In the first place it answers a wide-spread human love of the familiar and fear of change; but, more important, since a productive and distributive pattern which has emerged from a competitive process will be the most efficient and just of the known patterns for society, is it not sensible to stick with it? But the answer is that the conservative is making inconsistent assumptions. A social pattern which has not previously been consciously chosen will be better than the known alternatives only given the empiricist belief in the virtues of uncontrolled competition; but the conscious decision to stick in future with *any* fixed social pattern is sensible only given the rationalist assumption that we can know all the possibilities and consciously choose the best. If one can swallow rationalism, one can reasonably be a socialist, and if one believes in empiricism one may be a liberal, but the conservative can appeal to no consistent intellectual basis for his ideal. In the days when the Conservative party was conservative, it was justly nicknamed the 'stupid party'.[61]

There is a sense in which conservatism is an intermediate position between liberalism and socialism. If a conservative government maintains in being a pattern of society which was originally produced by free competition, then, although consciously imposed, this society will share features common to liberal societies. Capital will be distributed widely rather than concentrated in the hands of government, and all the pre-conditions for further progress will be present; indeed, it will be difficult for government to rein in the tendency to progress. A period of conservatism need be only a temporary hiatus in the life of an otherwise liberal society. Under socialism, on the other hand, society is reorganized in such a way that the tendency to progress disappears; government acquires a monopoly of capital and knowledge, abolition of competition removes the price yardstick against which innovations can be evaluated and the incentive to adopt them if successful. But, while in terms of its practical consequences conservatism may be viewed as a halfway house between liberalism and socialism, in principle the three ideals are most appropriately analysed in terms of two orthogonal dimensions. Conservatism differs from socialism as to how society should be organized, while liberalism differs from both these in denying that society should be consciously *organized* at all. If we contrast conservatism and socialism as 'right' versus 'left', then we ought to use some third direction – say, 'forward' – to indicate the liberal ideal.

Chomsky sees it as important to emphasize that the liberal/authoritarian dimension is not the only dimension along which diverse economic systems can be placed. He deals sarcastically with a statement in the standard textbook *Economics*, by the Nobel prizewinner Paul Samuelson, to the effect that 'the relevant choice for policy today' is to determine which position on the liberal/authoritarian scale the economy should occupy. 'No doubt one can place economic systems along this scale,' Chomsky comments, but it is a sad reflection on the current state of the academic social sciences that this question should seem so all-important.[62] What we really ought to be discussing is whether production should be controlled 'democratically', by the people actually doing the producing, or 'autocratically', by decisions passed down from higher authority whether this be government or private owners of capital. But Chomsky quite fails to see that the liberal/authoritarian dimension, while certainly not the only scale in terms of which an economy can be described, is logically prior to all others. If Chomsky's scale of 'democracy' v. 'autocracy' is not just liberalism v. authoritarianism under different labels, and we must assume from Chomsky's reaction to Samuelson that it is not, then it must refer to a difference in methods by which government is to arrive at a plan for production; to hold that there should be such a plan is to be an authoritarian. It is true that government in an authoritarian society could choose to formulate its plan for production in terms which make crucial reference to the wishes of the 'syndicates'. Thus, it might for instance ordain as a general rule that whenever two or more syndicates are rival contenders for the use of some good, the good is to go to whichever syndicate has waited longest since it last won such a conflict. But such a procedure for making economic decisions would be just as 'authoritarian', in our sense, as a system in which the central government handed down orders and rations of goods to the syndicates irrespective of their members' wishes (and the former procedure would presumably be a particularly inefficient variety of authoritarianism, since it systematically excludes the merits of the case from playing a part in resolving individual economic conflicts between syndicates). As already pointed out, an economy is no less authoritarian because the opinions to which the political system grants authoritative status are scattered over different parts of the society rather than concentrated in the capital city. Only a liberal society, as I have defined it, is not authoritarian, in that economic conflicts in such a society are ultimately decided not by any human authority but by the neutral arbitration of Nature.

Certainly Chomsky blurs the issue between liberalism and his own position, for instance by borrowing much of the rhetoric of liberalism. The words 'free' and 'freedom' occur repeatedly in the passages where he discusses his positive political ideals; he condemns his opponents e.g. by referring to 'capitalism and other authoritarian forms'.[63] Objecting to a passage in which Anthony Crosland states that socialism is about 'how we distribute our wealth and allocate our resources', Chomsky retorts that socialism should be about 'the liberation of the creative impulse and the reconstruction of society to this end'.[64] All this sounds as if 'socialism' might be simply Chomsky's private term for liberalism. But it is not. Chomsky's ideal society is described as having features which are wholly incompatible with liberalism. Thus, everybody's income should be equal. But, under liberalism, although we cannot predict in advance who will succeed in gaining a high income, we can be quite sure that incomes will never be equal. Among the 'workers' councils and other self-governing units' which make up the 'federal industrial republic' portrayed by Chomsky, some will succeed in finding more efficient methods of production or improved types of product, and in a free market these units will increase their incomes at the expense of units which stick with old products and methods of production, or whose innovatory experiments are unsuccessful. Incomes will be equal only if the federal government equalizes them by taxation or otherwise; by removing the rewards for successful innovation, such a policy would remove the incentive to progress (or even to maintain the progress achieved to date, since there would be no penalty for idleness or for failure to adapt to changing physical conditions).

We might, of course, interpret Chomsky as suggesting by his remarks about democratic control of production that the market should be free as between his self-governing economic units (so that economic conflicts between syndicates can be resolved without intervention by the federal government) and that work and income should be shared on an equalitarian principle only within them. In that case, the complexion of the resulting society would depend crucially on the size of the units. At the logical extreme, at which a 'self-governing unit' is an individual worker, we would in fact have a liberal economy. But Chomsky certainly intends his units to comprise more than one worker; the personnel of a single small factory might be about the size of group constituting a Chomskyan unit. In this case we would have moved some way, but not too far, from a liberal economy; in modern industrial conditions pay on a factory floor often has to be equal because conveyor-belt production makes it impossible to factor out different individuals' contributions and pay piece-work rates. But I cannot believe Chomsky's passionate rhetoric is aimed merely at levelling income differentials within individual factories while leaving great disparities of income between workers in neighbouring enterprises in the same town. Clearly he must intend equalization within the republic as a whole.

Indeed, not only does Chomsky intend income to be equalized society-wide as between different workers: he also advocates a kind of society-wide equalization of work. Replying to the obvious objection that equal incomes will result in a shortage of people willing to do the more unpleasant but necessary kinds of work, Chomsky explains that in his ideal state the unpleasant work would be shared equally among everybody, while economic incentives would not be needed to persuade people to do the enjoyable tasks.[65] One problem here is that a state in which men with very valuable talents were forced to spend part of each working day on unskilled labour would inevitably suffer a further drop in overall standard of living in addition to the drops entailed by absence of incentives for diligence and adaptability and absence of a competition-based system for rationing resources. More important, perhaps, the work of the world just cannot be categorized into a group of 'dirty jobs' which might reasonably be shared out equally as a matter of morality, together with a range of tasks which are so intrinsically enjoyable that people will do them voluntarily irrespective of financial inducements. There are certain kinds of work in the latter category: academic research, writing, the arts; but the great majority of jobs fall at intermediate points between the two extremes. Even if we had an objective measure of the pleasantness or otherwise of different tasks – and, under authoritarianism, we could have no such objective measure – it would obviously be quite impractical to share out all work other than research, writing, and the arts, in such a way that everybody did a fair share of work at each level of pleasantness. The value of given work, like the value of a good, derives from a balance between supply and demand, and the 'supply' side of the equation is a function of people's willingness to do work of that level of pleasantness, as well as of the number of people qualified to do the work. In a free market, wage rates will reflect this value. As R. J. Herrnstein points out against Chomsky, since it is pleasanter to paint the inside of a house than the outside, if the level of skill needed (and, one should add, the demand) is the same in either case then interior decorators will command lower fees than housepainters.[66] This leaves the choice open to the individual; in a liberal society no one is forced to contribute the maximum value of which he is capable to society (some people are hard workers, others prefer an easy-going life – these psychological differences are real and are entitled to our respect), but rewards will be in proportion to contributions.[67]

Even in the relatively authoritarian climate of opinion now obtaining, the substance of the last few paragraphs may seem too much a statement of the obvious to be worth writing. Socialists in the Marxist tradition, however, have an answer to it. I have taken for granted – what is plainly true in all the social spheres of which I have any experience – that the prospect of receiving a larger quantity of goods (in the broadest sense, including not merely consumable objects but e.g. the peace of mind provided by insurance, or the knowledge that one will bequeath enough to make a wide range of opportunities available to one's descendants) succeeds as an incentive to work, and that if this incentive were removed then people would do very much less work than they do at present (in the absence of governmental coercion). According to Marx, however, this fact is not a law of human nature but a mere by-product of a liberal (in Marx's terms, 'capitalist') economy; people's psychological attitudes are part of the 'superstructure' of a society, and this is determined by the particular stage of economic development which a society happens to have reached.

The mode of production of material life conditions the social, political, and intellectual life process in general. It is not the consciousness of men that determines their being, but, on the contrary, their social being that determines their consciousness.[68]

The notion of private property is tied to the 'capitalist mode of production'; when full socialism is attained, it may be that labour will not need to be motivated by incentives, and men will work selflessly on behalf of society in general as, now, they work selflessly on behalf of their narrow circle of family dependants. Non-socialists are of course likely to find this suggestion implausible on purely empirical grounds; and whether or not it corresponds to what Marx envisaged is quite unclear (Marx was much more explicit on the subject of the defects of capitalism than on the communist society which was to replace it).[69] But, even if socialists of other stripes do choose to avail themselves of this principle, the important thing for us to note is that Chomsky cannot do so. The essence of Chomsky's particular brand of rationalist politics is that human behaviour should not be controlled by governments because human nature is fixed rather than adaptable. So, if people are moderately selfish, and feel more responsibility for the fate of their own family than for that of outsiders, in contemporary society, then we must on Chomsky's premisses conclude (as many of us would conclude independently of Chomsky) that people will go on being moderately selfish and caring more for their family than for others in any future society.

It is of course open to Chomsky as a logical possibility to argue that his linguistic premisses show only that *certain aspects* of human nature are fixed, and to suggest that selfishness may be one of the traits which are affected by the nature of one's social environment. But for Chomsky to argue in this way would be to give up the match entirely. We have no empirical evidence to suggest that degree of altruism is one of the more malleable of human psychological traits; and the whole argument of Chomsky's with which this book is concerned consists of inferring, from observations of invariance in certain quite specialized aspects of psychology, that psychological invariance is valid as a relatively general principle. If Chomsky tried to escape through the logical loophole just discussed, his opponent would be equally entitled to reject Chomsky's argument *in toto* on the grounds that 'it is . . . a great intellectual leap from observations on the basis for cognitive development to particular conclusions on the laws of our nature and the conditions for their fulfill-ment'.[70]

Chomsky is aware that other socialists tend to believe that there is no such thing as a fixed human nature; he quotes statements by Antonio Gramsci and by Lucien Malson to this effect.[71]

He does not, however, seem to realize the central role that this tenet played for Marx himself; of Gramsci's paraphrase of Marx, 'there does not exist an abstract, fixed, and immutable "human nature" . . . but . . . human nature is the totality of historically determined social relations', Chomsky says that it is 'a questionable reading of Marx',[72] although it seems very fair as an exegesis of the passage in the *Critique of Political Economy* just referred to, or of various passages in Marx's *German Ideology* of 1845–6 – if Marx actually believed something different, as claimed by Engels after Marx's death,[73] this just means that Marx's theories were inconsistent (as they certainly were).[74] And Chomsky shows no sign at all that he appreciates how awkward invariance of human nature is for his own political ideal. Even in moderately authoritarian societies, the apparatus of graded rewards and punishments is commonly justified as a device for getting the work of the world done by people who by nature are selfish and lazy. Chomsky wants to sweep that apparatus away, while asserting that human nature is constant. If humans are *already* the saints which this programme suggests, why does Chomsky believe (as, realistically, he does)[75] that the prospect of his political ideal being realized is a remote one?[76]

Often as Chomsky uses the word 'freedom', then, his ideal, equalitarian society must be authoritarian. And the coercive aspect of authoritarianism is specially salient in Chomsky's version; whereas an orthodox Marxist can claim that a new society will produce a new man for whom the service of the State will be perfect freedom, Chomsky emphasizes that any society will be made up of the same kind of men that we know today. Thus Chomsky has simply misappropriated the term 'freedom'; if he means anything by it, it cannot be the usual meaning of the term, but the appeal of the word lies in the fact that people take Chomsky to mean what everyone else means by it.[77]

One might suppose that his inconsistency in using the rhetoric of liberalism to advocate socialism would make Chomsky less dangerous an opponent than other authoritarians, but quite the reverse is true. If a more straightforward socialist offers to provide equality in exchange for liberty, one will ponder the bargain and may realize that it is a bad one. When Chomsky offers equality and liberty too, people do not detect the inconsistency (or assume that if a man with Chomsky's philosophical credentials sees no inconsistency then they must be mistaken in suspecting one) and feel the offer to be one they can hardly refuse. Chomsky is far from the first to use this gambit, of course; many politicians have advocated 'libertarian socialism', as if the phrase were more meaningful than 'round square' or 'rainbow's end'.[78] But politicians often have no philosophical pretensions; from Chomsky we are entitled to expect better things. If a society opts for socialism and liberty combined, it is fairly clear which (if either) of the incompatibles it will get.

However, once one rejects the arguments for liberalism, the fact that a society is authoritarian ceases to be a criticism of it; and I certainly agree that if one accepts the need for or the inevitability of planning and coercion by government, then some version of socialism will be the only kind of authoritarianism that is not repugnant to our moral instincts. In the next chapter, we shall examine the light shed by the nature of language on the case for and against liberalism.

4 Linguistics versus Liberalism

We have clarified the distinction between two fundamentally opposed political ideals, liberalism and socialism; and we have seen that these two ideals rest on contrasting philosophical approaches to the nature of human understanding: liberalism being founded on empiricism, socialism on rationalism. Rationalism, as a philosophical theory in the tradition of Plato and Descartes, seems to have been straightforwardly refuted by the growth of scientific knowledge, so that those who advocate socialist modes of government appear to stand on very shaky intellectual ground. Many contemporary socialists certainly spend little or no time thinking about the philosophy of knowledge, and it is no doubt inevitable that this should be so. In the heyday of liberalism there were many statesmen who did much to further the cause of freedom while being empiricists only in the sense that empiricist assumptions formed the unquestioned background of their mental lives, rather than in the sense that they consciously reflected on philosophical problems – it is in opposition that one is forced to examine the foundations on which one's political creed is based.

However, Chomsky is as much philosopher as political theorist; and he claims to base his politics not on the old rationalism of Plato and Descartes, which fell victim to the increase of scientific knowledge about the exterior world of Nature, but on a new rationalism, which is emerging from the more recent growth of scientific knowledge about the interior world of Man. In this chapter, then, we turn to consider, in more detail than before, how far the specific facts revealed by modern studies of language and related phenomena support a particular view of human nature from which political conclusions can be drawn.[1]

As a preliminary to this, we should first clear out of the way some objections which Chomsky advances against liberalism that have relatively little to do with the deeper philosophical issues under discussion. Although, at the philosophical level, Chomsky attacks empiricism as a living and influential theory which needs to be overcome by careful arguments, in the political arena Chomsky shows no such respect for liberalism. We have seen that Chomsky prefers to neglect the issue of liberalism v. authoritarianism in favour of advocating one particular species of authoritarianism against its rivals. The reason for this is that, as far as Chomsky is concerned, liberalism is dead. 'Classical liberal thought . . . has been unable to survive the age of industrial capitalism.'[2]

This sort of remark could mean a number of things, and Chomsky takes fewer pains than he might to elucidate it. If by the term 'classical' Chomsky alludes to the fact that liberal ideas about the nature of societies and the proper functioning of governments have considerably broadened and deepened since the days of John Locke or Adam Smith, this is certainly true and very much as it should be. If Chomsky's remark implies, as in one's cynical moments one suspects it might, that he is simply unacquainted with such monuments of modern liberal thought as Popper's *Open Society and its Enemies* and *The Poverty of Historicism*, Hayek's *Road to Serfdom* and *Constitution of Liberty*, then Chomsky exposes himself as unqualified to discuss political theory; as well might one discourse on the origin of species who never heard of Darwin. Chomsky cites Rudolf Rocker's *Anarcho-Syndicalism*, published in 1938, and Karl Polanyi's *Great Transformation*, published in 1944, as having described 'the collapse of liberal doctrine in the nineteenth century'. Popper and Hayek are flourishing in our own day, and neither has yet seen fit to abandon liberalism.[3]

Liberalism, as we have seen, has 'collapsed' in the sense that it has gone rather far out of fashion in the intellectual world of the twentieth century; both Popper and Hayek write with the awareness that they are expressing what have become something like minority views. And, to a certain brand of socialist, this unmodishness of liberalism is less completely irrelevant to an assessment of its truth or falsity than the average reader may take it to be. There is a strand in Marx's thought, inherited from Hegel,[4] according to which not just our perception of truth but truth itself is a function of the historical stage of development reached by a society. There is no absolute morality independent of the economic basis; the productive relationships that obtain under 'capitalism', i.e. liberalism as a state of society, give rise to 'bourgeois morality', i.e. liberalism as a moral ideal, while the coming proletarian revolution will usher in not only a new form of society but a new morality to go with it. The advent of socialism, according to Marx, is made inevitable by a law of history, but though men have no power to choose whether or not socialism shall come into being, they can *and should* struggle to 'shorten and lessen its birth-pangs'.[5] But, if there is no absolute morality, why is it good to work for the proletarian revolution and wicked to work against it? The transition from healthy maturity to the decrepitude of old age is inevitable in a human body, but few of us feel that we are therefore morally obliged to speed up the process in ourselves or in others. (We all accept that birth-pangs should be shortened; but what Marx calls the birth-pangs of socialism might equally be called the death-throes of liberalism, a metaphor which would not work so well for Marx.) The answer seems to be that Marx felt that because everyone (as he thought) was coming to believe (or shortly would be coming to believe) that proletarian morality was right, therefore it *was* right.[6] To this kind of argument there is no reply; if someone believes that fashionable views are correct *because* they are fashionable, there seems little point in trying to convert him to an admittedly unfashionable view. As has often been pointed out, Marx's own life seems to refute these notions; he advocated socialism while leading a bourgeois and, in his later years, comfortable life (financed largely out of the profits of the cotton trade) in a society dominated by liberal ideology, thus demonstrating both that an individual's beliefs are not necessarily determined by his economic situation and that he recognized a standard of truth other than fashionability. And certainly Chomsky cannot use the fact that liberalism is out of fashion as an argument against it; in both his professional and political roles, after all, as he clearly recognizes, Chomsky has spent much of his life arguing points of view scarcely any more fashionable than liberalism is now. In linguistics, Chomsky has won the day; but readers familiar only with the reputation Chomsky now enjoys within the discipline should realize that the note of stridency which occasionally crops up in Chomsky's exposition of his theories on language derives from a time, twenty years ago, when views incompatible with his were taken so wholly for granted that he found it difficult to get a fair hearing.

There remains, of course, the possibility that Chomsky regards liberalism as 'dead' in the sense that events or earlier writers have refuted it so clearly that it can no longer be regarded by men of good faith as a tenable position – hardly flattering to scholars such as Hayek, but certainly a more intellectually respectable reason for Chomsky's curt dismissal of liberalism than the other possibilities mentioned. And Chomsky does refer to a number of such arguments against liberalism; but none of them hold water.

Thus, in the passage quoted above, Chomsky cites Ruldolf Rocker and Karl Polanyi against liberalism. Rocker's *Anarcho-Syndicalism*, while no doubt valuable as a brief history of the anarchist and anarcho-syndicalist movements, scarcely seems to contain serious arguments against liberalism.[7] Polanyi's book is weightier, but his objections to liberalism can easily be refuted. The essence of Polanyi's argument is that liberalism has been rejected because, in breaking down traditional social relationships, it made people aware for the first time of the importance of those relationships.[8] Although Polanyi claims not to be a Marxist, there is a clear echo here of the *Communist Manifesto*:

The bourgeoisie . . . has put an end to all feudal, patriarchal, idyllic relations. It has . . . left remaining no other nexus between man and man than naked self-interest, than callous 'cash payment'.[9]

(Marx and Engels are themselves echoing Thomas Carlyle, one of the chief British opponents of mid-nineteenth-century liberalism.) But no one who has read R. H. Tawney's *Religion and the Rise of Capitalism*, surely, will accept Polanyi's suggestion that the mediaevals were unaware of the importance to humanity of social bonds? The trouble is that in a society such as that of the Middle Ages, where the bonds of affection, respect, compassion, and the like which link individuals occupying neighbouring positions in a social structure take absolute precedence over the interest that society as a whole has in individuals' behaviour, progress is obstructed and therefore the life of Man remains 'nasty, brutish, and short'.[10] The operation of a free market does not destroy the bonds of affection between related individuals – nothing could, they are surely among the fixed elements of human nature whose existence Chomsky takes pains to stress; what it does do is to provide a channel through which society as a whole, with most of whose members the individual will be linked by no bonds of sentiment, can express its legitimate interest in the individual's actions, as one of the factors which the individual must balance in deciding how to lead his life.

Polanyi stresses that markets in the modern sense are not natural to Man, that they are a fairly recent development even in European history and are quite unknown to many of the peoples studied by anthropologists.[11] Of course that is so; open, competitive markets are no more 'natural' than life in houses rather than caves, or the use of drugs and painless surgery rather than magic to treat disease. Whatever the classical liberals may have imagined about the institution of society through an explicit social contract, modern liberals are well aware that markets, the precondition for so much subsequent progress, must themselves have been the unplanned outcome of an earlier stage of progress. Adam Smith himself anticipated Polanyi in pointing out that the propensity of humans to 'truck, barter, and exchange one thing for another' is probably not innate.[12]

Polanyi is more explicit than Chomsky in his redefinition of the notion of freedom. He writes:

Compulsion should never be absolute; the 'objector' should be offered a niche to which he can retire, the choice of a 'second-best' that leaves him a life to live. Thus will be secured the right to nonconformity as the hallmark of a free [sic!] society.[13]

Perhaps we may leave Polanyi at that point.

Even the very notion of 'progress', of course, has become suspect in our day. Many commentators on the contemporary world write as if twentieth-century man has discovered that progress is not all the Victorians cracked it up to be; in his discussion of the association between classical British empiricism and the notion of progress, Chomsky appears to have this idea at the back of his mind.[14] But, if so, the point can easily be dealt with, because it rests on a mere misunderstanding. Thus, for instance, people point to the pollution of the environment brought about by industrial 'progress' and suggest that it is too high a price to pay for the benefits derived. Society should care less about 'growth' and more about the 'quality of life'.

But, if the pollution caused by a particular industry really is too high a price to pay for the benefits provided by that industry, then the industrial innovation constitutes no 'progress' or 'growth' at all. The difficulty here lies in the fact that, when populations were less dense and technology less advanced than they are now, the operation of a free market was distorted very little by ignoring the 'neighbourhood effects' of industrial developments – that is, the adverse consequences on individuals who are not in traditional terms parties to the contracts involved in those developments, such as neighbours who breathe air which a new factory pollutes. In a liberal society enterprisers would be made to pay for their neighbourhood effects, and it is certainly a fair criticism of modern governments that they have devoted little effort to ensuring that this be done. And there is a further problem in that an industrialist could scarcely buy the right to pollute by making separate contracts with all the large number of individuals affected; clearly, even under liberalism, it must be local or national government that sells the right to pollute, and this does entail an addition to the activities of government. But the liberal acknowledges that there are some things which have to be done by government; government should make itself responsible for as little as possible, but this is not one of the avoidable responsibilities. It will certainly be appropriate to make the charge for neighbourhood effects much higher than the individuals affected would collectively be happy to settle for, in order to discourage industry from forcing government to expand in this way. But it would surely be odd to conclude, because certain classes of decision must nowadays be made by government rather than by the market, that market mechanisms ought to be replaced by government intervention throughout twentieth-century societies – as odd as it would be to argue, from the fact that certain medical conditions can be cured only by surgery rather than by drugs, that surgery should be preferred to drugs in treating all conditions. And it would be equally irrational to infer, from the fact that technological innovations almost invariably entail some undesirable consequences, that their benefits can never outweigh their drawbacks. As Chomsky himself says: 'Rejection of science is senseless. But it is a central problem of modern life to set the conditions under which scientific work will be undertaken.'[15] Since it is sensitive to so many more factors than any individual human mind, whenever it can be brought to bear the mechanism of the open market will provide the best solution to that problem.[16]

Another aspect of the modern loss of faith in progress has to do with the fact, apparently a new discovery to some, that the resources available to mankind are finite, and that some materials will be exhausted in the foreseeable future given the continuance, let alone increase, of present rates of consumption.[17] Economists, of course, have always known that our resources are finite – economics has nothing to say about resources which are available in unlimited quantities. In a situation where resources are particularly short, progress in the sense relevant here is not *less* but much *more* necessary, since it is progress that allows more value for humanity to be derived from the same quantity of physical resources. To take a simple example, if we know how to extract the chemical energy from a lump of coal by burning it we can use it to cook one man's meal; if we progress to the point of being able to extract the nuclear energy in it we can use it to cook very many men's meals.

An objection to progress that seems particularly cogent to some Americans is that, while there are pockets of poverty in the

U.S.A., the aggregate of wealth in that country is so great as to make the pursuit of more seem almost disgusting, particularly in view of the ocean of poverty that exists in much of the rest of the world.[18] This attitude does credit to the hearts of those that hold it, but less so to their understanding of the situation. The reason why America is so much richer than most other nations is that she enjoys a near-monopoly of liberal government and, consequently, a near-monopoly of economic innovation. Unlike those private institutions which monopolize the manufacture of a particular good, America as a nation would be very happy to see this monopoly ended; ever since the U.S.A. began to play an important role in international affairs in this century, its policy has been rather consistently one of encouraging the growth of liberalism abroad. American liberalism increases not only Americans' wealth but, in the measure as successful American innovations are taken up elsewhere, also the wealth of others; the greater the proportion of the world's population that is enabled and encouraged by liberal governments to realize the economic benefits latent in its creative powers, the more rapidly wealth everywhere will increase. In a world whose huge and increasing population is in the main desperately poor, and in which most nations, because of failure to understand the advantages of liberalism, show no signs of abandoning authoritarian government, it is all the more important that America should continue to progress as fast as possible in order to allow the poverty of non-Americans to be relieved by the parasitic process described in Ch. 3. American progress continues only because, fortunately, we have no authoritarian world government redistributing income from rich to poor across national boundaries;[19] since no such redistribution occurs (if we ignore the large charitable donations made by American individuals and government to foreigners), American progress inevitably entails great disparity of wealth as between Americans and others.

The point that seems to be missed by the opponents of liberalism is that economics, whether within a nation or internationally, is not a 'zero-sum game' in which a fixed quantity of goods are shuffled round so that X's gain must be Y's or Z's

loss.[20] There is a special case of the game of economic relationships which is zero-sum: this is the case where the various
players' moves are controlled by an overall plan, so that in effect
there is only one player and X, Y, and Z are merely pawns. The
more players in the economic game are acting as genuinely
independent competitors, the faster the total quantity of goods
to be distributed between them will grow.[21]

A point related to the last is that, according to Chomsky,
liberalism fails in its claim that the free play of market forces
organizes production as well as, or better than, it could be
organized by conscious planning.[22] Consider the proportion of
total effort devoted in modern societies to the production of
utterly unnecessary luxuries for the rich, while enormous
numbers of poor are in dire need of the basic amenities of life.
The straightforward answer to this, of course, is that the
luxuries are necessary as incentives to motivate the rich to do
things which benefit everybody, including the poor. We have
already seen that a society which hopes progressively to eliminate poverty in the absolute sense must be a society which
retains poverty in the relative sense – in which at any given time
some individuals will be considerably poorer than others; and, if
one accepts the need for relatively rich people, one must accept
that some productive forces must be devoted to meeting re-
quirements of theirs which may look frivolous to their relatively
poor contemporaries. To give people money in a world where
there was nothing to spend it on would be to give them valueless
pieces of paper. This reply to Chomsky's objection is, I believe,
quite adequate in logic, but it may seem emotionally unsatisfy-
ing. However, there is a further point which may make it easier
for one to reconcile oneself to the production of luxuries: this is
that the production of novel goods in small quantities for the
luxury market is a necessary step in the process by which those
goods eventually become relatively cheap necessities. Consider,
for instance, the history of the motor-car. Before the First World
War, cars were rich men's playthings, and very unreliable
mechanically. Thanks to the experience gained by manufacturing primitive cars expensively, mankind learned how to make

better cars more cheaply. Modern cars are highly reliable and within the means of very modest British and American families; and they bring their owners great benefits, not merely in making their leisure more enjoyable but in enabling them to commute to well-paid (therefore socially valuable) jobs that would previously have been out of their reach.[23]

A fourth reason for widespread disillusion with the notion of 'progress' as an ideal stems from the fact that many developments which are described as 'progressive' in the modern world are perceived by those affected as retrograde steps. Novel teaching methods in schools are an obvious example; those responsible for introducing them announce them as a step forward, but many parents feel that schools organized on the new lines are educating their children less well than traditional schools. But again, insofar as such feelings are justified, they constitute objections not to progress in the liberal sense, but to developments characteristic of authoritarianism. 'Progress' means not simply innovation but beneficial innovation; in a liberal society, however, it is not necessary to stress this distinction, since the only innovations that survive will be beneficial ones. Under liberalism, for instance, schools will be free to operate as their owners please, and parents free to send their children to whichever school they choose whose fees they are willing to pay. Thus it will be possible for one or a few schools to experiment with novel, perhaps expensive, teaching methods; if the new methods are successful, those schools will make a profit and others will imitate them, but if they are unsuccessful the schools that try them out will either abandon them or disappear for lack of customers. Under authoritarianism, on the other hand, there is every likelihood that innovations in a field such as school-teaching will be widely adopted without being on balance beneficial. In an authoritarian society, government will relieve parents of the responsibility for educating their children and private enterprisers of the job of running schools. It will need to entrust the task of exercising its new responsibilities to some body of planners, and will naturally select for this purpose people who lay claim to special expertise about the teaching process – i.e. men representing only one of the conflicting interests which, under liberalism, will jointly determine who teaches whom how. Since teaching, unlike, say, the supply of electricity, is an enterprise in which success or failure is not at all clearcut, the penalty for unsuccessful experimentation may be low (the planners can always argue that parents' complaints about poor schools reflect lack of specialized understanding of the nature of education) while rewards for the planners may be high. They may greatly improve career prospects in their profession, for instance, by recommending that government raise the age until which schooling is compulsory, or by requiring new teachers to study (at the taxpayer's expense) for an extra qualification, in addition to those previously thought adequate, involving courses taught by members of their profession. Or they may simply set out to make their reputation by changing the face of the nation's school system. Under authoritarianism, there will be no mechanism whereby the interests harmed by these innovations can offset the advantages to the planners of introducing them.[24]

I am not suggesting any dishonesty on the part of the planners here; we are all very good at persuading ourselves that things we should like to be so are so – that is why progress in the proper sense emerges only from the interplay between conflicting interests.

If under liberalism 'change' and 'progress' are in practice synonymous, then it is understandable that when liberalism gives way to authoritarianism, and changes cease in many cases to be beneficial, the word 'progress' may still be used for 'change' in general and disillusion with 'progress' will spread. But this argument against 'progress' is obviously no argument against liberalism.

A converse objection to liberalism is sometimes heard: that, given the present state of technology, further progress is so expensive as to require government intervention.[25] It is probably true that if Britain and the U.S.A. had retained the minimal government of the eighteenth and nineteenth centuries, then, for instance, no supersonic passenger aircraft would yet be in service, and men would not yet have walked on the Moon. But, although the Concorde and Apollo projects have provided a great deal of entertainment and some more tangible returns, it seems very questionable whether their total benefits in either case have matched their enormous costs; judged as commercial ventures, they are surely both failures. There may be some 'big technology' projects which only government has enough capital to undertake and which *would* be beneficial; but postponement of those projects until private holdings of capital become large enough to undertake them seems a small price to pay for avoiding the costly white elephants which often result from government enterprise.

All the above objections to liberalism, apart from being rather easy to refute, are perfectly standard ones – Chomsky allies himself with various of them to a greater or lesser extent but there is nothing original in his discussion of them. I have taken up these points not because either Chomsky or I have much new to say about them, but only because I know that, if I ignored them, it would undoubtedly be alleged that I had no answer to them.

What is interesting about Chomsky's work, clearly, is his claim to present novel empirical findings which are relevant to the issue. The liberal case depends on a fairly traditional notion of human creativity. According to Chomsky, that case is undercut by the deeper understanding of the nature of creativity which emerges from his and others' recent studies of its manifestation in linguistic behaviour; we can now see that human creativity is not, after all, the kind of faculty which the liberal's premisses presuppose.

Chomsky does not, certainly, suggest that we are wrong to think of the use of language as a creative activity. Quite the reverse: the word 'creative' is a key term in Chomsky's linguistic theorizing, and one of the chief points he and his followers make against Chomsky's predecessors in academic linguistics and psychology is that their attempts to account for human linguistic behaviour were hopelessly inadequate precisely because they ignored the creative aspect of language use. Statements to this effect occur in almost every book and major journal article which Chomsky publishes in his professional role. Thus, for instance:

> The most striking aspect of linguistic competence is what we may call the 'creativity of language', that is, the speaker's ability to produce new sentences . . . . Modern linguistics [i.e. the kind of academic linguistics in vogue at the time Chomsky began writing] . . . is seriously at fault in its failure to come to grips with this central problem. . . . Normal use of language involves the production and interpretation of sentences that are similar to sentences that have been heard before only in that they are generated by rules of the same grammar, and thus the only sentences that can in any serious sense be called 'familiar' are clichés or fixed formulas. . . .[26]

> Long accepted [psychological] principles of association and reinforcement . . . have been sharply challenged in [recent] theoretical as well as experimental work. . . . Ordinary linguistic behaviour characteristically involves innovation, formation of new sentences and new patterns in accordance with rules of great abstractness and intricacy. . . . There are no known principles of association or reinforcement, and no known sense of 'generalization' that can begin to account for this characteristic 'creative' aspect of normal language use. The new utterances that are produced and interpreted in the daily use of language are 'similar' to those that constitute the past experience of speaker and hearer only in that they are determined, in their form and interpretation, by the same system of abstract underlying rules.[27]

These passages seem to be powerful statements of the thesis that linguistic behaviour, speech and writing, is one of the aspects of human activity which offer clear evidence of our creative faculty – as the ordinary thinking man undoubtedly takes it to be, without even dreaming that the point might be called into question. What kind of features in the academic linguistics and psychology of the recent past have made it worth Chomsky's while to restate what might seem to be a truism so frequently and in such powerful language?

What Chomsky has in mind is an approach within both these subjects which, at its worst, suggested that a human language could be viewed as a large but finite stock of signals. Some animal species – various apes, for example – are said to have 'languages' which comprise a fixed number of different noises each with its set meaning.[28] Thus, one kind of sound could be translated as 'Watch out, danger about!', another as 'Food over here', and there might be half a dozen more. Now, while few if any linguists or psychologists of the 1940s and 1950s would have explicitly agreed with the idea, there is no doubt that running through much of their work was an unstated assumption that human languages were, essentially, phenomena of this kind – that English differed from ape-talk in that it contained many thousands of words rather than a handful, but that this difference was merely quantitative rather than a difference of principle. Those aspects of human language which fitted this paradigm were studied in detail, whereas the characteristics which make human language seem rather different from ape-talk were shuffled off into a corner – perhaps alluded to in a line or so near the beginning or end of one's contribution to the learned literature, but not brought into focus as an important subject for investigation. Thus, psychologists interested in language analysed the way in which a child learns an individual word by coming to associate the sound of the word with features common to the various situations in which he has heard the word.[29] Of course the adult does not speak by merely stringing together at random words expressing concepts connected with what he has in mind – he orders his words in a quite particular way, and supplements the nouns and verbs with words like *if* and *the* which can scarcely be treated as learned by association with particular features of the environment; but this was often felt to be something of a minor detail. Linguists went about describing the grammar of a language by collecting a large 'corpus' of utterances observed to have been produced by speakers of that language, and then looking for a simple, generalized form of description that neatly accounted for each sentence in the corpus.[30] Any such description invariably also fitted other sequences of words that had not actually turned up in the corpus; this was inevitable, but it was no part of the linguist's intention – if anything, it had to be apologetically explained away.

Now what Chomsky is saying – and, as against the brand of linguistics and psychology that I have been describing, he is of course perfectly correct – is that such an approach is utterly inadequate as an attempt to come to grips with human language as a distinctive phenomenon. What makes human language 'special' – what makes us rightly reluctant to think of our languages as merely ape-talk writ large – has nothing to do with number of words in the vocabulary, or the like; rather it has to do with precisely those considerations which are being swept under the carpet here. Humans differ from apes, not so much in their ability to acquire word-concepts by associating sound with situation – to a limited extent, at least, apes seem to be able to do this too – but in their ability to organize these concepts into logical structures of unlimited complexity.[31] A corpus-based description of English which managed to account for all the sentences in the corpus while avoiding the inclusion of other, unobserved sentences would not be the ideal description the linguist should be seeking – it would be a description utterly irrelevant to the language as it is used in real life, since a man's ability to use his mother tongue, though acquired from exposure to some finite set of instances, is in no way limited to those instances. There are some 'clichés and fixed formulas', such as *How do you do?*, which we learn by hearing those precise words used in given situations; but such cases cannot be regarded as the typical ones from which an account of language should set out, and in fact we recognize them as clichés precisely because they do not quite fit the normal patterns of our speech (we do not commonly say such things as *How do they do?* or *When do I do?*). The appropriate description for a language will consist of a set of general principles, or 'rules', which must define a range of sentences including not only those that have been observed but countless others, because when someone has learned a language the particular instances from which he learned it have no special status with respect to his subsequent use of the language. Most sentences we produce or encounter are new to us, and even if we meet one that we happen to have come across before we may quite possibly not realize the fact.

Furthermore we cannot justify omitting discussion of the syntactic rules of a language on the grounds that they are simple and self-evident, for they are not. In the first place they are not simple but highly complex (and, while I have suggested that Chomsky and others exaggerate the syntactic complexity of human languages, even when this exaggeration is allowed for I agree that considerable complexity remains); and secondly, our feeling that many properties of the rules are self-evident merely stems from failure to appreciate the logical possibility that human languages might have had syntactic properties quite other than the familiar ones which they in fact possess.

As a criticism of the trend in linguistics and psychology that I have described, all this is absolutely right. On the other hand, though, the terms in which Chomsky expresses his quite justified criticism of that trend involve a very odd use of the word 'creative'. Remember that we regarded the production of novel works of art, or new scientific theories, as 'creative' activities because of the fact that, at any given time, it is impossible in principle to delimit the range of potential future products of those activities – there is no saying what might one day count as a worthwhile work of art or scientific theory. This is what we *mean* by calling the arts and sciences 'creative'; although the products of some individual artists and scientists may be nothing more than new examples of antecedently recognized ranges of possibilities, such individuals do not attract the respect or homage which we feel to be the due of genuinely 'creative' talents. To be creative is to produce something which falls outside the class implied by any set of principles that might have been proposed to account for previous examples.

In this sense of 'creativity', the above quotations from Chomsky clearly presuppose that the utterance of new sentences is *not* a creative activity. 'Normal use of language involves . . . sentences that are similar to sentences that have been heard before *only* in that they are generated by rules of the same grammar;' 'The new utterances that are produced and interpreted in the daily use of language are "similar" to those that constitute . . . past experience . . . *only* in that they are determined . . . by the same system of abstract underlying rules' (my italics). But if future sentences do indeed conform to rules that can be established on the basis of previous experience, that is quite enough to make speech a non-creative activity.

Chomsky is saying that possible utterances in a language do not form a finite class which are learned case by case, but rather form an infinitely large class which can be learned only by mastering a system of general rules. One might similarly contrast a young child's ability to carry out multiplication problems up to 12 x 12 by rote-learning of multiplication tables with our more sophisticated ability to solve relatively complex problems, say 3924 x 678, by means of general rules which in principle cover an infinitely large range of cases. In the days when clerks rather than machines were employed to carry out this latter kind of computation, should their work have been classed as 'creative'? I think not.

The rules for multiplication are rather simple, of course, and Chomsky lays great stress on the fact that the grammar-rules of a human language are far from simple. But this does not affect his case. Musicologists have recently written computer programs which generate novel examples of such well-recognized musical genres as Mozart concertos or Bach fugues. I have no doubt that these programs are highly complex; does that entitle us to say that a computer which produces a new 'Mozart concerto' is acting creatively? Surely not; once the genre is well-defined, a composer is not being creative unless he goes beyond it in at least some small way.[32]

In other words, Chomsky has misappropriated the term 'creative' as he misappropriated the term 'free'. In each case he uses the term in a sense that conflicts with its standard usage; but, by contrasting 'freedom', or 'creativity', in his impoverished sense with something that is even further removed from the notion usually associated with the respective word, he invites us to overlook the fact that what we usually mean by the word is something different from both his alternatives. A

Chomskyan society will be 'free', if I understand him, in that an individual's economic niche will be determined by a plan drawn up on the basis of his own as well as others' suggestions, rather than imposed on him without reference to his wishes; but for a liberal one is only free if one has the option of constructing one's own economic niche independently of any overall plan. A Chomskyan speaker is 'creative' in that his utterances are usually new examples of a range defined by general principles, rather than being copies of a familiar, limited stock of proto-types; most of us have supposed that speakers are 'creative' in the broader sense that what they say commonly fails in certain respects to conform to any principles that might have been laid down to account for past utterances. And the same contrast of views extends from the question of utterances made by mature speakers to that of the acquisition of language by infants. Chomsky argues that a child is born with psychological machinery which implies a definite, though no doubt infinitely large, range of 'possible languages' from among which the child must identify the particular language being spoken around him;[33] others have supposed that nothing in our inherited neural apparatus predisposes us to speak languages of any particular kind (or even predisposes us to 'speak a language' at all), and that in deciding what to make out of the verbal be-haviour which surrounds him an infant faces the same 'open-ended' range of possibilities which (as most of us think) face a scientist searching for a hypothesis to account for some novel observations.[34]

In my first chapter I described Chomsky's thought as dangerous on the grounds that it tends to deflect the energies of those who might help to overthrow the scientistic fallacy which mars so much of modern life. We see here the justification for this criticism. The adverse consequences of scientism stem from its assumption that all human phenomena can be analysed by the scientific method; creativity is an exception, since acts which are truly creative cannot, by definition, be predicted. To the question 'Who, in the contemporary intellectual world, most stresses the importance of human creativity?', the answer must undoubtedly be Noam Chomsky. (Thinkers primarily connected with literature and the arts, who might be expected forcefully to advance the claims of creativity, seem too much on the defensive nowadays to do so with much success.) Yet, when we ask what Chomsky means when he calls men creative, he turns out to refer to our ability to behave in conformity to certain fixed, rigorous rules. This is indeed scientistic pseudo-opposition to scientism.

Socialists have long recognized the clash between two concepts of 'freedom': they accuse liberals of advocating 'formal' rather than 'material' freedom,[35] an accusation to which liberals proudly plead guilty as charged, while suggesting that since the liberal notion of freedom was first in the field it might be more honest of the socialists to use for their notion some word which has accumulated a less overwhelming stock of goodwill. Chomsky shows some awareness that his notions of creativity and freedom are contentious. Thus he writes:

without a system of formal constraints there are no creative acts; specifically, in the absence of intrinsic and restrictive properties of mind, there can be only 'shaping of behaviour' but no creative acts of self-perfection.

The many modern critics who sense an inconsistency in the belief that free creation takes place within – presupposes, in fact – a system of constraints and governing principles are quite mistaken. . . .[36]

But Chomsky gives us no grounds for accepting his bland dismissal of his critics, who seem absolutely right here. It is of course true that activities which are rule-governed in some respects may nevertheless be creative in other respects. An architect may be creative when he designs a house, despite the fact that his design conforms to the code prescribing how building materials may safely be used. Language contains obvious analogues of this – original poems written in strict metres, for instance; and one might well suppose that ordinary speech or written prose should be seen as another case in point. I shall argue that this is indeed so; but for Chomsky, as we shall see, this account of the situation is inappropriate.The point is that the architect or poet is creative *despite* the rules, not because of them. The building code, for instance, permits creative architecture only because it is nowhere near complete enough to define a class of all possible future buildings. Many haphazard structures containing a couple of walls here, an archway there, could be designed so as to meet the safety code while having no conceivable use as buildings. An architect is creative when he successfully extends the notion 'building' to include a type of structure not previously conceived of – the fact that the structure conforms to the safety code is irrelevant, since the vast majority of structures conforming to the code never will be buildings, and there are no rules distinguishing, among structures permitted by the code, between those which might be and those which never will be worth bringing into existence. The case of poetry is similar – nothing is easier than to write doggerel or worse in strict metre. But Chomsky envisages the rules of English as distinguishing between those sequences of words which might in some circumstances be worth uttering and those which will always be nonsense. To claim that there are such rules, and simultaneously to claim that our use of language is creative, is as sensible as to announce that someone gets through a bottle of whisky daily while simultaneously describing him as abstemious.

Again, consider the following passage:

Creativity is predicated on a system of rules and forms . . . determined by intrinsic human capacities. Without such constraints, we have arbitrary and random behavior, not creative acts. The constructions of common sense and scientific inquiry derive . . . from principles grounded in the structure of the human mind. Correspondingly, it would be an error to think of human freedom solely in terms of absence of constraint. . . . A libertarian social theory will try to determine [the] laws [of human nature] and to found upon them a concept of social change and its immediate and distant goals.[37]

Despite the attacks on 'authoritarian social forms' which immediately precede and follow this statement, the latter part of it can as far as I can see mean only that liberty should consist of determining what social and economic arrangements best suit human nature and constraining people to accept those arrangements. I shall not reiterate the objections to this view; what is more interesting here is the first part of the statement. Chomsky suggests that the class of creative acts is determined by human nature; to suggest that a scientist creating a novel theory, or a painter producing a novel work of art, is doing something other than realizing one more of a range of possibilities that an adequate scientific knowledge of human psychology would enable us to define is to suggest that such people are behaving arbitrarily, striking out at random.

Certainly many will agree that creative behaviour is not arbitrary or random. But the opposition Chomsky sets up here is surely a quite false one. The question whether it is in principle possible to specify rules which define in advance the range of potential creative acts that humans may perform is independent of the question whether such acts are performed at random. For creative behaviour to be random would mean, presumably, that it was as likely to be bad of its kind as good; no greater a proportion of the novel hypotheses propounded by scientists would be true, no greater a proportion of the novel products of artists beautiful, than one would expect to happen by chance. Insofar as I can understand this ('expect to happen by chance' is obviously a problematic phrase in this context), it seems to me not to fit the facts; Albert Einstein did not merely propound novel theories, he propounded *good* novel theories – we will never be able to say for sure that his or any other scientific theories are true beyond the possibility of refutation, but Einstein's have shown great ability to survive criticism. Of course it is possible to take the other line and say that Einstein was in no way more inherently talented than crowds of unknown physicists – he just happened to hit the jackpot, and we are familiar with Einstein's name for the same sort of reason as we may be familiar with that of a man who filled in his football coupon using no special judgement and won half a million pounds. I do not believe this; Einstein showed such infinitely greater skill in exploiting his fundamental insight than winners of football-pool fortunes do in exploiting their sudden wealth. But this question is surely quite independent of the question whether behaviour that we think of as creative is drawn from a specifiable range like the range of possible Treble Chance entries, rather than being called 'creative' precisely because it conforms to no antecedent norms.

Chomsky appears to suggest that we think of some kinds of behaviour as creative because, being still very ignorant about the machinery of mind, we are not as a matter of contingent fact familiar with the ranges of possibilities which they exemplify. But, if future psychological investigation reveals that some aspect of behaviour previously regarded as creative consists of realizing various instances drawn from a specifiable range, my reaction (and, surely, that of many others) would be not 'Now I understand the neural basis of this kind of creativity' but 'Now I see that we were wrong to think of this kind of behaviour as creative.'

Chomsky sometimes writes as if a view of creativity which implies that it is not a phenomenon that can ever be the subject of scientific predictions is itself an irrational, anti-scientific attitude.[38] But in fact the claim 'No prediction about the class of possible future scientific theories which is narrower than the class of sequences of declarative sentences will be compatible with the future development of science' exemplifies a kind of statement which is recognized by philosophers of science as having an important role to play in human understanding.[39] Chomsky begs the question whether language acquisition or scientific discovery are 'creative' activities in the 'rich' sense by taking it for granted that we can increase our understanding of how humans perform them by asking ourselves how a computer might be programmed to do them.[40] A computer can formulate only such hypotheses as are provided for in its program, so to assume that human 'creativity' can be simulated by a computer is to assume that humans are not truly creative.[41]

Having established the distinction between the two notions of creativity, I do not wish to labour the point that Chomsky's usage is abnormal, although (as in the case of 'freedom') one feels that discussion could have been clearer if Chomsky had chosen a new term for his new notion. What is more important is to ask whether Chomsky is right in suggesting that humans are 'creative' only in this new, impoverished sense? Are we wrong to think of our species as characterized by creativity in the richer sense?

If so, the case for political liberalism founders. Liberal government, in this case, might be valuable as a temporary expedient – a device which, by offering rewards for enterprise in the field of production, and by fixing prices for goods in response to competition between individuals with very diverse incomes, gives us the data we need for planning the ideal society of the future. Since the techniques and objects of production would form a well-defined range, in principle it ought to be possible to work out on paper how to maximize production, but we will certainly find it easier and make fewer mistakes if we let a liberal society show us how; and, since it would be very difficult to get people to *tell* us their preference-functions as between different amounts of different goods, we will do well instead to note the prices thrown up by an open market. It would be immoral to set up such an experiment, of course, but by great good fortune the wicked capitalists are operating one already; all we need to do is, as it were, quickly to copy down the figures, before erasing it and replacing it with a new society, in which rewards will be equal, and production arrangements will differ from those of the old society only in ways needed to cater for the fact that everyone now exhibits the preference-function which, under liberalism, characterized the few whose income happened to fall at the mean. Under the new regime, obviously, there will be no room for the 'bourgeoisie'. The liberal justified the returns available to the enterpriser as an incentive to take part in gambles which benefit society as a whole when successful; but even the liberal knows that a gentleman does not bet on a certainty.

An argument much like this underlies Marx's advocacy of socialism. Before liberalism, no one had any idea what 'productive forces slumbered in the lap of social labour'; but a century or so of liberalism had well and truly woken those forces up. The bourgeois had done their stuff, but now had no further useful role to play. Competition between capitalists would involve concentration of capital in fewer and fewer hands as the weaker were eliminated by the stronger; this would swell the number of proletarians competing for the decreasing number of jobs which resulted from the tendency to mechanize production, so that the contrast between the rich few and the poor many would grow ever wider – until the system broke down in revolution.[42]

The crucial point overlooked by this is that, when Marx and Engels in 1848 described how the forces of production had been aroused during the preceding hundred years, there were still plenty of economically beneficial ideas yet to be invented. New ideas offer new investment opportunities which give rise to new jobs, thus tending to raise wages as well as increasing total production. If novel investment opportunities continue to materialize, then Marx's argument that capital will be concentrated in ever fewer hands falls to the ground, and with it falls his doctrine of the progressive immiseration of the proletariat. That argument depended on the assumption that, once the full range of conceivable or useful goods were being produced, mechanization and other economies of scale were the only factors that could enable an enterprise to succeed in competition with its rivals, so that the biggest enterprises would get bigger and wipe out their rivals. In fact, small firms succeed by exploiting novel and more efficient production techniques or by producing novel products, superior to those of established enterprises; innovative thinking of these kinds regularly outweighs the advantages of size. Monopolies can exist only when they are actively protected by government policy; in a liberal society a monopoly which is profitable ensures its own disappearance, as new enterprises seek to gain a share in the profits to be made in that business, using capital which is constantly being created by the exploitation of new ideas.[43] The tendency of successful established industries to generate unemployment through automation is counteracted by the tendency of innovative enterprise to produce labour shortage, and there is no reason to predict the formation of a 'reserve army of the unemployed'. As Marx's life continued (he was thirty in the year of publication of the *Communist Manifesto*), he began to notice that investment opportunities were not drying up as he had predicted, and that the proletariat was correspondingly failing to sink deeper into misery – in fact their standard of living was improving, and the bourgeois class was expanding rather than contracting; accordingly he substantially revised his estimate of the timetable for revolution, which he had originally expected to occur almost immediately.[44] By a late stage in his life Marx is reported as having said privately more than once – although we do not know what precisely he meant – that 'All I know is that I am not a Marxist';[45] one wishes, for the sake of the hundreds of millions who have been made to suffer in his name, that Marx had been a man who found it easier to admit openly that he was wrong.

The liberal takes it for granted (or, perhaps more accurately, holds as a matter of faith) that humanity will never run out of things to invent.[46] To a rationalist, of course, it is always open to suggest that Marx was merely premature. The rationalist need not do so; he can, for instance, stress that the range of cognitive possibilities implied by some aspect of our mind, though well-defined, is infinite and can therefore never be exhausted. Chomsky appeals to this notion at one point:

> Notice that these . . . views on the scope and limits of knowledge set no finite limits on human progress. The integers form an infinite set, but they do not exhaust the real numbers. Similarly, humans may develop their capacities without limit, but never escaping certain objective bounds set by their biological nature.[47]

This reply seems rather unimpressive; if progress continues indefinitely in a given sphere of human activity it is normally only because new possibilities are continually thought up, and in 'uncreative' situations where the range of possibilities is given us in advance we can usually discover which is correct in a finite time even if the range is infinitely large. (We know the approximate mass of the Sun, even though there are infinitely many possible hypotheses about its mass.) But this passage is untypical, and in the immediately following passage Chomsky expresses a view that seems much more consistent with his rationalist idea of Man:

Suppose that the social and material conditions that prevent free intellectual development were relieved. . . . Then, science, mathematics, and art would flourish, pressing on towards the limits of cognitive capacity. . . . If cognitive domains are roughly comparable in complexity and potential scope, such limits might be approached at more or less the same time in various domains, giving rise to a 'crisis of modernism'. . . . It may be that something of the sort has been happening in recent history.

In other words, what Marx prematurely took to be happening in the economic sphere in the mid-nineteenth century, namely exhaustion of the possibilities for innovation, Chomsky expects to happen in the sphere of the arts and sciences, and he thinks it may be happening right now. The signs of this are that, having run out of serious new work to invent, artists and thinkers will descend to frivolity, and to 'professionalism' by which the individual artist or thinker claims to be producing material that appeals not to the general educated public but only to a small coterie of like minds (who will presumably profess to recognize each other's talents for mutual benefit).[48] 'Mockery of conventions that are . . . grounded in human cognitive capacity might be expected to become virtually an art form in itself, at this stage of cultural evolution.'

[margin note: Chomsky on limits to creativity & the crisis of modernism]

Chomsky makes his belief that mankind is running out of things to invent more explicit with respect to the domains of art and science than with respect to the economic domain. Nevertheless, it is fairly clear that for Chomsky, as for Marx, what is wrong with capitalism is that it has already completed the task of discovering the range of beneficial investments (so that further competition can lead only to ever-increasing monopolization and immiseration of the proletariat). Chomsky writes, for instance, that

Vast disparity in wealth and power [is] tolerable to the underprivileged and dispossessed if there are reasonable prospects that with the growth of the economy, each share will grow. . . . as prospects of limitless growth fade, those deprived of wealth and its concomitant benefits no longer have such reasons to tolerate the existing system of inequity. . . .[49]

There is no logical absurdity in the claim that we will one day – or perhaps already have – run out of worthwhile innovations, whether in the arts and sciences or in economic life. Nevertheless, what Chomsky is saying will strike many readers as grossly implausible, even with respect to the purely intellectual, non-economic domains where our judgement is less apt to be biased by our political prejudices. The sciences seem to be making progress about as rapidly as they ever have. Chomsky's own empirical work on linguistic universals, after all, is but one of many wholly novel scientific theories that have emerged and met with acceptance in the recent past. In all such cases it is possible, after the fact, to descry vague links with earlier ideas, as Chomsky has linked his work with that of the seventeenth-century French grammarians of Port-Royal;[50] but it would be a serious misrepresentation to claim that Chomsky's theory was merely a working-out of earlier ideas, or was anything less than a genuinely original intellectual creation.[51]

It is true that many things are currently being greeted as 'art' which are very difficult to accept as having any value whatever, but one can easily quote less apocalyptic reasons than Chomsky's for this state of affairs. In the first place, the process by which innovations succeed in winning acceptance is always a long-drawn-out affair, in art as much as in science or the business world; even innovations that come to be generally recognized as valuable always, at an early stage, appeal only to a small group of converts – the kind of comments that I and, as I infer from his remarks, Chomsky make about aleatory music or op art were made in their day about Beethoven and Cézanne. Admittedly, I believe with Chomsky that most of what is happening in contemporary art really is rubbish and will in due course be generally recognized as such. But then most new scientific hypotheses are quickly falsified and most business innovations do not pay; and if the proportion of dross in contemporary art is unusually high, it is easy to explain this by pointing to special factors in contemporary society. (Thus, high rates of inflation force people to seek non-depreciating alternatives to government currency for their savings.Works of art happen, largely as a matter of arbitrary convention, to have acquired this role, and the large rewards that consequently accrue to their producers have attracted mediocre talents into the field.) However, we need not waste much time on these general speculations of Chomsky's, since we can decisively refute his rationalist view of human nature in the particular area of human activity where Chomsky feels he can back up his assumptions with solid, detailed evidence: that of language.

There is little doubt to my mind that Chomsky is correct when he suggests that, from the syntactic point of view, our use of language is uncreative, or that it is 'creative' only in Chomsky's impoverished sense (but from now on I shall use 'creative' only in the 'rich' sense, since Chomsky's distinction between behaviour-patterns learned case by case and behaviour-patterns which involve mastery of a fixed set of rules covering many cases will not be relevant in what follows). The syntactically well-formed, or 'grammatical', sentences of a language form a set which is in principle definable, if moderately difficult to define in practice, and speakers of a language do not normally go outside this set to use syntactically novel forms. Syntactic innovation does occur, of course – otherwise it would be easier to read Chaucer. But, apart from the fact that such innovations are relatively infrequent in the history of a language, they are arbitrary in the sense that changes in fashionable length of skirts or in the livery of a railway company's rolling stock are arbitrary. Rather than extending the range of message-structures or 'logical forms' available in a language, syntactic innovations (such as replacement of case-endings by fixed word order) merely provide novel means to express the same logical forms.[52] Likewise, Chomsky seems to be right in claiming that the range of humanly possible syntactic systems forms a class which is in principle definable, and it may well be reasonable to suggest that individuals could come to speak a language whose syntax falls outside this set only as a result of a genetic mutation, of a kind that we are unlikely to observe given the time-scale available to us. I accept that Chomsky has made his case here, and I believe that his discovery is one of great interest to psychologists and to logicians.

But grammaticality and its opposite constitute only one of two important ways of categorizing word-sequences in a language, the difference between which has been stressed by Chomsky as much as by anyone.[53] We may distinguish the grammatical sequences of English words from sequences which are mere 'word-salad', such as *The in go elephant whether*; but, among the grammatical sequences, we may further distinguish those which are 'sensical' (to use a neologism) from those which are nonsensical. Many word-sequences will be perfectly grammatical and yet perfectly nonsensical; Chomsky's famous example is *Colourless green ideas sleep furiously*. Syntactically speaking, this is a well-formed sentence: its subject is a certain kind of ideas, namely those which are both colourless and green; it says of such things that they sleep in a certain way, namely furiously (notice that one can say nothing of this sort about *The in go elephant whether*); but *Colourless green ideas sleep furiously* makes no sense, i.e. what it asserts could not possibly be true – ideas have no visual appearance and do not sleep, nothing can be both colourless and green, and so on.

Now a Chomskyan 'grammar' – the set of principles that define a range of possibilities open to a given individual which that individual will not extend, and that vary between individuals of different speech communities only within definite limits – is concerned with grammaticality, not with sensicality. 'The fundamental aim in the linguistic analysis of a language L is to separate the *grammatical* sequences which are the sentences of L from the *ungrammatical* sequences which are not sentences of L. . . . the notion "grammatical" cannot be identified with "meaningful" or "significant" in any semantic sense'.[54] But it is with respect to sensicality, not grammaticality, that the liberal needs to claim that language-use is creative, and that there will be no specifiable limits on the ways in which the usage of various communities may differ. To invent a novel scientific theory, mechanical device, social institution, or the like, is *inter alia* to render sensical some word-sequences which were previously grammatical but nonsensical. *Horseless carriages travel rapidly* was nonsensical in 1700 but is a mere truism today. The sentence was not just *false* at the earlier date: it was *nonsensical*, provided that the idea of self-propelling machines had not yet occurred to anyone, and provided that *horseless* is understood to mean 'not designed to be harnessed to a draught animal' (as it did when *horseless carriage* became a common phrase) rather than simply 'not at present harnessed to a horse'. Before the invention of the locomotive, to speak of a carriage which needed no horse was as self-contradictory as it is today to speak of an idea as green, or to call anything green and colourless too. Again, consider *The elements of which water is composed burn furiously*. When water was itself taken to be one of the four basic constitutents of matter few statements could have sounded more paradoxical; even today it is difficult to convince oneself that the sentence is true, yet who does not know that it is? Moving away from the fields of science and technology for a final example, consider how a phrase such as *aggressive benevolence* has been robbed of its air of paradox by modern developments in social psychology.

The notion that linguistic behaviour is *syntactically* uncreative, despite its great interest for the psychologist and logician, is of no relevance for the political liberal; syntax provides merely the framework on which to hang any idea, novel or well-known, useful or pointless. The liberal will be no more concerned by the fact that it is possible to specify the range of potential grammatical English sentences than by the fact that it is possible to specify the range of potential arrangements of pigment on canvas; the liberal will however insist that it is not possible to predict a division of the grammatical sentences into sensical and nonsensical, just as it is impossible to predict where the borderline between works of art and daubs will in future be seen to run. Similarly, the liberal will not be concerned by invariance between human languages in the field of syntax; but he will insist that there are no limits to the ways in which vocabulary can develop, and therefore no limits to the ways in which the vocabularies of various societies may differ, since the vocabulary of a society encapsulates the stock of ideas which that society has produced. *Locomotive, insurance, playgroup, Oedipus complex, gravity* – these are not convenient short expressions for concepts which Chaucerian English could express only by cumbersome paraphrases, they are expressions for concepts which in Chaucer's day did not yet exist; and, according to the liberal, the potential existence of these particular concepts was in no sense implied by the stock of concepts which did exist in the fourteenth century. Furthermore, words such as those just cited differ from more 'basic' words such as *tree* or *child* only in a matter of degree, not in principle – only in that mankind formulated the concept 'tree' very much earlier than the concept 'gravity', for instance.[55]

Nothing in Chomsky's linguistics does anything to suggest that the liberal is wrong in making these claims. A Chomskyan grammar, as we have seen, explicitly aims to define grammaticality and to ignore sensicality;[56] Chomsky's linguistic univerals are universals of syntax and have nothing to say about vocabulary. Philosophically speaking, it might be appropriate to describe the picture of human cognition suggested by Chomsky's linguistics as rationalism of a kind; but, if so, it is the rationalism of Immanuel Kant, who held that there are structural properties which characterize all possible human beliefs, and that there is a method by which these properties can, with considerable effort, be discovered – not the rationalism of Descartes, who held that there are certain particular beliefs which we innately know to be true and certain particular word-concepts which we innately know to be applicable. Rationalism as weak as that is in no way incompatible with the liberal political ideal. Indeed, it is not clear that Kantian rationalism is opposed to classical British empiricist philosophy; if Kant is called a 'rationalist', it is rather because he stressed that there are certain invariant properties of thought than because he claimed to be invariant any properties which the empiricists regarded as variable. To return to Chomsky's version of rationalism: a liberal will be happy to agree that any way of increasing wealth that may be invented in future will involve producing some object describable by a noun by applying some process describable by a verb to materials describable by other nouns (or will otherwise fit the range of logical forms provided for by Chomsky's theory of linguistic universals); but the liberal will deny that the particular nouns and verb will necessarily belong to a vocabulary which can now be specified, or that, even if the words already exist, we will necessarily know now that it is not nonsense to arrange those words into a sentence in this way. The notion of making nylon stockings out of oil would have been both meaningless and paradoxical in 1800: meaningless because the concept 'nylon' had not been invented, paradoxical because obviously stockings of any sort could not be made out of a liquid; yet nowadays the process so described is a very valuable one, in view of the high price of silk.

The specific discoveries which Chomsky has made about language, then, by no means render the liberal position untenable. But Chomsky has an answer to this sort of objection. Although Chomsky is the leading figure in the movement away from belief in the empiricist view of human nature at the philosophical level, he himself regards his work on language as only one of a number of recent pieces of evidence, all of which point in the same direction:

I think it is fair to say that these empiricist views are most plausible where we are most ignorant. The more we learn about some aspect of human cognition, the less reasonable these views seem to be. No one would seriously argue today, for example, that our construction of perceptual space is guided by empiricist maxims.[57]

There are two points here, one specific and one general: the specific point being Chomsky's allusion to recent discoveries about the perception of space, the more general being the suggestion that empiricism remains appealing only because we remain ignorant. Let me first deal with the specific point.

The research Chomsky is referring to is that being carried out within a paradigm of enquiry represented most notably by Chomsky's M.I.T. colleagues David Hubel and Torsten Wiesel.[58] Hubel and Wiesel examined the functioning of the brain in cats, and discovered that the part of the brain which processes visual signals includes neurons sensitive to relatively sophisticated properties of a visual stimulus. Thus, there might be one neuron which fires when and only when the cat's field of vision contains a diagonal line oriented top-left to bottom-right: and this neuron will always fire for such a line, despite the fact that the image of the line might be at many different places on the retina, so that there are no particular retinal cells which such a line must always stimulate to produce the effect. If neural circuitry which includes such sophisticated arrangements is determined by our genetic blueprint (and, obviously, what is true of cats in this area is likely to be true of men also), then we have something close to the Cartesian notion that the stock of concepts which we use to categorize the world is innate. Descartes suggested that the notion 'triangle' must be innate because we see a roughly drawn triangle as a triangle despite the fact that it is only approximately a triangle while it is quite exactly the irregular figure that it actually is;[59] neurophysiology may now be able to turn this philosophical speculation into hard fact by discovering that human brains contain a neuron which fires for triangles and which, perhaps, fires less actively for near-triangles, but no neuron which fires preferentially for near-triangles. Thus we might be able to say that our neurology determines a fixed range of simple, elementary concepts, and all other possible concepts are constructed in some way out of these fixed elements; work subsequent to that of Hubel and Wiesel has shown us more of this neurological basis for cognition.[60]

The empiricist reply to this sort of finding has to do with the continuity which exists between biological evolution and the evolution of human knowledge.[61] A biological species is faced with the problem of survival in its environment. It throws up various mutations; most of these are unsuccessful and perish, but occasionally one represents an advance on its ancestor and survives, to mutate in its turn – and so species evolve. One enormous biological advance has been the development of the human brain. This enables us to continue the evolutionary process of adaptation to our environment *within the individual* – rather than death being the penalty for unsuccessful innovation, humans can throw up hypotheses to 'perish in our stead', as Popper puts it.[62] The labourer can conjecture that his best move might be to get a job with a railway, the enterpriser can conjecture that there may be a market for a supersonic passenger aircraft, the scientist can conjecture that light may consist of oscillations in an ether; they can press their respective conjectures far enough to discover their falsity, and can then abandon them for alternative hypotheses having wasted only a small part of their capital of earning time, wealth, or thinking time respectively. An animal born with an unfavourable mutation in one of its instincts or organs, on the other hand, has no second chance.

Now animals which lack creative minds must have evolved sense-organs which impose some kind of categorization on sensory stimuli; if salmon instinctively snap at flies then they must inherit some piece of neural circuitry which picks fly-like images out of the varied visual stimuli impinging on their retinas (though, if their fly-catching behaviour is purely instinctive, then individual salmon will not be able to evolve a more refined categorization scheme when the environment begins to include artificial flies attached to fish-hooks). Men, too, will inherit the categorization scheme evolved by our ancestors through the ages before we acquired the ability to think creatively; but, now that we have acquired this ability, we owe no special respect to the primitive conceptual schema we inherit. This inherited schema consists not of innate ideas out of which our more sophisticated concepts are all assembled, but of innate prejudices which in many cases human thought will have rightly rejected. Thus, we seem to be innately inclined to classify lines perceptually as straight or non-straight, and this innate inclination may well be useful; but we are also innately inclined to classify perceptually the shimmer that occurs above tarmac or sand on a hot day with the visual impression produced by a body of water – we see them as the same – and this is an innate prejudice which we have risen above. We know that a mirage is not the same as a lake, and we behave accordingly.[63] The relationship between humanity as a whole and the concepts and beliefs implied by our neural anatomy is like the relationship between an individual and the concepts and beliefs inculcated in him by parents and teachers. We have to start with some working hypotheses, but our task is to rise above them rather than to echo them uncritically; the concepts and hypotheses we create in the process of rising above our innate prejudices cannot in general be predicted from the nature of those prejudices.

Therefore neurological phenomena such as those discovered by Hubel and Wiesel, although, again, they are of great interest to the psychologist, are neither surprising nor at all worrying to the empiricist philosopher – certainly not to the brand of empiricism on which the liberal relies.

But what of Chomsky's general point, that empiricism is 'most plausible where we are most ignorant'? Chomsky's suggestion here is reminiscent of the argument against religious belief, popular fifteen years or so ago, which objected that the God of the modern believer was merely a 'God of the gaps'. At a time when the inherent limitations of the scientific method were less widely appreciated than they are now, it was felt by many that science had offered an independent explanation for many of the phenomena traditionally explained in religious terms; as fast as one such phenomenon was brought into the orbit of science, the believer would say 'Yes, but science still has not explained such-and-such another phenomenon', but the sceptic suspected that the 'gaps' unexplained by science would continue to shrink until there was no room left for God at all. Similarly, Chomsky suggests that research is showing one after another of the aspects of human behaviour that are traditionally regarded as 'creative' not in fact to be creative (in the 'rich' sense) after all; we may reasonably extrapolate to the conclusion that no aspect of human behaviour is creative.

The argument deserves some respect, but I do not believe it is just (in either case, although I shall not discuss the religious case further here. The two cases are of course related: the notion that creativity is one of the respects in which human behaviour manifests the divine is an old and familiar one[64]). The argument as it bears on language might perhaps have some force, if those who think deeply about language had long taken for granted that our linguistic behaviour is creative and were now for the first time asking themselves whether the assumption is in fact valid. But quite the reverse is the case. Those who think to most purpose about the semantic aspect of human linguistic behaviour (who have been, and still are, in most cases philosophers rather than linguists) have for a very long time assumed that we are semantically *un*creative; only in recent decades has the assumption been examined, and those who have examined it have argued forcefully and, to my mind, incontrovertibly, that it is false.

Those who have argued this case – not always using the same terminology – include, in Britain, Karl Popper[65] and Ludwig Wittgenstein,[66] and in America Edward Sapir[67] and Benjamin Lee Whorf[68] (who were linguists, though this aspect of their work is not highly regarded by the contemporary linguistic 'establishment') and the philosophers Morton White[69] and Willard van Orman Quine.[70]

Thus, White and Quine have approached the issue by arguing that there are no grounds for distinguishing, among sentences of a natural language such as English, between those which are 'analytic' and those which are 'synthetic'. Traditionally, philosophers have distinguished analytic sentences, whose truth depends solely on their meaning, from synthetic sentences, whose truth-value can be ascertained only by checking whether what they assert about the world does in fact obtain: thus Aristotle regarded *A man is a rational animal* as analytic – that he is a member of that animal species which possesses the power of reason is what we *mean* by calling something a 'man' – and *A man is a featherless biped* as synthetic – men do in fact have these properties, but these are not the properties by virtue of which they are called 'men'.[71] But by what right do we say that 'men' are *by definition* animals but only as a matter of fact bipeds? A man's use of his mother tongue does not involve mastery of a set of explicit definitions for words; we pick up most of our vocabulary by encountering it used in context, and who can say what contextual features we will seize on as most relevant to the use of a given word? The link between the objection to the analytic/synthetic distinction and the notion of semantic creativity is fairly clear. If our semantic behaviour were uncreative, so that the borderline between nonsensical and sensical sentences was determinate, then the borderline between analytic and synthetic sentences should be equally determinate. The analytic sentences would be all those sentences which contradict the nonsensical sentences, and the others would be the synthetic sentences.[72] But in fact grammatical sentences are continually shifting across these borderlines as our knowledge grows: *Horseless carriages run rapidly* has shifted from nonsensical to synthetic (or even to analytic – might one not suggest that these days one of our criteria for calling movement 'rapid', in everyday life, is 'car or train speed rather than foot speed'?), while *John's father is a man* is shifting from analytic to synthetic as sex-change operations become a recognized fact of life. Just as we cannot specify a definite class of sensical sentences, so within the range of sensical sentences we cannot pick out a well-defined range of analytic sentences (apart from the mere logical truisms, such as *Red things are red*).

What Quine does for sentences, Wittgenstein does for word-concepts. If semantic behaviour were uncreative, then, as we have seen, there should be some definable range of 'possible word-concepts'. Such a range might be specified in terms of a fixed stock of elementary concepts together with rules by which these could be compounded to form more complex concepts, and any given word would represent one of these simple or complex concepts in a clearcut way – the only unclarities would be cases where a word is actually polysemous (has two or more clearly distinct meanings), or where a word undergoes a definite change in its meaning by acquiring or dropping one or more elementary concepts. But is this really the way words work, asks Wittgenstein? Surely it is not.

Consider for example the proceedings that we call 'games'. I mean board-games, card-games, ball-games, Olympic games, and so on. What is common to them all? . . . if you look at them you will not see something that is common to *all*, but similarities, relationships, and a whole series of them at that. . . . Look for example at board-games, with their multifarious relationships. Now pass to card-games; here you find many correspondences with the first group, but many common features drop out, and others appear. . . . Are [all games] 'amusing'? Compare chess with noughts and crosses. Or is there always winning and losing, or competition between players? Think of patience. . . . we can go through the many, many other groups of games in the same way; can see how similarities crop up and disappear. . . .

I can think of no better expression to characterize these similarities than 'family resemblances'; for the various resemblances between members of a family: build, features, colour of eyes, gait, tempera- ment, etc. etc. overlap and criss-cross in the same way.[73]

There is no fixed stock of simple concepts, from which we can pick out a few as those criterial for use of the word *game*. The properties which any particular thing or phenomenon can be thought of as possessing or lacking are endless, they are limited only by our imagination (which means that they are not limited at all), and there is no telling what properties will be seized on to extend the applicability of the word *game* from those phenomena which have previously been called games to novel phenomena needing to be named – just as, given some novel phenomenon, we have no way of predicting which existing word will have its meaning extended by society to cover it. We may confidently predict that the word *game* will in future be used for things different in kind from any of our contemporary games, but we cannot predict what features of those novel things will cause them to be called games. And, if the earliest games were, say, ball games, with board games such as chess being a later invention, then although after the fact it might look 'obvious' that *game* was the appropriate general term to cover chess, before the extension of meaning occurred it was in no way determinate – rather than noticing the similarities between chess and football, one might have noticed the turn-taking behaviour of chess and extended the word *conversation* or *dialogue* to cover it instead, for instance.

The analogy with family resemblances is an apt one; we expect new members of a family to resemble their parents and ancestors in some ways, but we do not know what features will be retained in the next generation or what innovations will appear – just as, in the case of evolution of species, we expect the descendants of a given species to show some similarities with that species while we have absolutely no idea what particular novel organs or instinctive behaviour-patterns they may acquire.

This view of semantics as creative has not gone unchallenged by linguists. Chomsky himself has had very little of substance to say on the matter, but he has given his blessing to the work of those, particularly his M.I.T. colleague Jerrold Katz, who have considered the subject.[74] Katz has supposed that the vocabulary of a language *can* be analysed in terms of a fixed stock of sematic primitives which are assembled into various complex structures. There are a number of unclarities in Katz's technical exposition of his system;[75] but what is quite clear is that his attempts to meet the general philosophical objections to any such system of analysis are inadequate, to put it kindly.

Thus, Katz points out how his system reflects a sharp distinction between analytic and synthetic sentences; to Quine's objection that no such distinction exists Katz replies by describing an empirical test of native-speaker's behaviour by means of which the distinction may be established. But, although Katz specifies the results which the test would yield, he makes no pretence of having himself carried out any such test, and the many people who *have* performed similar experiments (some of which were cited by Quine) have uniformly reported quite different results which suggest that Quine is correct in attacking the analytic/synthetic distinction.[76]

After this, it is rather difficult to take Katz's subsequent discussion of semantics seriously; and few other linguists who discuss semantic analysis even show that they are aware of the philosophical objections to their project; they simply take it for granted that the semantics of natural languages ought to be accessible to the same scientific descriptive techniques which they rightly hold to have been successful when applied to syntax. It has become commonplace for linguists to bewail the fact that attempts to apply scientific techniques of description to the field of meaning have not yet actually met with much success, but very few seem to suspect that there may be reasons of principle why they never will.[77]

Linguists who discuss semantics commonly give the game away, in fact, by saying at the outset that they aim to describe only the semantics of words used literally, rather than metaphorically or figuratively, as they would be understood in normal rather than exceptional circumstances.[78] But no circumstances are wholly 'normal', and there is no difference other than a difference of degree between literal and metaphorical usage. We are constantly faced by at least slightly novel things and circumstances to which we have to adapt our given stock of words, and we do so by creatively extending their senses. If the extension is especially great, and particularly when a poet wilfully uses a conceptually 'distant' word where a 'nearer' word was available, we recognize the case as one of semantic innovation or metaphor; but this kind of creative extension of meaning is the essence of normal semantic behaviour, not something unusual (like innovation in syntax) which can reasonably be ignored at a first approximation.[79] Setting out to describe the functioning of a semantic system when it is not unpredictably changing is like setting out to describe the functioning of the heart when it is not beating. It is not because we have not examined linguistic behaviour closely enough that it seems to us 'creative': on the contrary, those who have thought about it seriously rather than taking ancient myths for granted have emphasized its creativity, and nothing said by Chomsky or his followers gives us any reason to dispute this finding. The facts of language strongly support the liberal view of Man; only the short-sightedness of contemporary linguistics has given rise to illusory scientistic arguments against liberalism.

5 Chomsky, Race, and Foreign Policy

While Chomsky attacks the empiricist view of human nature in a spirit of disinterested scientific enquiry, his enthusiasm for the task does not stem only from a wish to establish the truth: as we have seen, Chomsky believes empiricism to have provided the intellectual foundation for an immoral political system. And the burden of guilt which Chomsky places on empiricism is indeed heavy. We have examined the relationship between empiricist philosophy and an economic ideal which Chomsky regards as indefensible; but, in addition to this, Chomsky holds empiricist philosophy to be in a certain sense responsible for the appeal of racialism to the British and American mind, and hence for episodes such as the war in Vietnam, and other manifestations of American power in distant countries.

The existence of a connexion between racialism and empiricist views of language and mind, and the notion that Cartesian rationalism provides an intellectual bulwark against racialism, were argued in an article by H. M. Bracken;[1] and Chomsky has strongly endorsed Bracken's views.[2] Bracken's argument, briefly, runs as follows. One aspect of Descartes' thought was what is known as 'dualism'. Whereas an empiricist might be inclined to think of the term 'mind' as referring to one part of the human body, namely the brain, as considered from a functional rather than from an anatomical point of view, Descartes on the other hand regarded mind and matter (or body) as two radically distinct 'substances' characterized by distinct properties – mind by thought, matter by extension in space. Brute beasts are pure matter, but humans involve mind as well as matter. If one accepts the Aristotelian distinction between the 'essence' of a thing and its merely 'accidental' properties, then one may well feel, as Descartes did, that the mind of a man is his essence – what he really is – while his bodily characteristics are merely accidental, and could be other than they are without the essential man being changed. And, according to Bracken, this is enough to make racialism an untenable intellectual position:

if one is a Cartesian, a defender of mind/body dualism, it becomes impossible to state a racist position. Man's essential properties reside finally in his spirit. His color, his language, his biology, even his sex – are in the strictest sense *accidental*.[3]

For an empiricist, on the other hand, there is no distinction between essence and accident – all the properties of a man are logically on a par with one another, and his skin-colour, for instance, has as much right to be considered an 'important' property as any of his other characteristics. Empiricism provides no intellectual barrier to the formation of racialist attitudes; and Bracken claims that empiricists such as Locke and Hume supported institutions which would certainly today be condemned as racialist, such as the enslavement of negroes. Empiricism is a 'manipulative' doctrine: it teaches that human behaviour is determined by interaction with other humans, rather than autonomous:

. . . thinking of people as conditionable reserves a place for those who must do the conditioning. Which is to say that the empiricist model of man provides room for experts. Once in power they have a clear vested interest in the theories and categories they employ in talking about men and women.[4]

Bracken even comes close to claiming that racialism, in the sense of belief in the inferiority or wickedness of groups of humans distinguished by genetic rather than e.g. by religious criteria, *started* with British empiricism in the seventeenth and eighteenth centuries, and Chomsky adds his authority to this allegation[5] – although Bracken himself admits the persecution of the Marranos by the Spanish Inquisition at the end of the fifteenth century as one forerunner, and I should have thought that belief in the inferiority of groups of humans identifiable by *any* criteria as 'strangers' was one of the instinctive prejudices which is common to all men, and which we must all strive to overcome.[6]

Bracken and Chomsky both admit that the connexion between empiricism and racialism is 'historical' rather than 'logical'; the empiricist view of Man does not make racialism inevitable, though it does nothing to hinder it, and the bulwark against racialism provided by rationalism is only a 'modest' one: 'ingenious   rationalists   could . . . have   articulated   racist theories'.[7]

But none of this stands up for a moment. Bracken's and Chomsky's disclaimers to the effect that the link between empiricism and racialism is 'only historical' and that Cartesianism   provides   only   a   'modest'   bulwark   against racialism merely conceal the fact that they have in reality done nothing whatever to suggest why an empiricist should be more inclined than a rationalist towards racialism. It is difficult not to entertain the notion that their writing might in part be motivated by a desire to link their trend in philosophy with the 'right' side in an issue which happens currently to be a focus of intense public controversy. It is vexatious for an empiricist to be told that his views are one step away from racialism, particularly when, as we shall see, the boot is in fact very much on the other foot.

In the first place, it is straightforwardly untrue that a Cartesian who was for independent reasons inclined to believe in the inferiority of certain races would need to apply any ingenuity to reconcile this belief with Descartes' dualism. It is true that body and mind are distinct substances for Descartes, but they are not *disconnected* substances; after all, we normally do things because we will to do them, in other words our physical actions are controlled by our thought. If minds and bodies are intimately related, then presumably it is open to anyone to argue that people with different kinds of body are likely to have different, possibly unequally valuable, kinds of mind. Dualism is a claim purely about the *logical* relationship between mind and body, not about their substantive nature; this particular strand in Descartes' thought is as irrelevant to the issue of racialism as it is irrelevant (and Chomsky himself has pointed this out[8]) to psychological theory.

It is certainly true that France can claim a better record than Britain in recent years with respect to the degree of tolerance shown by the indigenous population towards immigrants of other races. One could suggest a number of explanations for this, but the fact that the British are by tradition empiricist and the French rationalist surely can have little to do with it; Germany has a fairly strong rationalist tradition, yet it has not been noted as a home of racial tolerance in our century.[9]

Bracken and Chomsky are right to say that empiricism focuses attention on the external influences on a man's behaviour, rather than on the respects in which his behaviour is autonomous. But one cannot possibly infer from this that empiricism sanctions the proposition that members of one race are justified in 'manipulating' the behaviour of members of other races. The gap in logic here seems so very wide that I am unsure how best to answer anyone who questions its existence. Empiricism suggests that *every* man's behaviour is determined by the actions of other men, as well as by non-human influences; nothing in empiricist theory leads us to divide men into 'determiners' and 'determinees' – still less to identify the 'determiners' with one particular ethnic grouping. In political theory, the notion that certain specified individuals should be discriminated against economically, and still more the institution of slavery, are examples of authoritarianism and are utterly alien to the liberal ideal, as should be obvious from material in earlier chapters.

And it should be obvious also that the notion of entrusting the government of a society to 'experts' with a vested interest in the accuracy of their pet theories is a notion which flies in the face of empiricist teaching. For the empiricist there can be no such thing as an infallible expert. As far as possible (which is quite far), governors should act not as 'social engineers' but as neutral umpires, holding the ring while their subjects battle to establish what social arrangements work best, and blowing the whistle only when the rules of fair fighting are breached. Government is a job for amateurs: experts should be 'on tap, not on top'.

What is one to say, then, of the support which Locke, in particular, is alleged to have given to the enslavement of negroes?

In the first place, the evidence quoted by Bracken for saying that Locke held negro slavery to be philosophically justified is extremely thin (and Chomsky says nothing to suggest that he has found independent evidence). Bracken quotes Peter Laslett's critical edition of Locke's *Two Treatises of Government*.[10] But, while the *Treatises* do contain two short passages arguing that 'captives taken in a just war', who have forfeited the right to life and liberty, may be used as slaves instead of being executed, I see little reason to conclude with Laslett that Locke included these passages as a justification of the trade in negro slaves. Locke seems to be arguing that perpetual penal servitude is an appropriate alternative to the death penalty for cases such as the war crimes tried at Nuremberg, and Laslett gives no evidence for the belief that Locke held such a gross misconception of the nature of the slave trade of his time as to suppose that the negroes transported to America had fought on the wrong side in just wars. The fact is that neither Locke nor his contemporaries appear to have seriously considered the philosophical implications of negro slavery.[11] Locke, as secretary to the slave-owning proprietors of Carolina, might be thought to have had more reason to do so than other philosophers; but it seems clear that Locke in fact took the enslavement of negroes completely for granted – it probably never occurred to him that it raised a moral problem.[12]

That negro slavery should not have raised a moral problem for Locke may appear to us grossly inconsistent with his liberalism. But it is important here to appreciate that the implications of a philosophical principle for concrete action will always depend crucially on one's knowledge of the facts of the situation in which one has to act. Liberalism prescribes that all people should be treated by government as on a par in the competition to secure economic well-being. To the modern Briton or American, accustomed every day to encounter members of other races on the street or at his place of work, having many opportunities to become personally acquainted with individuals whose ancestors lived in some of the most distant parts of our planet, it is entirely obvious that the negro, the Chinese, or the Indian are 'people' as much as are the inhabitants of Devon or Vermont. To the Englishman of the late seventeenth century, the facts on which this judgement are based were simply not available. Liberal philosophy prescribes that all who are fully human should be treated as equal under the law; but it is not philosophical theory, only factual knowledge, that shows us that the class of 'fully human' individuals – which will include normal adult Europeans but exclude, for instance, dogs, horses, monkeys, children, and mental defectives – should include rather than exclude normal adult negroes. As recently as a century ago, Charles Darwin regarded the question whether the races of Man were separate biological species as one on which people could reasonably disagree (although, contrary to a statement by Bracken, he did not say that they were – he explicitly argued that they were not).[13] To Locke, negroes must have been almost as unknown as life-forms revealed by the Mars probes might be to us, and it seems merely anachronistic to accuse Locke of failing to acknowledge their right to be counted as fellow-humans.

The linguist, of course, will be inclined to point to the possession by all human races of languages as the most obvious, tangible evidence that they all possess the faculty of reason, which brutes lack, and which entitles those who have it to the privileges of full membership in society. But, living in the seventeenth century, it seems very improbable that Locke would have been in a position to know, as we know today, that the indigenous languages of Africa, Asia, and the New World were systems comparable in complexity and richness to the classical and modern languages of Europe and the Middle East. The former languages were utterly unknown to the scholarship of the time; and stories about languages of primitive peoples being poor things of a few score words and little or no grammar – being, in fact, little different from the ape 'languages' discussed in Ch. 4 – remained current in educated circles until a much later period.[14] Locke's 'racialism', in all probability, was a consequence not of his philosophical principles but of his factual ignorance. It may possibly be, of course, that evidence can be adduced to show that Locke knew negroes to be fully human; in that case his toleration of slavery would have been grossly inconsistent with his liberal principles – this would not be the first time that Locke has been accused of inconsistency.[15] But my brief is to defend liberalism, not Locke, and the incompatibility of liberalism with racialist policies is very clear.

What is also clear is that, when negro slavery and the treatment of the sparse aboriginal populations in the remaining colonies of settlement did become live issues in Britain, with the campaigns leading to the abolition of the slave trade in 1807 and of slavery in 1833, and the controversy of the 1830s between Exeter Hall and the Colonial Reformers, it was the Liberal side of the political spectrum which pleaded the cause of the alien races. The Colonial Reformers argued in favour of greater freedom for the colonists; but such freedom was in practice largely freedom to coerce the aborigines, and therefore not the sort of freedom of which a liberal approves. Accordingly, the liberals of Exeter Hall opposed the Reformers, and the Colonial Office sided with Exeter Hall. Exeter Hall favoured the extension of empire, but this was consistent; one of the important aims (and achievements) of the extension of the British Empire in the nineteenth century was suppression of the slave trade where it still flourished.[16] One might well argue that these issues ought to have been taken up earlier than they were, and that there must have been many liberals who hypocritically avoided drawing the conclusions which their principles implied with respect to the treatment of other races; but that is very different from saying that liberalism encourages racialism.

The truth is that the respective implications of empiricism and rationalism for our attitudes to race are precisely contrary to what Bracken and Chomsky suggest.

The empiricist, as we have seen, thinks of the human mind as originally a mere blank slate. The rich organization of an adult's mind is wholly the product of interaction with his environment since birth: exposure to the teachings of his elders, broadened and corrected in the light of his own experience. It is a clear consequence of this that the empiricist will think of intellectual diversity among the various groups into which mankind is divided in terms of cultural rather than biological differences. The two variables will tend to coincide, of course, since culture is transmitted primarily by parents to children; but it is the continuity of teaching and example, not biological heredity, which ensures that an ethnic group usually resembles its ancestors in the nature of its intellectual life. One blank slate is the same as another, so a newborn Chinese or Zulu adopted by English parents would grow up intellectually indistinguishable from a native Englishman (and *vice versa*), although of course physiologically he would remain a Chinese or a Zulu.

Furthermore, empiricist philosophy strongly suggests, at least, that different human cultures cannot be compared and ranked as 'superior' and 'inferior': they will be merely different. The evolution of human cultures, after all, is logically parallel to the evolution of biological species. A chart of the relationships between biological species shows not a single line of evolution from lower to higher, but rather a constantly branching tree; a given species at any one time produces many descendent species at a later age, each of which has departed in a different and unpredictable direction from its ancestor. It makes sense to say that a species is 'higher' than the species which are its direct ancestors, but it is meaningless so to compare species at the tips of different branches: the shrimp, the blackbird, and the dandelion constitute very *different* solutions to the problem of survival, but what would it mean to call one 'higher' than another? (This point is somewhat obscured in practice by the special biological position of Man; we feel we have good grounds for regarding our own species as superior to all others, because of the enormous advantage conferred by our faculty of reason, and we consequently incline to rank other species as 'higher' or 'lower' depending on their nearness to Man in the evolutionary tree.

The special position of Man is a standard problem for Darwinian evolutionary theory – the co-discoverer of biological evolution, A. R. Wallace, argued that the general theory needed to be supplemented by extra principles to account for the human mind[17] – but, for the present analogy, this point is best ignored; think of the tree of evolution as it must have been before the emergence of Man, when there really would have been no grounds for ranking any one 'twig' of the tree above any other.) So we may envisage the cultures of different human groups constantly being enriched by the activities of successive generations, and frequently branching in unpredictable directions as growing populations split and found divergent traditions, without our having any grounds for calling any one of the cultural traditions existing at a given time 'superior' or 'inferior' to the other traditions existing at that time. (This model is of course less applicable to the history of the last few centuries, in which the development of communications has made cultural traditions much less separate from one another than they used to be.) The empiricist may well regard it as literally meaningless to compare diverse cultures, since we have no 'neutral' conceptual system in which different cultures can be described – every culture has to be described in terms of the conceptual system appropriate to it.[18] And the empiricist will certainly see cultural diversity as desirable, as a source of strength; just as knowledge grows fastest when many individuals are trying out different hypotheses, so human happiness increases fastest if many human groups are experimenting with different forms of life (always provided, in each case, that the experiments which do not work out well are abandoned in favour of the more successful ones).

It would be possible for an empiricist to avoid the conclusion that human cultures were unrankable, e.g. by suggesting that the different races had originated separately and at widely different periods, so that the cultural evolution of one race had not proceeded as far as that of another. But, while this sort of notion was widely believed before Darwin, it was difficult to reconcile with his biological theory, which made it clear that all men descend from common ancestors.[19] A modern empiricist seems therefore to be debarred from ranking cultures, except with respect to the degree to which they permit or encourage innovation and hence cultural progress.

For the rationalist, on the other hand, who believes that the important features of our intellectual life are inborn rather than learned, purely cultural differences between groups will seem relatively uninteresting; and, since the ultimate truth is already available to the introspection of the philosopher, there will certainly be no *value* in cultural diversity. Quite possibly different cultures may be rankable according to their respective closeness to the ideal social system as defined by the infallible intuition of the philosopher-king; but there is little point in dwelling on relative degrees of imperfection, what matters is to remove the imperfections and bring cultures into conformity with the ideal.

Historically, the attitudes of different nations to matters of race have conformed to this logic. Compare, for instance, the colonial policies of empiricist Britain and rationalist France. Obviously the very assumption by Britain of governmental authority over an alien people inevitably entailed a considerable degree of modification of that people's culture. But, that admitted, British policy – in theory, and to a great extent in practice – was to refrain as far as possible from tampering with indigenous cultural patterns. Thus, for instance, when possible the British governed through local rulers rather than directly; in the period immediately before Independence, about one in four of the inhabitants of the Indian Empire were ruled by Indian princes to whose administrations British political advisers were attached. The French, on the other hand, aimed to bring the cultural patterns of their colonies into conformity with their view of the fixed ideal, which meant in practice turning them into departments of France in all but geographical location.[20]

In the field of language study, Chomsky's work differs from that of his empiricist American predecessors very much as one might predict from these philosophical considerations.

The father of linguistics in America was Franz Boas, for

whom the study of language was one branch of the study of culture, i.e. anthropology, and Boas makes it clear that cultures can only be studied each in its own terms rather than being classifiable by some neutral conceptual schema:

The history of inventions and the history of science show to us in course of time constant additions to the range of inventions, and a gradual increase of empirical knowledge. On this basis we might be inclined to look for a single line of development of culture. . . . The knowledge of today makes such a view untenable. Cultures differ like so many species . . . of animals. . . . It seems impossible, if we disregard invention and knowledge, the two elements just referred to, to bring cultures into any kind of continuous series.

. . . the material of anthropology is such that it needs must be a historical science, one of the sciences the interest of which centers in the attempt to understand the individual phenomena rather than in the establishment of general laws. . . .[21]

. . . a system of social anthropology and 'laws' of cultural development . . . are unattainable. . . . [I oppose] speculative theories based on the imposition of categories derived from our culture upon foreign cultures. . . .[22]

Boas, and his successors in the great flourishing of linguistic research which occurred in the U.S.A. from the 1930s onwards (many of whom made their commitment to the empiricist view of human understanding much more explicit than Boas does in the first sentence quoted above) stressed that the categories in terms of which we are accustomed to discuss the familiar languages will often not be applicable to 'exotic' languages such as the Amerindian languages on which much of their research was concentrated. (Indeed, they regarded the traditional categories as not necessarily constituting an ultimate truth even with respect to the languages to which they are customarily applied; thus, Charles Fries analysed English in terms of 'Class 1 words', 'Class 2 words', etc., in order to avoid prejudging the issue by using the terms 'noun', 'verb', 'adjective', and the like.[23]) Although the languages of the world are very different one from another, there is no sense in which they can be described as relatively 'primitive' or 'advanced'; to choose one at random from the very many passages where this point is made, R. A. Hall states that:

All languages spoken at present, even those of American Indian, African, or Australian Bushman tribes, have reached substantially the same stage of development and are equally susceptible of linguistic analysis.[24]

For Chomsky, on the other hand, a principal aim of linguistic research is to establish a fixed system of categories in terms of which any human language can be described. Thus:

a *generative grammar* . . . is a system of rules that relate signals to semantic interpretations of those signals. . . . the theory of generative grammar must provide a general, language-independent means for representing the signals and semantic interpretations that are inter-related by the grammars of particular languages.[25]

. . . to develop a substantive linguistic theory we must provide . . . a specification of the class of potential generative grammars. . . .[26]

(Chomsky adds: 'Before going on . . ., let us reassure ourselves about the uncontroversial character of what has preceded. Is there, in fact, anything in this account to which exception can be taken?' – a question which he answers in the negative.)

Furthermore, one of the components of a linguistic theory which aims to account for the ability of an infant to acquire his mother tongue will be an 'evaluation measure': a function which ranks the class of possible grammars, and hence the class of possible languages, into a linear sequence.[27] The reason for this is that, as Chomsky points out, the limited amount of data on the language surrounding him which is available to an infant at any given time will never, logically, be sufficient to determine the structure of that language uniquely – there will always be questions left open which are not decided by the data that have come in so far, no matter how long the child goes on attending to examples. If the child is ever to stop learning and plump for a particular language as the one he will himself speak, he must have some means of choosing between the various languages which are all compatible with a limited quantity of data.[28] The problem will be partly solved by the fact that the range of 'humanly possible languages' is narrow relative to the range of logically conceivable languages; but Chomsky feels that this will not be enough, that the data available to a child during the years of language-acquisition will not even eliminate all but one of the humanly possible languages. Therefore our psychological machinery for language-acquisition must involve some ranking of humanly possible grammars, and we will plump for the 'best possible grammar' compatible with what we have heard.

Since Chomsky discusses this notion of ranking in connexion with the problem facing, say, an English infant who does not know whether what he is hearing is what we know as English or is some other humanly possible language, similar to English, which no human community in fact speaks, Chomsky himself does not stress the notion that the languages actually spoken in the world can be ranked relative to one another. But his theory certainly implies this, and some of his followers have developed this aspect of his work in more concrete detail. Thus Theo Vennemann argues in recent work for a syntactic evaluation criterion which treats, for instance, Japanese as an unusually 'good' language and German (Vennemann's own native tongue) as an unusually 'bad' language.[29] (English occupies an intermediate position.)

Genetic inheritance does not, as far as we know, predispose particular individuals to learn one of the world's languages rather than another; a child of Japanese parents adopted by Germans will learn German as readily as a child of German parentage, and a biologically German child (if we may so speak) reared in a Japanese environment will learn Japanese as readily as a biologically Japanese child. Therefore Chomsky might argue that his notion about ranking of languages does not conduce to racialism, strictly defined. That is, the rankability of languages implies not that some ethnic groups inherit psychological structure inferior to that inherited by other ethnic groups, but only that (certain aspects of) the learned cultural patterns of some nations are (in some sense) inferior to (the corresponding aspects of) the learned cultural patterns of other nations – which may, perhaps, be regarded as a less unfortunate finding; no biological factors prevent the speakers of a 'bad' language learning to use a 'good' language instead. (Here and below, I should make it clear that I am not concerned *primarily* with the truth or falsity of the doctrines discussed – as it happens I regard Vennemann's development of the notion of grammar-ranking as highly insightful and very probable correct; the point I am aiming to stress is that Chomsky is in a peculiarly awkward position from which to accuse his empiricist opponents of providing an intellectual foundation for racialism.)

However, while Chomsky may dismiss the prima facie racialist implications of his notion of grammar-ranking on the grounds that it concerns an aspect of inherited psychological machinery which is assumed to be identical for all men, if we turn to consider the general theory of human nature for which Chomsky is arguing we may find that it is less easily acquitted of the same charge.

The essence of Chomsky's view of Man, remember, is the claim that an individual's intellectual faculties are largely acquired, as his physiology is, by the mechanisms of genetic inheritance, and that environmental influences will normally affect a man's intellectual life only in certain limited respects. (The word 'normally' here is intended to exclude the kind of major traumas which may radically affect either the physiological or the intellectual nature of an individual. Thus, we are all 'genetically programmed' to have two legs, but the accidents of war and the like leave some individuals with fewer; and similarly an injury to the brain can rob a man of the faculty of speech altogether.) Now we are rather well aware of the general pattern of physiological attributes produced by the mechanisms of genetic inheritance. Except for a small proportion of individuals with congenital defects (and ignoring sexual differences, which are irrelevant here), all individuals inherit much the same broad physiological structure – two arms, two legs, head with eyes above nose above mouth, and so on – but we find differences of detail: some individuals have slightly longer legs than others, some have blue eyes while others have brown, and so forth. Furthermore, where we find groups of people who, for geographical or other reasons, have tended to breed more with one another than with outsiders (what we commonly call 'races' or 'stocks', although these terms suggest the possibility of sharp categorization in an area where we can in reality speak only of statistical tendencies), we find consistent trends in the distribution of variable physiological traits. Thus, the inhabitants of Japan tend to have shorter legs than the inhabitants of Germany (although many individual Japanese have longer legs than many individual Germans), a much higher proportion of Germans than of Japanese are blue-eyed, and so on. There is no great mystery about this; not only are the visible facts well known, but the genetic mechanisms which give rise to these facts are reasonably well understood.

Now, if the nature of human intellectual faculties is largely determined by biological inheritance, and if there is any variability in those faculties as between individuals (as there clearly is), then the obvious corollary is that there will be statistical tendencies for intellectual attributes to differ as between the races. In particular, if any variable aspect of human intellect can be expressed in terms of a linear scale, as can length of legs, for instance, in the domain of physiology, then we will expect the members of different races to cluster round different mean points on that scale. Psychologists have produced evidence that there is an intellectual variable which they call g, for 'general intelligence' (meaning something closely akin to what the layman means by intelligence), which can indeed be measured on a linear scale and can be expressed as an 'I.Q.';[30] therefore, if Chomsky's view of human nature is correct, we will expect races to differ in average level of general intelligence or I.Q.

For a thoroughgoing, Lockian empiricist, such a possibility is literally unstatable. If minds begin as blank slates, we can hardly say that newborn German minds are blanker or less blank than newborn Japanese minds. If all our cognitive dispositions, including those that we regard as manifestations of 'intelligence', are built up by interaction with the environment, then any differences in intelligence between individuals or be-

But this sort of empiricism is absurd - note the creative engine has now dropped out.

tween races must by definition be the product of differences in environmental factors.

Of course, it would be quite possible for Chomsky to argue that his theory of human nature is compatible with lack of racial differences in intelligence – as indeed, logically, it is. Chomsky does not and could not argue that every detail of human mental functioning is determined genetically (my ability to name the capital of Australia correctly is clearly not, for instance), and it might be that just those characteristics of our minds which contribute to our being regarded as more or less intelligent are among the characteristics that the genetic blueprint leaves 'open'. But the whole tendency of Chomsky's approach to mind consists of arguing that we ought to assimilate our account at least of the 'important', 'central' human mental phenomena to our relatively well-established account of physiological phenomena in terms of genetic determination; and the fact is that statistical variation between the races is part of that well-established account – there are few, if any, complex physiological phenomena which are completely invariant throughout the human species while nevertheless differentiating our species from others. Indeed, from the physiological point of view the idea that species are demarcated by sharp borderlines one from another and that racial differences are on a clearly separate level from differences between species is as much a fallacy as the non-linguist's idea that 'languages' are sharply separate from one another and that there is a real distinction to be drawn between 'languages' and 'dialects'. The truth is that one taxonomist will divide a group of related biological organisms into ten species where another taxonomist may divide it into fifty species, and there are no good grounds for calling one right and the other wrong. For the Popperian philosopher, Man is an exception to the general rule that species boundaries reflect arbitrary decisions by biologists; humans really are special, because all of them have creative minds – things which are not amenable to analysis by the scientific method, and therefore are not adequately explained in terms of biological evolution – while, it is (rightly or wrongly) supposed, all other species are biological organisms and nothing more. But if Chomsky argues that psychology should be assimilated to biology this Popperian account is not available to him; intelligence seems to be about as 'central' a human mental phenomenon as any, so it would be wholly perverse of Chomsky not to predict racial variation in intelligence.

If we were very lucky it might turn out that in intelligence, unlike other aspects of human biology, there was no variation correlated with descent; but for Chomsky this would be a highly surprising finding running counter to the general tendency of his thought. If we ask which of the two approaches to human nature, empiricism or rationalism, does more to provide an intellectual foundation for the drawing of invidious distinctions between the races, the answer is plain enough. I do not mean to accuse Descartes of arguing for such distinctions – when he claimed that certain ideas were innate he obviously did not mean that they were encoded in our genes or anything of that sort, and it seems quite unlikely that he ever thought about inherited differences between men. But Chomsky's genetically sophisticated version of rationalism is in a different case. As we have seen in Ch. 3 in connexion with authoritarian government, Chomsky can avoid being convicted of the tendency which he imputes to others only by means of an *ad hoc* resort to a logical loophole.[31]

And in any case, it is known independently of Chomsky's work that, with respect to the issue under discussion, we are not lucky. Arthur Jensen of the University of California, and other psychologists, have shown that level of general intelligence is largely determined by heredity rather than by environment, and that levels of intelligence do vary statistically as between the races. Of the inhabitants of the U.S.A., for instance, whites are on average more intelligent than negroes but less intelligent than orientals; the average Canadian Eskimo is more intelligent than the average white Canadian.[32] (But let me stress that the differences which are found are small relative to the degree of variation found *within* groups – so that there is a high probability that the difference in intelligence between a randomly chosen pair of individuals of unlike races will be opposite in direction to that predicted by the overall statistics.)

Jensen's work has been attacked, often with great vehemence, by people who would like his findings not to be true. But the attacks are very unsuccessful. In many cases they are simply based on misunderstanding or misrepresentation of what Jensen and others have said. Certainly this is not always so; but those who have brought more serious intellectual effort to bear on the task of reconciling the observations of Jensen and others with the hypothesis that there are no genetically determined differences of intelligence between the races have had to resort to an increasingly and perversely complex structure of special assumptions. Just as no scientific theory can be decisively confirmed, so no hypothesis can be irrevocably refuted; if one is sufficiently anxious to believe that the Earth stands still and the Sun moves round it, it is possible even today, by piling epicycle on epicycle, to reconcile the Ptolemaic system of astronomy with observation; but the Copernican system offers so very much more straightforward an account of the data that no respectable astronomer suggests retention of the earlier theory. In this sense, one who studies the controversy about heritability of intelligence in a spirit of neutral academic enquiry can scarcely avoid the conclusion that Jensen is right and his opponents wrong.[33] If it is 'racialist' to believe that certain ethnic groups are intrinsically somewhat less intelligent, statistically speaking, than others, then I believe that anyone who examines the evidence in good faith must be a racialist (although I take it that to be a racialist is to hold unwarranted prejudices rather than scientifically based beliefs about racial differences, so that the term would be inapplicable here). Notice that while I accept Jensen's theory, I do so not *qua* empiricist; to accept that theory is to reject empiricism in its most thoroughgoing form, and to admit that there are some aspects of mental functioning which are inborn, as the rationalists claim. We have already seen that both empiricism and rationalism in their most extreme forms are untenable, and that Chomsky has provided satisfactory arguments for a strictly limited version of rationalism.

In contrast to many other contemporary *bien-pensants*, but consistently in view of his rationalist approach to human nature, Chomsky does not suggest that Jensen's theory is false. Chomsky does not say explicitly that he accepts Jensen's interpretation of his data; instead, he attempts to sidestep the issue by arguing that it is an unimportant one which would be better not raised in the first place. Thus:

> it seems that the question of the relation, if any, between race and intelligence has little scientific importance (as it has no social importance, except under the assumptions of a racist society). . . . It is . . . surprising to me that so many commentators should find it disturbing that I.Q. might be heritable, perhaps largely so.[34]

Given 'the assumptions of a racist society', on the other hand, to choose such a topic for academic research is as mischievous as would have been a decision by a psychologist in Nazi Germany to investigate whether Jews have a genetically determined tendency towards usury and domination:

> there is the likelihood that even opening this question and regarding it as a subject for scientific inquiry would provide ammunition for Goebbels and Rosenberg and their henchmen. Were this hypothetical psychologist to disregard the likely social consequences of his research (or even his undertaking of research) under existing social conditions, he would fully deserve the contempt of decent people.[35]

For the latter comment one can have considerable sympathy, although I believe it is misguided. Were it possible, it might have been a very humane action to initiate an impartial scientific investigation in Nazi Germany into the possibility that Jews inherit a disposition to usury, since one would expect the result to be negative (there are, after all, well-known historical reasons why Jewish communities were forced through no choice of theirs into money-lending as a way of life in Christian countries), and to establish that negative result firmly might possibly have done something to stem the tide of race-hatred in Nazi Germany. The trouble with Jensen's work is that it has produced the 'wrong' answer; but obviously the whole point of the scientific method is that one cannot specify in advance how the results are to turn out. And, while Jensen's results are not as pleasing as would have been the discovery that there are no intelligence differences between groups, they are nevertheless a welcome corrective, surely, to the bigoted attitudes to race which both Chomsky and the liberal deplore. I am not an American, but I doubt whether many white Americans of the kind who regard opprobrious epithets as the appropriate vocabulary for talking about negroes feel at the same time that their fellow-citizens of oriental ancestry would be justified in referring to whites in similar terms; and I question whether such people envisage intellectual differences between races in terms of largely overlapping distributions about slightly differing means. What is very clear is that once the question had been raised, if the qualified scholars had all refused to investigate the issue, then the bigots, and indeed more open-minded people too, would certainly have drawn conclusions much more unpleasant than those which turn out to be correct.

It is clear also that questions such as the one investigated by Jensen will arise much more regularly and acutely in an authoritarian society, such as Chomsky advocates, than under liberalism. The original motive for Jensen's research, after all, was the failure of very expensive Federally-funded experimental programmes of compensatory education, designed to raise the educational attainments of children from impoverished backgrounds (who tended also to be negroes) closer to the national mean. The suggestion was that the programmes might be attempting the impossible; the children might be poor learners, statistically speaking, not because they happened to be brought up in a poor environment but because they were intrinsically less educable than average. Since large amounts of public money were being spent on the programmes, this was an entirely legitimate public concern; taxpayers are entitled to expect that their money should not be wasted by governors who place considerations of sentiment before those of fact. In an extreme liberal society, on the other hand, parents will be responsible for the education of their children, and no third party will have an interest in knowing how much and what sort of education parents choose to buy for their children. The more liberal a society is, the fewer reasons of public policy there will be to decide issues such as the one investigated by Jensen.

To say that the issue of correlations between race and intelligence 'has little scientific importance' is to express a personal opinion about which scientific questions are worth investigating, and as such one cannot quarrel with it (although it is perhaps a surprising opinion to be expressed by someone who has spent his entire professional life arguing for the thesis that human intellectual faculties are largely genetically inherited). To say that it is of 'no social importance' is less acceptable: Chomsky's own work includes a rather clear analysis of one reason why it is of considerable social importance. Consider the problem confronting someone who has the task of selecting a candidate for some desirable position requiring high intelligence – say, a demanding but enjoyable job, or a place in an excellent but small graduate department in a university. The task of the selector is logically quite analogous to that confronting an infant in learning its mother tongue: the selector has to make a prediction about the candidate's future performance on the basis of the limited quantity of data available by the time of decision, just as the infant has to predict the nature of the language spoken by his elders on the basis of a limited number of instances; in both cases the data are logically insufficient for the prediction, but it must somehow be made. Now, racial membership of candidates is usually a very salient datum in these situations; so, if it is known that race is statistically speaking a predictor of intelligence, then the obvious danger is that the selector's intuitive 'evaluation criterion' (and such subtle decisions can only be made intuitively) will assign considerable weight to racial membership, so that dull orientals will regularly be chosen over bright whites and negroes.

Chomsky suggests that this undesirable effect can arise only in a racialist society. 'If, say, it were determined that mental capacity correlates with height, no social consequences would ensue, since our society does not suffer under discrimination by height.'[36] But this is clearly false; if it became known that short people tend to be more intelligent than tall people, then, since an individual's height is much easier to determine than his level of intelligence, bright but tall people would certainly find themselves regularly passed over. Chomsky quite fails to grasp the relevance to this issue of his own discussion of the problem of making decisions on the basis of logically insufficient data.[37]

Under authoritarianism, there would appear to be no escape from this difficulty. One can pass laws forbidding selectors to take racial membership into account in making their selections (and such laws have come into being recently in Britain and the U.S.A.); but the usual problem, surely, is not that selectors are *unwilling* to discount this particular factor in making their intuitive decisions but that they are *unable* to do so. Different selectors' intuitive evaluation criteria will no doubt vary in the relative weightings assigned to diverse factors, but one cannot will oneself to adopt a particular intuitive criterion. Under liberalism, of course, the problem (like so many others) is self-correcting; a firm whose selectors have inefficient criteria will become less profitable and therefore jobs in it will become less attractive, a graduate department whose selectors have inefficient criteria will become less excellent and thus a less desirable department. (It is true that this self-correction mechanism acts only over a relatively long term: but at least it exists.)

Chomsky, then, is disingenuous in suggesting that he cannot see what all the fuss over Jensen is about. But there is worse to come.

I have argued in earlier chapters that the facts of language do justify a kind of rationalism, but a very restricted kind. The logical forms of our utterances are universal, and I accept Chomsky's suggestion that they are universal because they are inherited; but nothing we inherit limits the word-concepts we can formulate, or the ways in which we can assemble those word-concepts into sensical propositions. These matters are not determined by heredity or by anything else, and it is in the nature of human beings to formulate genuinely novel concepts and genuinely novel propositions. Now this very restricted kind of rationalism allows room for belief in inherited intellectual differences, but it requires that such inherited differences must themselves be of a very restricted kind. Thus, it is possible that some people inherit a propensity to formulate novel concepts or propositions more frequently than others, or a propensity to formulate concepts and propositions which are more original – further removed from existing concepts and propositions – than those typically formulated by others, or a propensity to draw inferences from their novel propositions more rapidly and to better purpose than others do. All these conceivable differences of inherited intellect, which are purely quantitative, seem quite compatible with the restricted kind of rationalism that Chomsky has justified (although they are not, certainly, necessary consequences of that restricted rationalism); and they seem to correspond fairly well to our notion of 'intelligence', at least in the layman's sense and I believe also in the psychologist's.[38] But the facts of language are *not* compatible with what we might call 'qualitative differences' in inherited intellect. That is, if we accept the limitations of Chomskyan linguistic nativism for which I have argued in Ch. 4, then we cannot consistently allow that some people inherit a propensity to formulate *certain types of* novel concepts or novel propositions. This is surely fairly clear; what we mean by calling an activity 'creative' is that its products do not fall within an antecedently specifiable class. If we could predict that certain individuals tend to formulate concepts or propositions of a kind which we could describe, then, by describing them, we would ensure that any such mental acts were not 'creative', in the 'rich' sense. If one accepts the argument that our mental lives are creative in that sense, then one must accept that any inherited intellectual differences between men will be only quantitative, not qualitative.

For Chomsky, of course, the situation is rather different. Chomsky does believe that a reasonable goal for linguistic research is to formulate a 'universal semantic alphabet', in terms of which one will be able to specify the range of potential word-concepts which men are biologically capable of acquiring; and, although Chomsky himself has not done much in this connexion, he has expressed his approval of research by others which aims to state systematically the range of sensical sentences, that is, the range of potential propositions which men are biologically capable of formulating.[39] Chomsky quite explicitly sees it as likely that the potential ideas which humans are biologically capable of producing are only a small subset of those which would in some sense be available but for the limitations of our intellectual equipment:

An intellectually significant science, an intelligible explanatory theory, can be developed by humans in case something close to the true theory in a certain domain happens to fall within human 'science-forming' capacities. . . . the class of humanly accessible sciences [is] possibly a small subset of those potential sciences that deal with matters concerning which we hope (vainly) to attain some insight and understanding.[40]

I must confess that I cannot understand this. I do not see what Chomsky can mean by writing of theories which are sensical or even true but which we are constitutionally incapable of formulating or understanding – in what sense would these mysterious entities count as 'theories'? One might interpret Chomsky as thinking in terms of a body of true theories in the mind of God, only some of which can be grasped by the minds of mortals; but Chomsky does not write in these terms, and a theory which *no* mind can grasp seems to me to be a contradiction.[41]

But let us suspend our scepticism, and let us suppose that Chomsky may be right in suggesting that there are genetically determined boundaries to the range of ideas which men can formulate. Then the almost inevitable corollary would surely be that these inherited bounds, while broadly similar for all men, will differ somewhat as between individuals; and that there will be a tendency for the location of the boundaries to be relatively constant within an ethnic group but to vary more widely as between groups. It would make sense to use such phrases as e.g. 'German mathematics', 'Jewish physics', meaning not 'mathematics within the tradition that happens to have grown up in German universities', 'physics of the sort which tends to appeal to individuals who have been brought up as Jews', but rather 'mathematics of the kind German minds are innately

capable of grasping', 'physical theories which Jews are biologically predestined to mistake for truth'.

Forty years ago, such phrases were used seriously – although
not in the English-speaking world. The empiricist Britons and
Americans took them to be self-evident nonsense. I should be
sorry to think that that judgement was mistaken. Fortunately,
since I do not believe in semantic predictability, I do not for a
moment believe that it was mistaken. I accept that some
individuals may be rather slower than others in matters of
intellectual innovation – that some will be leaders in the task of
increasing practical and theoretical human knowledge, while
others will be followers; but I do not believe there are any
barriers to the continuation of that task (although *at any given
time* there will of course be limits to our knowledge), and I do not
believe that some people are genetically incapable of grasping
particular ideas which others can understand. If such are the
consequences of rejecting empiricism, then perhaps we may
hope to hear rather less in future about empiricism being the
next best thing to racialism.

A defender of Chomsky might object here that I am putting
words into Chomsky's mouth in a quite irresponsible way. It is
true that Chomsky does not say explicitly that he believes
individuals or ethnic groups to exhibit qualitative differences of
intellect. But, first, that thesis is such a straightforward inference from what Chomsky does say about the inherited intellectual limitations of mankind that we can hardly absolve him
of responsibility if those who trust him as an intellectual leader
go on to draw it. One who leads a blind man to the edge of a
precipice does not escape censure merely because he refrains
from pushing the blind man over. And secondly, while Chomsky
does not make the thesis explicit, much of his discussion of
foreign policy suggests strongly that it is lurking not far below
the conscious surface of his mind. To see this, let us consider
Chomsky's arguments against American participation in the
Vietnam war.

There is a considerable difficulty in writing about the war in
Vietnam. Whatever one's beliefs about the political issues

involved, this was one of the most barbaric episodes in human history, and it occurred far too recently for its horrors to have faded for those who experienced them. To refer to this war in order to illustrate an academic argument about political theory may seem to be the height of callousness. I have better reason, perhaps, than most to be sensitive to this problem; such reputation as I possess in the field of substantive linguistic research is based largely on analyses of the Vietnamese language carried out in the cosy security of various English and American university towns during the years when the speakers of the language were enduring the war at its most savage, and I am a citizen of a country whose role in the conflict was an exceptionally ignoble one.[42] Chomsky has argued movingly that to discuss the rights and wrongs of so barbaric an episode as if it were a serious intellectual issue is degrading – as degrading as it would be to hold a sober, neutral debate about the ethics of exterminating several million Jews and others in Nazi Germany.[43] Chomsky thus puts anyone who disagrees with his attitude to the war in the position of appearing the kind of moral animal who might be prepared to argue in favour of genocide.

This is a false position; any analogy between the ethics of the Nazi 'Final Solution' and those of U.S. participation in the Vietnam war is entirely specious.[44] As an empiricist, I believe that men can (though they often do not) learn from their errors; if by thinking soberly about the issues of principle raised by that war we can improve our understanding of how governments should function, that may be a tiny scrap of good to set in the balance against the great weight of evil which the war entailed. Certainly I would be happier to discuss foreign policy in connexion with examples from the comfortably distant past; but Chomsky discusses Vietnam, so that is the arena in which I must take issue with him. Chomsky's discussion of the war presupposes a false, and objectionably false, attitude to human nature. If the horror of the war is taken as making any questioning of that attitude unthinkable for decent men, then those who fell in Vietnam will have done worse than die in vain.

While I disagree with Chomsky over some of the principles

involved in the Vietnam episode, I would not dispute his main practical conclusions. I believed at the time and still believe that America should have withdrawn from Vietnam and allowed the Communists to take over many years earlier than they did (although, unlike Chomsky, I cannot claim to have done much to make this view more widely accepted). Even when a cause is just, those who take on themselves the responsibility of prosecuting it by military means are morally obliged to strike some sort of balance between the degree of suffering entailed by the war, on the one hand, and the 'weight' of the cause and the chances of success on the other. I have no idea how that balance is to be struck (although I cannot accept the pacifist position that *no* cause justifies war, and Chomsky does not write as a pacifist either); but I feel sure that the enormous suffering caused by the Vietnam war from the mid-1960s onwards could only conceivably be outweighed by a cause which was morally about as 'weighty' and clearcut as any in the history of human conflict, and in which the chances of a victory by the right side were at least approaching evens. I did not and do not think that the Thieu/Ky regime had anywhere near this weight of justice in its cause. Unlike Chomsky, I regarded it as somewhat superior to any government likely to be installed in South Vietnam after a Communist victory (since it was a government with somewhat better prospects of evolving towards the liberal ideal), but the difference was surely not outstandingly great, when measured against the overwhelming level of horror of the war;[45] and furthermore it seemed unlikely (unless they invaded and occupied North Vietnam, an option which was presumably ruled out by the danger of starting a global war with the big Communist powers) that the Americans could achieve any permanent victory in Vietnam.

The fact that very many of us are likely to agree with Chomsky about the wrongness of prolonging the war after the mid-1960s makes his discussion of the theoretical issues raised by the war all the more insidious.[46] One who is not alert to the logical fallacy is in danger of supposing that, because we all now see that Chomsky was right in concluding that the war should be abandoned, therefore we probably ought to admit that he was right with respect to the principles on which he based that conclusion. It does not follow, of course – false premises often have true consequences; and in fact Chomsky's reasons for opposing the war are very different from the reasons which I have listed. Indeed, Chomsky is fairly contemptuous of those who, like myself, use the misery caused by the war as an argument against it: 'The principle that we should retract our claws when the victim bleeds too much is hardly an elevated one.'[47] This is of course a highly tendentious way of paraphrasing the argument – the cat-and-mouse metaphor suggests that it is their enemies' too obvious suffering which bothers the hypocritical liberals, whereas in fact the liberal was concerned about the suffering of innocent individuals who were not responsible for the existence of a state of war, rather than of the North Vietnamese and N.L.F. leaders who made the decisions to prosecute the war on the Communist side. But it makes the point that Chomsky has no sympathy for those – whom he rightly characterizes as 'liberals' – who opposed the war primarily because of the human costs, or because of the poor chances of victory.[48]

Nor does Chomsky seriously argue against the war on the grounds that the Thieu/Ky government was no better than the government with which the Communists were likely to replace it. True, Chomsky makes passing comments on undesirable aspects of the Thieu/Ky regime, many of which I have no doubt were justified; and he sometimes suggests briefly that the organization of the N.L.F.-controlled areas of South Vietnam approximated in some modest degree to the loose syndicalist federation which is his governmental ideal.[49] But Chomsky nowhere, as far as I know, sets out systematically to compare the virtues and vices (according to his own or anyone else's political ideals) of the then governments of South and North Vietnam, which is what he would presumably have had to do if he wished to argue that the Communists should be allowed to take over in the South on the grounds that they would govern it at least as well as the Thieu/Ky regime. (I will surely not be accused of wisdom after the event in taking it for granted that North Vietnam was a better guide that the 'liberated areas' of South Vietnam to the shape of government after a Communist victory in the South? The Communists never made any secret of their aim of reuniting Vietnam, and even the most naïve must surely have realized that the 'loosely federal' character of N.L.F. administration in the South was an inevitable consequence of the 'underground' nature of the N.L.F. organization.) I have no doubt that Chomsky did and does believe that the government installed by the Communists in South Vietnam would be and is a better government, in an absolute sense, than the Thieu/Ky government; but that is not the reason why Chomsky thought America should get out of the war.

Chomsky's principal reason for opposing American participation in the Vietnam war was quite different: it was that the Communist side represented a movement with genuine roots among the Vietnamese people, while the Thieu/Ky regime was a puppet government – it was manned by native Vietnamese, but if one looked at the realities below the surface, Chomsky suggests, it was government by an alien nation. Never mind counting up the misery caused by the war, Chomsky argues: 'What about opposition to the war on the grounds that we have no right to stabilize or restructure Vietnamese society?'[50] After quoting from a number of discussions by liberal American scholars of methods of combating Communist insurgency in South Vietnam and elsewhere, Chomsky comments:

. . . notice how perverse is the entire discussion of the 'conceptual framework' for counter-insurgency. The idea that we must choose between the method of 'winning hearts and minds' and the method of shaping behaviour presumes that we have the right to choose at all. This is to grant us a right that we would surely accord to no other world power.[51]

An obvious reply is that Chomsky is factually wrong in contrasting the Vietnamese Communists with the Thieu/Ky government as representing indigenous and alien political movements, respectively. But let me ignore this, since the point I want to make against Chomsky is independent of it.

The general assumption concerning political relations between peoples which underlies the quoted comments by Chomsky is one which has become very fashionable in recent decades; but it seems to me a shocking assumption to be voiced by a thinker who prides himself on working out his own code of political morality independently of the fashion of the day. The assumption is that it is wrong for one people or nation to attempt to influence the political arrangements of another. The fact that, in the Vietnamese case, such influence was exerted by military means is for Chomsky irrelevant to the principle, as the second of the above quotations indicates; he points out that 'In fact, the liberal experts have been dismayed by the emphasis on military means in Vietnam and have consistently argued that the key to our efforts should be social restructuring and economic assistance,'[52] but he clearly regards that as no excuse.

The notion that it is permissible or even laudable to attempt to influence the politics of one's own country (and Chomsky has gone to great lengths to shift the policies of the U.S.A. in directions which, as he admits, are quite alien to the desires of very many of his countrymen) but impermissible to do anything to help a foreign country avoid what one sees as bad government – which is what Chomsky is saying – may seem an arbitrary and perverse notion; of what possible relevance is it whether the flag that flies over my neighbour's head is or is not patterned like the flag that flies over me? But Chomsky's view of human nature offers an intellectual foundation for the notion. If the races inherit qualitatively differing patterns of thought, then it may be quite appropriate to suggest that what form of government is good or bad will depend in part on the genetics of the governed; nations should avoid meddling in each others' politics because what is bad for 'us' may be good for 'them', and we are not likely to appreciate this.

Thus, the traditional conceptual schema shared by the Chinese and Vietnamese includes no words for 'free', 'freedom', 'liberty', 'liberal'. The Chinese *tzu yu* (in Vietnamese transliteration, *tu do*), originally a phrase of no philosophical interest meaning 'following one's own bent' or the like, was pressed into service in the nineteenth century to translate the Western concept of liberty, and it seems fair to say that the concept has never yet really 'taken' in the Far East.[53] For instance, the standard Chinese encyclopaedia-dictionary *Tz'u Hai*, published in 1938, calls *tzu yu* a 'legal' (rather than 'political') term, and its definition includes the phrase 'not subject to illegal restraint' (*pu shou fei fa chü shu*) – the qualification 'illegal' clearly makes the definition empty as a definition of political liberty. (It is known that one of the difficulties which faced Chinese who began to read Western political theory in the late nineteenth and early twentieth centuries lay in comprehending that the term translated *tzu yu* was not intended by the Western authors as a pejorative one – so deeply permeated by authoritarian assumptions is Chinese culture.[54])

The empiricist will see the Chinese lack of the concept of liberty as essentially a historical accident – the evolution of ideas in Europe happened to throw up and develop the notion of 'liberty', the independent evolution of ideas in China happened never to produce this particular notion and indeed developed well-entrenched principles incompatible with the liberal ideal.[55] (The empiricist might explain the fact that Western material and intellectual progress has in the last few centuries suddenly overtaken the previously far more advanced civilization of China by saying that the growth of liberal ideas in the West preceded technological advance, while in China material progress enabled thought to be relatively successfully regimented before the disadvantages of such regimentation were appreciated, so that the rate of progress decelerated.) In that case, the only barrier preventing the Chinese or Vietnamese enjoying the benefits of liberty is one of education, and it will be a generous as well as a self-interested policy to do whatever is needed to teach them that lesson while meanwhile standing in the way of their unenlightened politically-minded countrymen who wish to destroy the preconditions for a liberal society.

One who believes in genetically inherited qualitative differences in intellect, on the other hand, may explain the facts quite differently, by saying that liberal concepts are incomprehensible to the Oriental mind for biological reasons which cannot be affected by education. From that it might well be felt to follow (this is no doubt arguable) that liberal government is inappropriate or impossible for Orientals – although liberalism may be the political ideal for people of European descent, for Orientals the choice is and must be between alternative versions of authoritarianism. In other words, whether Chomsky appreciates it or not (and I am strongly inclined to believe that he does not realize these natural consequences of his ideas), what he has provided is an intellectual justification for the notion that some given form of government may be quite appropriate for a distant nation even though it would never do for 'us' – a notion so often used, without any such justification, by 'progressive' intellectuals in Britain and America to condone the vile tyrannies which exist elsewhere.[56]

It is in any case somewhat disingenuous of Chomsky to suggest that his philosophical position rules out interference by nations in each others' affairs. Chomsky is an equalitarian; and he cannot logically refuse to extend his equalitarianism from the national to the international level. If the annual output of consumer goods in one country ought on moral grounds to be divided equally among the consumers of that country, then the same moral principles surely suggest that the production of the various countries of the world should be pooled and divided equally among the population of the world, so that individuals will not be made to suffer merely because they were unlucky enough to be born in Chad or Bengal rather than in the U.S.A. or Britain. (To speak of 'the' production of the world ignores the fact that any such equalitarian distribution would clearly entail a considerable drop in production apart from the drops discussed in earlier chapters – thus if Americans could not afford cars to drive to work in that relatively spread-out country, their production would clearly diminish even if their will to produce remained constant.[57] But we have already seen that this sort of consideration does not bother Chomsky.) Only a minority of those who advocate socialist measures in Britain or the U.S.A. add the rider that redistribution should occur at a world rather than national level; but then many socialists do not have Chomsky's high moral ideals. In order to carry out such international redistribution, a world government – only a small minority of whose members could be drawn from any one country – would have to have the authority to tax richer-than-average nations in order to subsidize poorer nations: Britain might be taxed at a rate of about 50 per cent of G.N.P., the U.S.A. at a rather higher rate. Since the voluntary overseas aid donations currently made by the governments of our countries are of the order of 1 per cent of G.N.P., it is clear that many Britons and Americans would view such a system of international taxation as a very serious interference by foreigners in their affairs. But for Chomsky it would be wholly inconsistent not to regard such a system as desirable, indeed essential, in an ideal world.

Chomsky might argue, however, that while incomes should be redistributed internationally, his principles forbid interference by one nation in other nations' democratic control over their internal affairs (other than overall standard of living). Given international taxation this principle would lose much of its apparent force: if poor countries were living largely off subsidies paid involuntarily by rich countries, then rich countries would have a good moral case for insisting that poor countries should progressively reduce the need for such subsidies by adopting political systems which enabled them to grow richer, i.e. liberal systems. But let us leave that point aside. I suggested a few pages ago that, if Chomsky tries to influence the policies of his own country, then he ought to allow nations to influence other nations' policies. An opponent might well object that this is a wilful equivocation; it ignores the distinction between the kinds of 'influence' which are permitted by the principles of democracy and those which are not. The opponent might suggest that Chomsky attempts to influence his nation's policies only by persuasion, not by coercive means; he would have had no objection if the American liberals who wished to protect Vietnam from Communism had set about doing so e.g. by sending the Vietnamese anti-Communist literature through the post, but in fact they advocated measures which, even if not military, were in lesser ways coercive.[58]

Chomsky himself does not agree with the principle that only persuasion rather than coercion may be used to influence the nature of actions of government. Discussing issues raised by the use of violence in a campaign to dissuade scientists from contributing professionally to the American war effort, he writes:

> By counterpoising 'reasoned discussion' to 'confrontation', [a writer quoted by Chomsky] might be taken to be suggesting that reason and action are to be seen as alternatives. . . . Clearly [this view] is irrational. Reason may dictate that some form of direct action, even violence, is appropriate in certain circumstances. . . . the methods employed [to attain legitimate policy objectives] cannot simply be dismissed, without further argument, as a violation of a commitment to reason. Rather, one must show that these were not the methods dictated by reason to attain legitimate objectives, a different matter.[59]

Certainly, Chomsky did not use military means to attempt to force the U.S. government to end the Vietnam war, but then he would presumably have had little opportunity to do so or hope of success if he had. Probably the most effective thing a citizen of a modern state can do to attempt to coerce his government is to refuse to pay taxes and to persuade as many of his fellow-citizens as possible to do likewise; Chomsky did just this.[60]

I agree with Chomsky's principle here; ends can justify means. For a liberal, the aim of freeing a large population and its posterity from a highly authoritarian government may justify a limited amount of violence. But, although Chomsky himself cannot appeal to the democratic principle that persuasion alone may be used to influence government, others may do so.

The liberal reply is that it is a typical authoritarian heresy to treat democracy as something desirable in itself, rather than as a more or less efficacious means to an end. What matters about a government is not whether it is democratically chosen but whether it is a good government. Ultimately the authoritarian recognizes this also; a government which sanctioned enslavement of negroes, for instance, or which decided for no good cause to shower bombs and napalm on a distant nation, would not be regarded by a socialist as in that respect a desirable government even if it enjoyed the support of a majority of the population (as it might). But it is understandable that democracy seems relatively important to an authoritarian, who believes that government should decide the way of life of the governed with respect to all manner of details: such decisions will seem more tolerable if those whom they affect control those who make them. For the liberal, who believes that government should merely 'hold the ring' and allow the governed to create their own ways of life, the issue of who installs the governors is a clearly subsidiary one. In a boxing match, after all, there is no advantage in the referee being under the control of the fighters.

Other things being equal, the liberal does of course regard democracy as highly valuable. For one thing, liberalism is an ideal; the most liberal government attainable in practice will have to decide *some* aspects of the way of life of the governed, and to the extent to which it does so the authoritarian argument for democracy will have force. And, given a population in which liberal ideals are deeply engrained, democracy is a very efficacious means of ensuring liberal government. A benevolent despotism may govern liberally at a given time, but if it loses its liberal character there is no means of replacing it except by revolution; revolutions rarely produce liberal governments.

But other things are often quite unequal. If a nation, because of its cultural traditions, has no serious chance of throwing up a liberal government from within itself, then it is far better for that nation to be governed liberally by aliens than to suffer authoritarian government by its own nationals. Imperialism is, certainly, not an activity to be lightly undertaken. Any colonial relationship is sure to involve some modification of the culture of the colonized nation beyond the mere replacement of authoritarian by liberal rule; since the liberal values cultural diversity, this is a serious objection, and can be outweighed only by a very great difference in degree of liberalism as between colonial power and subject people. Where governors are entirely independent of governed, there is clearly a standing temptation for the governors to exploit the situation to their own advantage; any such actions are to be condemned.[61] And, since empiricism teaches that any people can learn any ideas, a liberal will have little respect for an empire which regards its authority as anything more than a temporary trust, to be handed back to the subject peoples when they have adequately learned the lessons of liberalism.[62] Given these qualifications, the liberal has no objection to imperialism, which may indeed in certain circumstances be a highly desirable world order. It would certainly be an excellent thing for the Vietnamese and for everyone else concerned if the U.S.A. were administering North and South Vietnam in place of the authoritarian government now in control there. To say that, in such circumstances, Vietnam would not be free would be merely to make a bad pun: nations are not free or unfree, only people are.

Put baldly as I have put it here, this last remark is surely a banal truism. There is certainly room for argument about what 'freedom' means, but it seems scarcely arguable that the entities which are endowed with a will that they may or may not be free to exercise are individual human beings, rather than aggregates of individuals (such as nations). If we speak of a nation as having a 'collective will' this can only be a metaphorical way of saying that all the members of that nation individually will the same thing. (There have been thinkers, including for instance German Romantics of the early nineteenth century and, later, the French sociologist Emile Durkheim, who held that nations have 'collective minds' in some more than metaphorical sense, but to me such a suggestion is pure mysticism – my judgement here is surely not seriously controversial?) Furthermore, the great majority of any man's wishes are sufficiently specific and idiosyncratic that the notion of 'collective will' will have very little application in practice even as a metaphor; any statement that 'the Ruritanian people unanimously desire X' is likely to be a falsehood foisted on the Ruritanians by a government which claims to know their wishes better than they do themselves, unless 'X' is some state of affairs so vague and general as to lead to no specific prescription for particular action. Chomsky quotes

Rudolf Rocker's remark that 'Our social system has "sacrificed the general interests of human society to the private interests of individuals"' as a (true and important) 'near cliché';[63] but a society has no interests other than the several interests of the private individuals who compose it, and Rocker can mean only that our social system has sacrificed the private interests of some, perhaps most, individuals to the private interests of other individuals.[64]

I have therefore been rather surprised to find that the paragraph before last is regarded by some readers as one of my more controversial passages. It is put to me that the desire of the inhabitants of various former colonies for 'independence' and 'freedom' – the two terms often having been used more or less synonymously during the campaigns for decolonization in various African and Asian countries – showed that there *is* a sense, and an important sense, in which a nation can be free or unfree.

But, if people really have supposed that national independence and freedom are synonymous, it is surely obvious that they were mistaken? In some cases the two will amount to the same in practice; if a nation is governed tyrannically by colonial masters but is ready to give itself a liberal government when the colonizing power withdraws, then a member of that nation who seeks national independence is simultaneously seeking freedom. Conceptually, however, the two notions are quite distinct, and it is by no means inevitable that they will coincide. If the colonizing power rules relatively liberally but the colonized nation is incapable of throwing up a liberal government from within itself, then to call for national independence is to call for the reduction or extinction of freedom (except for the small group of people who succeed in grasping power in the independent nation). The twentieth century has seen examples of each of these patterns (as well as of the third pattern in which authoritarian imperial rule is replaced by authoritarian national independence); to my mind the cases in which decolonization has led to liberalization have been in a very small minority (though, since the degree of liberalism of a government is very much a more/less rather than all-or-nothing issue, there can be no question of treating the various patterns as rigidly distinct and exhaustive categories). Clearly, those who have campaigned for national independence have often, understandably enough, compared the imperfect freedom of life under colonial rule not with the reality of future independence but rather with a utopian vision of a life in which freedom was untrammelled – we are all good at finding scapegoats to blame for evils which are in reality inevitable.

I do not wish to downplay the humiliation that is suffered by the subjects of a colonial power, which may seem to be one of the strongest arguments against imperialism. But much clearly depends on the alternative. Other things being equal, it cannot be pleasant for any man to know that his governors regard him as unfit to exercise the power they have assumed. But, in the first place, this applies not only to imperial rule but equally to rule by a native élite; and, more importantly, if he knows that a govern-ment formed by men of his own nation would be likely to tyrannize over him, then he might well feel colonial rule to be the lesser evil. Furthermore, a government does not need to be manned by aliens or even by a native élite to be humiliating to its subjects. Those Britons who stress this aspect of imperialism seem to be people who for one reason or another have not felt the humiliation of living under the kind of governments that have ruled us in recent decades.

People who argue in favour of democracy and national 'self-determination' as absolute goods irrespective of the nature of the government which results tend to rely on the systematic ambiguity of reflexive pronouns which refer to plurals. Thus we find Lord Blake writing that:

Nineteenth-century England was probably better governed than twentieth-century England, but we cannot expect to repeal the Re-form Acts of 1867 and 1884. Rhodesia is better governed than Uganda, but it does not follow that Rhodesian Africans prefer being ruled by Europeans. *The right to mis-govern oneself is as valid as any other political right* and is exercised more often than most.[65]

To say that a group of people A, B, C, . . . 'misgoverns itself' or 'misgovern themselves' can mean either of two things, and English syntax is not sensitive to the distinction. It may mean either that A runs A's life badly, that B runs B's life badly, and so on, or that the group collectively run the lives of all members of the group badly. If we construe Lord Blake in the former way, then he is correct to say that individuals have a right to run their own lives badly but wrong to say that they commonly do; all the evidence I am aware of suggests that, as one might expect, normal adult humans can run their lives, not infallibly, but better than anyone else can do it for them. On the other hand, if we construe Lord Blake's reflexive pronoun in the second way then the 'right' he speaks of is a most bizarre one. He is giving a group in which A is a tiny minority the 'right' to run A's life badly, a group in which B is a tiny minority the 'right' to run B's life badly, and so on. But where did the group get any such right? Plainly, they have none; only the equivocal nature of the reflexive pronoun allows us to delude ourselves into thinking that such a right might exist. If it is true that the lack of a property qualification in the modern English franchise is the cause of the relatively illiberal government from which we suffer nowadays, then we ought to devote our political energies to the reintroduction of a suitable property qualification; to say that the disenfranchised citizens would prefer a less liberal government is to say that they would like greater coercion to be imposed on their fellow-men, and such wishes should be ignored on moral grounds. Similarly it is irrelevant that Rhodesian Africans would prefer to be ruled by members of their own race, if such rule is bound to be thoroughly illiberal (as Lord Blake apparently believes, assuming that his notion of 'good' government resembles mine): that would mean that they wish their co-nationals to be coerced in unnecessary ways, and no one has a right to get such an objectionable wish realized.

Chomsky writes with some scorn of 'the mentality of the colonial civil servant, persuaded of the benevolence of the mother country and the correctness of its vision of world order'.[66] But he quite fails to explain what is objectionable about this mentality, provided that the man in question is right in thinking that the mother country has a correct vision of world order and that it is ruling its colonies in their own interests. The liberal is the first, of course, to argue that no one should seek to organize other people's lives; tyranny is the cardinal political sin. But tyranny means authoritarian government; to abolish tyranny is not itself tyranny. If I see a man horsewhipping his baby, I cannot justly be accused of assault because I take away the whip by force – even though I am not a member of that family, and even though neither child nor, perhaps, even father knows that what he is doing is wrong.

The liberal willingly acknowledges that his own opinions about how societies should be organized may be quite wrong (and this attitude of mind is one of the principal factors which is causing liberalism to decline in the face of rationalist authoritarians who believe that they have infallible intuitive guarantees of the rightness of their opinions – what has been said of the French to explain their disproportionate influence over the evolution of the E.E.C., that they 'have the kind of intellectual training which produces people who are better at winning an argument than finding the right solution',[67] might stand as a comment on the rationalist mind in general). But the liberal should not extend the area within which he admits that he may be wrong from his opinions about particular economic and social arrangements to his belief that those governments are best which permit their subjects maximum freedom to experiment with diverse economic and social arrangements. (Similarly, the empiricist scientist readily accepts that any of his particular hypotheses may be false, but he does not go on to say that the system of allowing individuals freely to propose and defend novel hypotheses may be inferior as a knowledge-increasing method to the mediaeval system of arguments from authority.)

To this theoretical defence of imperialism Chomsky might be inclined to object that it ignores the practical shortcomings of human nature; a liberal empire might be justifiable in liberal terms as a theoretical ideal, but any real empire, even if controlled by a power which practises liberalism at home, will invariably rule its alien subjects in ways that cannot be defended even by a liberal. But such a suggestion would be false, because the 'Second', post-mercantile British Empire which grew up in the late eighteenth and the nineteenth centuries was a rather clear counter-example.

This is certainly not to say that the Second British Empire was governed at all times and places in full accordance with liberal ideals; that was far from being so. Many individual acts of tyranny were inflicted by Britons on their alien subjects, or were tolerated by the British rulers when inflicted by some subjects on others; every such case was wrong and constitutes a shameful blot on British history. But, accepting that the Empire was very far from perfectly liberal, it nevertheless is surely almost unquestionable that the incidence of authoritarian or tyrannical actions within the territories governed by Britons over the two hundred years between Clive's activities in India and the recent dissolution was very much lower, and the societies inhabiting those territories came considerably closer to the liberal ideal of free markets in goods and ideas, than would have been the case if they had been left to their own and their neighbours' devices. (Even Chomsky would presumably agree that there is nothing to choose, morally, between an act of tyranny by a European over aliens and an otherwise similar act in which tyrant and tyrannized belong to the same race.[68]) I have never seen it suggested that any of the alien subjects of the Second British Empire had independently discovered the virtues of liberalism or were likely to put liberalism into practice without Western influence. In the case of India, this was certainly not so. A British statement here might be tainted by imperialist prejudice, so let me quote that useful source of liberal arguments, Karl Marx:

. . . we must not forget that these idyllic [Indian] village communities, inoffensive though they may appear, had always been the solid foundation of Oriental despotism, that they restrained the human mind within the smallest possible compass, making it the unresisting tool of superstition, enslaving it beneath traditional rules. . . . We must not forget that these little communities were contaminated by distinctions of caste and by slavery, that they subjugated man to external circumstances. . . .[69]

After all, Britons only came to rule alien nations in the first place because of the absence in their cultures of the institutions on which a liberal society and economy depend. The original policy of the East India Company was 'peaceful trade without territorial responsibilities'[70], and the territorial responsibilities, in India and elsewhere, tended to accumulate (often very much against the will of the British government and of liberal British public opinion) as an unlooked-for by-product of trading relationships with people having no tradition either of peace or of free trade – a pattern of empire symbolized by the fact that control of much of the Indian Empire was not transferred from the Company to the Crown until 1858, after the Mutiny.[71] It has been argued that this pattern remained constant until the end of the growth of the British Empire.[72] Others have felt that the somewhat strident imperialism of the last quarter of the nineteenth century represented a policy of deliberate national self-aggrandizement; but, significantly, jingoistic imperialism emerged at a time when liberalism and empiricism were themselves losing their hold on British thought.[73]

Chomsky, unsurprisingly, does not share my respect for the Second British Empire. He gives his verdict by quoting an Indian, H. D. Malaviya:

the British, in the process of their domination over India, kept no limits to brutality and savagery which man is capable of practising. Hitler's depredations, his Dachaus and Belsens . . . pale into insignificance before this imperialist savagery.[74]

But the reasons cited for this extraordinary judgement are highly specialized ones. Apart from the familiar general charge that Britain exploited India financially, which (in the non-question-begging sense of 'exploit') is simply a myth,[75] the main grounds for alleging that British rule over India was 'savage' are that individual Britons were allowed to practise free trade with individual Indians, which damaged the interests of certain other individual Indians (particularly weavers, who were put out of business by competition from Lancashire).[76]

It is mysterious to me how anyone can regard it as immoral to permit individuals to make bargains which both sides regard as advantageous. Would Chomsky think it wrong for A to sell some good to B at a lower price than B's previous supplier C can match, given that A, B, and C are all white residents of Cambridge, Massachusetts? Surely not; the logical conclusion of such a morality would be that we should return to the primitive, miserable state of society in which there is no division of labour and everyone is his own farmer, tailor, architect, etc.[77] Is the situation morally altered if A differs in skin colour and place of residence from B and C? It would surely be true racialism to suggest that this affected the ethics of the situation.[78]

(Consider the awkward consequences which Chomsky's apparent principle would entail for his attitude to other historical movements. Thus, the closest Britain has come in modern times to violent revolution by the working classes was the Chartist movement of 1838–48. One would expect Chomsky to have considerable sympathy for the Chartists, as do most socialists, and as I do myself. But the distress which largely fuelled Chartism had to do with the high cost of food stemming from the Corn Laws which protected British agriculture against importation of cheap foreign grain; and, although the Corn Laws were introduced by aristocratic land-owning interests, it was tenant farmers who had most to lose by repeal.[79] For Chomsky, therefore, the hungry workers who rioted in the 1840s must presumably be likened to the blackshirted thugs of the 1930s: one group directing their 'brutal savagery' towards the tenant farmer, the other towards the Jew.)

It might be thought immoral to adopt a policy which one knows in advance will destroy the livelihood of a specifiable group of individuals. If the policy is one of free trade then I am not clear that this *would* be immoral; those who produce some particular good inefficiently have no right to expect to be subsidized by a captive market (with the implication that mankind as a whole has less goods to share out than need be so). But anyway that did not apply in the case under discussion. The British liberals who argued for free trade with India did not expect Britons to be able to undercut the Indian weavers' prices.[80] Furthermore, while they were delighted as well as surprised when, through technological innovation, Lancashire managed to lower its costs enough to conquer this new market, their delight was not unalloyed since they had no wish for India to be impoverished – such an outcome would obviously have made trade with India less valuable.[81] A liberal does not hope for his country to become wealthy at other nations' expense, since he knows that this is impossible; in a free trade economy, nations enrich each other in enriching themselves. The free-trader predicted that as India gave up one occupation which it carried out inefficiently it would develop new and more success-ful activities, and this did indeed happen; the business of Dacca, the textile centre, dwindled, but at the same time Calcutta grew 'from a village on a mudflat to the "City of Palaces" teeming with a prosperous Indian commercial community'.[82]

All this seems a far cry from 'brutal savagery'. Let us examine the thought of one of the chief architects of the British raj, to see how far it is imbued with tyrannical, Hitlerite racialism. In 1826 Sir John Malcolm wrote:

The most important of the lessons we can derive from past experience is to be slow and cautious in every procedure which has a tendency to collision with the habits and prejudices of our native subjects. We may be compelled by the character of our government to frame some institutions, different from those we found established, but we should adopt all we can of the latter into our system. . . . Our internal govern-ment . . . should be administered on a principle of humility not pride. We must divest our minds of all arrogant pretensions arising from the presumed superiority of our own knowledge, and seek the accomplish-ment of the great ends we have in view by the means which are best suited to the peculiar nature of the objects. . . .That time may gradu-ally effect a change, there is no doubt; but the period is as yet distant when that can be expected; and come when it will, to be safe or beneficial, it must be . . . the work of society itself. All that Govern-ment can do is, by maintaining the internal peace of the country, and by adapting its principles to the various feelings, habits, and character of its inhabitants, to give time for the slow and silent operation of the desired improvement, with a constant impression that every attempt to accelerate this end will be attended with the danger of its defeat.[83]

Is this the attitude to racial differences which we associate with the names of Dachau and Belsen? If so, the Nazis have been grievously maligned. It is true, of course, that Malcolm was not wholly representative of all the men who grappled with the problem of replacing Oriental despotism with liberal government in India. A liberal who finds himself responsible for governing people whose traditions are thoroughly illiberal faces a real dilemma: on the one hand liberalism enjoins respect for alien traditions, on the other hand it opposes despotism.[84] Malcolm was one of the 'paternalists' who tended to favour the claims of native tradition over those of libertarianism where the two were evenly balanced. He was writing in reaction to the policies of men such as Lord Cornwallis, Governor-General from 1786 to 1793, and Lord Wellesley, Governor-General from 1798 to 1805, who had hoped to create a liberal society in India by breaking sharply with despotic native governmental traditions; thus, Cornwallis replaced the system of land tenure at the whim of the feudal overlord with a European system of secure proprietary rights in land.[85] Chomsky describes Cornwallis's policy, with heavy sarcasm, as if Cornwallis aimed to impose English institutions on India because he assumed English society to represent 'the only civilized form of social organization';[86] in fact, Cornwallis and Wellesley aimed to anglicize India exclusively in those ways which they believed to be necessary in order to permit the success of minimal government.[87] With hindsight, we can see that Cornwallis and Wellesley were wrong and the paternalists right – men cannot shake off millennia-old traditions of despotic government and learn to exploit free institutions overnight; and the empiricist will not be surprised or disappointed that the British did not pitch on the ideal formula for governing India immediately. But it is not clear to me that Cornwallis's and Wellesley's error was not a noble one, contrary to Chomsky's suggestion; they over-estimated their subjects' ability to live free. And both their and the paternalists' views are surely greatly preferable to that of Chomsky, who seems to imply that tyranny by Asians over Asians is better than non-coercive government of Asians by Europeans.[88]

Chomsky's comments on the British colonial mentality in fact confuse two entirely separate issues. It is one thing to say that imperialists who pay lip service to liberalism in practice govern subject nations less liberally than they suggest (or, indeed, than they sincerely believe); this is undoubtedly true, and is one reason why the liberal will see empire as justified only if the traditions of the governors are not just somewhat but very much more liberal than those of the governed. The Second British Empire surely fulfilled this requirement, but, if evidence to the contrary can be adduced, then I am perfectly willing to concede that that empire was a bad one, without accepting that empires are intrinsically bad.[89] It is a quite different thing for Chomsky, as an authoritarian, to argue that even if the condition just mentioned were fulfilled imperialism would be immoral; the liberal simply rejects this argument, since he sees liberalism as the supreme virtue of a political system and democracy as valuable only insofar as it conduces to liberalism – and the liberal will counter-attack by pointing out that an authoritarian's commitment to democracy, as we have seen, is itself highly conditional and equivocal.

Certainly the British Empire did not achieve all that a liberal would have hoped of it; in particular, few of the former colonies retained liberal government for very long after their independence. This does not mean that these territories might as well never have been ruled liberally at all – any period of liberal government is pure gain. In particular, the post-Imperial experience certainly does not demonstrate that liberals were wrong to hold that all men are educable. The British Empire dissolved when it did, not because the governors believed their task had been achieved (pious hopes were expressed, but they were surely never very sincere?), but partly because the growth of authoritarianism in Britain had combined with two world wars to rob Britain of the power to continue its rule, and partly because that growth of authoritarianism made the continuation of British rule unjust by anyone's standards; even a liberal recognizes that if the mother country is no longer teaching liberal lessons she has no business running her school. If intellectually influential Britons themselves have been turning to authoritarianism in this century, it is scarcely surprising that our former subjects also show little faith in the liberal principles which nineteenth-century Britain tried to inculcate. Had we kept faith with our own liberal heritage, and had we retained control over the Empire for somewhat longer than we did, I know of no reason to doubt that we could in time have converted our Asian and African subjects into as complete parliamentary democrats as were ever found in Victorian Westminster – to their own, as well as everyone else's, immense advantage.[90]

For historical reasons, American liberalism has traditionally opposed empires. But the American Declaration of Independence was a rejection by a group of highly liberal Britons in America of what, by the refined standards of the eighteenth century, was seen as unnecessarily authoritarian rule by the British administration, which was still thinking in mercantilist rather than free-trade terms. The argument for self-determination in such a case has no validity as against a liberal empire whose subjects' own cultural inheritance includes no inkling of liberalism. Chomsky criticizes various American liberals for suggesting that it is a mistake to limit U.S. action in support of liberalism abroad to backing for relatively liberal indigenous political leaders where these appear, and to eschew any suggestion of direct political control.[91] Chomsky writes as if he has only to collect together and render explicit hints to this effect scattered in various liberal publications for them to be seen as self-evidently wicked. On the contrary – particularly in view of the regularity with which foreign political leaders backed by the U.S.A. have turned out to be illiberal tyrants whose only virtue is opposition to socialism – one wishes very sincerely that these hints had been made earlier and more loudly, and that they had been acted on. If the Pax Britannica had been replaced and extended by a true Pax Americana, the world would be a much happier place for all of its inhabitants today; but one does not achieve peace by calling out to the children in the next room that it would be nice if they stopped bullying one another.

The idea that nations which are relatively enlightened and powerful should act as international policemen-cum-school-teachers obviously depends on the empiricist belief that everybody has the ability to learn better then he now knows – that unenlightened, poor nations are in the position of children who, given suitable training, will become responsible, self-sufficient adults, rather than of mental defectives who cannot be cured but must be endured and supported. (And, if unen-lightened nations are compared to children, the liberal nations should be seen not as parents but as brothers who happen, purely as a matter of luck rather than because they are the eldest or cleverest of the family, to have stumbled on the solution to the problem of good government.) Chomsky's approach to human nature, on the other hand, seems to suggest that the view of unenlightened nations as mental defectives is the more appro-priate one. Both metaphors will be rejected, of course, by the modern cant according to which only those governments may be criticized whose members are of European ancestry; the reader may decide for himself which of the two views better deserves the pejorative epithet 'racialist'.

6 What We Know and How We Know It

One of the earliest pieces of writing through which Chomsky came to the notice of the academic world was a critique of the ideas of the Harvard psychologist B. F. Skinner.[1] Skinner is an experimentalist who has worked mainly with animals (it was chiefly of Skinner's work that I was thinking when I referred in Ch. 2 to the possibility of training pigeons to play ping-pong by means of a suitable schedule of rewards for ping-pong-like behaviour); but, like Chomsky, Skinner sees his concrete professional discoveries as evidence for a structure of beliefs of much more general interest concerning the nature of language, of the human mind, and of the ideal society.[2]

Skinner is an empiricist, of a quite extreme form; but his idea of human nature, and his notion of the ideal society, are both very different indeed from the liberal's views. They also conflict sharply with Chomsky's beliefs, and Chomsky has continued to attack Skinner's work warmly.[3] There is no doubt that many who have encountered the Skinner – Chomsky controversy without, perhaps, much prior interest in the abstract philosophical issues underlying the debate have felt – as I feel myself – that in their relatively concrete beliefs about human nature and the ideal society Skinner is patently wrong and Chomsky at least nearer the truth; and they have concluded that, if Skinner represents the position to which empiricism leads, then Chomsky must be right to prefer rationalism.

Chomsky has done nothing to discourage this line of argument, which has been one of his most fruitful sources of converts. But the argument is in fact quite fallacious. Skinner *is* an empiricist, but he is an empiricist of a very odd (although not altogether uncommon) breed. It is only through an attractive but quite indefensible error of logic that one can infer Skinner's objectionable views on human nature and society from the premisses of empiricism. And Chomsky is the last one who is entitled to criticize Skinner for this logical error, since, as we shall in due course see, it is an error which lies also at the heart of Chomsky's own structure of thought.

Skinner is perhaps the most notable contemporary representative of a trend in psychology known as 'behaviourism', which emerged in the early years of this century, under the leadership of J. B. Watson of Johns Hopkins University, as a reaction against a (largely German) school of psychologists who attempted to fathom the workings of the human mind by introspectively observing the interior phenomena of their own minds in various circumstances. The main objection to 'introspectionism' (there are other objections) is surely fairly obvious: if the 'data' of our enquiry are internal, uncheckable phenomena, then there will be no neutral method of settling the issue when different psychologists evolve incompatible views about mental processes – and, since we all have vivid imaginations, and since our imaginations are largely controlled by the faculty of wishful thinking which we all possess, it is certain that rival introspectionists soon will come up with incompatible theories, none of which will willingly be abandoned by its inventor. D. E. Broadbent gives an example: certain introspectionists suggested that the experience of fear involved nothing more than experience of the bodily changes, such as a faster heartbeat, which are induced automatically by the sight of a fearsome object and which have obvious survival value, e.g. in helping one to run away.

This suggestion was sharply criticized, because some people hold that when one is afraid, there is something in consciousness as well as these sensations. Other people support the [quoted] theory; and it is probably fair to suspect the existence of a third group who get more and more confused the more they think about the question. Introspection did not seem able to solve this problem.[4]

The empiricist, as we know, does not hold with the idea that scientific knowledge can be derived from introspection; situations such as that described by Broadbent demonstrate that the empiricist is right. Accordingly, Watson insisted that psychological theories must be based on interpersonally observable phenomena: physical behaviour, and the physical stimuli which impinge on the behaver. An experiment such as the ping-pong one already discussed, in which it is shown that a given pattern of stimuli impinging on an organism (in the shape of food pellets presented when it carries out given behaviour-patterns) leads to a specified subsequent pattern of behaviour, is clearly precisely the kind of research which conforms very well to the behaviourist principle.

Quite a lot is known about the ways in which various patterns of stimulation, particularly pleasant stimuli such as food and unpleasant stimuli such as electric shocks, evoke responses in organisms such as pigeons and rats. The questions that one can ask about the subject are not wholly trivial – it is not obvious beforehand, for instance, whether rewards for producing the 'right' behaviour will be a more or less efficacious way of inculcating that behaviour than punishments for the 'wrong' behaviour, nor is it obvious to what extent the introduction of a certain percentage of deliberate 'mistakes' into a training schedule will increase the time taken by the organism to learn a given complex behaviour-pattern. And, on the other hand, it is fairly clear that the notion of behaviour being 'shaped' by the rewarding or punishing stimuli which it evokes has some applicability to human language. I have read somewhere of an audience who 'trained' a lecturer to return more and more frequently to some unimportant topic by deliberately donning expressions of intense fascination and attentiveness whenever he mentioned it by chance; and although that may be apocryphal, we surely all find ourselves talking shop to one colleague and chatting about gardening to another because our past history of verbal interactions has shown us (without our necessarily being conscious of the fact) that these are the kinds of conversation that go down well with the respective individuals.

But most of us feel that there is a very great deal more to linguistic behaviour than this. We speak, in many cases, because we want to express our ideas or to seek knowledge possessed by others. It is true that the results of speaking will often *ultimately* include pleasant stimuli impinging on the speaker; by explaining to a new employee how to do his job now, I initiate a chain of events which may result in higher profits made by my firm in several months' time, and the sight of the numbers on the bank statement, or if not that then at least the consumption of the goods which I buy for myself out of those profits, could reasonably be described as 'positively reinforcing' me, to use Skinner's terminology. But, in the first place, such an account will be fairly unenlightening unless it discusses in detail the *intermediate* steps in the chain, which will be largely a matter of the mental phenomena induced in the employee by my explanation; secondly, if I use the money, say, to buy books or to put myself through university, we will not be able to understand why even the ultimate result of my talk to the employee 'reinforced' my action unless we appreciate the importance of unobservable mental activity to humans. Furthermore, Skinner's paradigm is good at explaining why one does something *again* when one has had good results from doing the same thing or something closely similar before, but in the case of linguistic behaviour this is often not the case. Thus, some men utter the words 'Will you marry me?' just once in their lives; and, although others are less fortunate, in many cases they continue to make proposals while the responses are unsatisfactory and cease after the first 'Yes', which is precisely opposite to the pattern predicted by Skinner. We can hardly hope to understand what is going on unless we reckon with the fact that utterances have *meanings*, which are not always connected with the stimuli impinging on the speaker at the time of utterance. The behaviour of rats and pigeons may be fully describable in terms of propensities to act in certain ways in response to food pellets and similar observable stimuli (though even with respect to rats and piegeons this is in fact debatable), but a psychologist's account of human behaviour, and particularly of linguistic behaviour, will tell us far less than any layman knows unless it refers to the workings of the mind.

According to Skinner, this is an error. 'Ideas', 'knowledge', 'meanings' are the kind of notions that appeal to introspectionists, but the behaviourist can have no truck with them; they are mere myths, convenient fictions. Human verbal behaviour may be more complex than pigeon behaviour, but it is not qualitatively different; in principle it should be explicable in all details in terms of the same battery of technical notions (reinforcement, contingency, and the like) which are used to describe the shaping of rat or pigeon behaviour. In his *Verbal Behavior* Skinner set out to provide just such an account of human language.

Skinner's account satisfied its author, but it will satisfy few others. The technical terms which have very concrete uses in the context of pigeon-and-rat behaviour are stretched until they seem empty of any meaning in Skinner's account of language; and, where his account does include definite, non-trivial statements, over and over again those statements turn out to have the most bizarre consequences. Thus, Skinner suggests that to confirm a scientific hypothesis is, essentially, to increase the probability that it will be uttered and the 'strength' – i.e. loudness and pitch – with which it will be uttered;[5] as Chomsky points out, this implies that a good way to confirm a hypothesis would be 'to train machine guns on large crowds of people who have been instructed to shout it'.[6] Chomsky takes Skinner to pieces chapter by chapter, and his demolition job is, in my view, entirely justified.

Skinner's error of logic is surely clear enough. Behaviourism is a rule of scientific *method* which tells us that our theories about human behaviour, like any other scientific theories, must be based on observation rather than introspection; it is not itself a *theory* about the nature of behaviour or of the mind – it does not deny that there is anything to be introspected. In the days before breakdown of marriage was a legal ground for divorce, private detectives spent many hours gathering evidence by hanging round hotel corridors noting who went through which bedroom door with whom, and how much time elapsed before they came out again. Provided that they were genuine detectives rather than blackmailers they did not attempt to get direct evidence about what was actually happening behind the closed doors;

but one would not, I think, have much respect for a detective who believed that 'adultery' was a myth, or merely a layman's way of talking about people walking through doorways. What keeps us outside the door behind which mental processes occur is not modesty but ignorance; if there are potentially observable, physical events corresponding to our introspections they must presumably be processes occurring in the brain, but we know little about the workings of living brains, and we cannot intrepret much of what we do know.

Many behaviourist psychologists were well aware of this distinction between empiricism as a method and empiricism as a theory. Broadbent, for instance, draws the distinction explicitly[7] and then goes on to point out that, if behaviourist method has any implications for psychological theory, the implications are that we are likely to be able to form theories only about relatively simple aspects of behaviour – we may have to forgo theories about the subtler aspects of human behaviour indefinitely for lack of objective data. Leonard Bloomfield, probably the greatest name in twentieth-century linguistics before Chomsky and certainly the linguist whose commitment to empiricist methodology was most explicit and most sophisticated, made very much the same point.[8] It is not Skinner's empiricist method, but only his confusion of method with theory, that allows him to believe that linguistic behaviour can be adequately described in terms of the parsimonious battery of concepts which may, possibly, suffice for rats and pigeons.

Skinner's ideal society – which he has described both in a utopian novel, *Walden Two*, and in a theoretical work, *Beyond Freedom and Dignity* – is certainly one which many of us would find repugnant. Human behaviour, for Skinner, consists of automatic responses to the 'contingencies' of the immediate situation; our belief in free will is an illusion. Therefore society must be planned by wise and benevolent psychologists in such a way that 'contingencies' promote those kinds of behaviour which are in fact beneficial to society, rather than socially desirable behaviour being left to 'chance'. Skinner's objection to liberal society is not that enlightened self-interest leads to injustice, as socialists claim; for Skinner 'enlightened self-interest' is a myth, since there is no mechanism by which humans could decide their actions in the light of long-term goals.

> Probably no one plants in the spring simply because he then harvests in the fall. Planting would not be adaptive or 'reasonable' if there were no connection with a harvest, but one plants in the spring because of more immediate contingencies, most of them arranged by the social environment. The harvest has at best the effect of maintaining a series of conditioned reinforcers.[9]

That is, the real reason why a farmer plants in the spring is that his family and neighbours have trained him to do so; his family look kindly on him if he does and nag him if he does not, his neighbours greet him with respect if he does but draw aside from him in the pub if he does not, and so forth. It is true that if we then ask how family and neighbours have come to behave in these ways the answer, at the end of a long chain of responses acquired by individuals to more or less immediate stimuli, will ultimately have to do with harvests; but we cannot say that the farmer plants because he knows that planting is a necessary precondition of harvesting, since 'knowledge' is the kind of psychological term that does not refer to observable behaviour and therefore, for Skinner, does not refer to anything at all. It would scarcely be a distortion to say that, for Skinner, men do not have minds – the machinery needed to learn to behave in ways that have been immediately followed in the past by pleasant experiences will surely scarcely be complex enough to deserve the honorific title 'mind'.[10]

Let me not waste time discussing the inadequacy of Skinner's theory of behaviour to explain the facts of human life, which we have already considered in connexion with his account of language. (Notice for instance that Skinner could not account for long-term plans executed by an isolated Robinson Crusoe unless by saying that Crusoe 'reinforces himself', which reduces the notion of behaviour shaped by reinforcement to emptiness.) Once we appreciate the logical fallacy underlying Skinner's feeling that human behaviour *ought* to be explicable without recourse to talk of minds, any plausibility in his attempt to do so disappears.

As we might expect from one who does not believe in the human mind, Skinner utterly fails to comprehend the liberal's objection to planned societies. Skinner addresses himself to this objection, as voiced by Joseph Krutch:[11]

> The threat in a designed culture, said Mr. Krutch, is that the un-planned 'may never erupt again'. But it is hard to justify the trust which is placed in accident. It is true that accidents have been re-sponsible for almost everything men have achieved to date, and they will no doubt continue to contribute to human accomplishments, but there is no virtue in an accident as such. The unplanned also goes wrong. . . . The only hope is *planned* diversification, in which the importance of variety is recognized.[12]

If men were not creative, this might make sense; we might ask psychologists to discover the range of innovations which human minds were capable of inventing, and then plan a series of experiments designed to winnow the useful from the valueless ones as rapidly as possible. But men are creative. 'Planned diversification' must be restricted diversification; even the wisest and noblest of psychologists will be able to specify only a negligible fraction of the innovations waiting to be invented, so, if our experiments are planned by a group of people smaller than society as a whole, fewer possibilities will be tried than when every citizen is his own experimentalist.

We see, then, that while Skinner's social ideal and that of the liberal are both offshoots of empiricism – they both stem ultimately from the notion that we can discover truth only by experience, not by introspection – they are utterly incompatible with one another. The liberal agrees with Chomsky as against Skinner that men have minds, and Skinner's disagreement on this score can be derived from empiricism only by fallacious reasoning. Where the liberal differs from Chomsky as well as from Skinner is in the recognition that men's minds are creative, so that men's potential can be harnessed only by a free society, which encourages unforeseen innovation. For Skinner, as for

Chomsky, the only alternative to rule-governed behaviour is random behaviour, 'accidents'; but creative behaviour, though not governed by rules, may be very purposeful.[13]

Chomsky explicitly comments on the logical flaw in Skinner's reasoning.[14] But, ironically enough, Chomsky commits the same fallacy. Whereas Skinner moves illegitimately from empiricism as a method to empiricism as a theory – from the belief that mental phenomena are no evidence to the belief that there are no such things as mental phenomena – Chomsky moves illegitimately in the reverse direction, from rationalism as a theory for which he has found a certain level of support to rationalism – reliance on the data of introspection – as a method of research. As a result, Chomsky's thought on both academic and political issues suffers from a fundamental failure to appreciate the logical distiction between what is right and what people believe to be right.

As we have seen in Ch. 2, Chomsky has shown that the facts of human language provide evidence for a limited version of rationalism – for the belief that certain restricted aspects of mental functioning in humans are the way they are because they are 'built-in' by the same genetic mechanisms which determine physiological structure. Chomsky infers innateness from universality; all human languages share certain properties, therefore the psychological 'hardware' characteristic of our species must impose those properties on our linguistic behaviour. The universality of the syntactic properties in question is discovered by comparing descriptions, or 'grammars', of the various languages which linguists have studied; so the *data* on which Chomsky's theory is based might seem empirical enough. Languages are abstractions, but they are manifested by phenomena such as speech and writing which are perfectly concrete and interpersonally observable. So it might seem that Chomsky's rationalist theory is constructed on a basis of empiricist method. But according to Chomsky himself this is not in fact so.

For Chomsky, the data on which a grammar is based are not the utterances which speakers of the language in question are

observed to produce; rather, Chomsky's data consist of the
beliefs of speakers as to the properties of their language. 'The
empirical data that I want to explain are the native speaker's
intuitions.'[15]

This early remark of Chomsky's is contradictory, of course; if
'empirical data' is anything more than a high-sounding synonym
for 'data', it means 'data derived from experience of the external
world, *as opposed to* introspection or intuition'. But it is clear from
many other things that Chomsky has said that it was the word
'empirical' which was out of place in the quoted remark, not the
word 'intuitions'; Chomsky believes that it was a fallacy of his
empiricist predecessors in linguistics to think that a grammar
should be regarded as answerable to the observable facts of
speech and writing.[16] The following quotation from Chomsky's
follower D. T. Langendoen states just what kind of introspective
knowledge speakers are supposed to have about their languages
rather more fully that Chomsky does in any passage I have come
across, but it represents Chomsky's views fairly accurately:

It is . . . possible to elicit from fluent speakers of English judgments
not only about the . . . grammaticality of linguistic objects [i.e. word-
sequences], but also about the internal structures of those objects
judged to be grammatical sentences. The simplest judgments that one
can elicit concern classification of the words of sentences into 'parts of
speech,' such as NOUN (N), VERB (V), CONJUNCTION (C), and the like, and
of the groupings of these elements into PHRASES and CLAUSES.
   . . . what we are claiming is that English speakers' grammatical
intuitions include the ability to parse sentences, or at least to recognize
and give assent to correct parsings of sentences.[17]

In other words, speakers know the relatively low-level, specific
facts predicted by a grammar – they know that certain word-
sequences are grammatical in their language, that others are
ungrammatical, and they have some inklings about the hierarchical structure which the grammatical rules impose on
sentences; but in the mind of a layman this knowledge is un-
organized and ungeneral – the linguist's task is to organize it

and reduce it to a maximally simple, general system of rules.[18]

We may be able to understand where this notion of speakers' intuitions as data came from if we recall the discussion of pre-Chomskyan, corpus-based linguistics in Ch. 4. Many empiricist linguists fell into the trap of thinking that, because their methodology prescribed that only observations were relevant to the truth or falsity of theories, therefore their theories about languages (i.e. their 'grammars') should, ideally, not go beyond the corpus of observations that they had amassed about the languages. This is as if, say, a chemist investigating the properties of iron were to drop three pieces of iron into sulphuric acid under different conditions of temperature, lighting, etc., find that all three dissolved, and then published *as his theoretical conclusion*, not 'Iron dissolves in sulphuric acid', but 'Lumps a, b, and c of iron dissolved in sulphuric acid under conditions X, Y, Z respectively'. In science, obviously, we are interested in the general rather than the particular; 'Iron dissolves in sulphuric acid' is a worthwhile chemical statement, while the more specific statement is valueless except as a means to an end. But the fact that scientific theories go beyond the empirical observations on which they are based does not mean that they are not answerable to empirical observation; all it means is that scientific theories constitute *predictions* about observations yet to be made. I see three pieces of iron dissolve in certain conditions, and I hypothesize that any piece of iron will dissolve in any conditions. Similarly, I observe utterances of several English sentences in which verbs ending in *–s* are preceded by third-person-singular subjects, and I hypothesize that there is a general rule by which verbs in the present tense always take *–s* after such a subject. In both cases my hypotheses constitute predictions about future observations (and in both cases the predictions may have to be modified in the light of experience; there may be circumstances – e.g. very low temperature – in which iron fails to dissolve in sulphuric acid, and there are certainly verbs – e.g. *must* – which do not take – *s*). In neither case does the fact that our theories run beyond our experience render those theories in any way unempirical.

Chomsky, unconsciously, is arguing as follows: grammars are clearly not based on observations of utterances, since they always run beyond such observations and we can all see that it is right for them to do so; therefore they must be based on something else, and the obvious candidate is native speaker's intuitions. But this is as if a chemist were to conclude that, because chemical theories regularly generalize beyond their data, therefore what they are really based on is someone's intuitive beliefs about the interactions of diverse substances.

In the case of chemistry no one would make this mistake, and the reason is clear; people do not have many 'intuitive beliefs' about chemical interactions – most of our beliefs about chemistry are obviously derived from formal teaching (and hence, ultimately, from other people's experiments), and the few which are not are mostly fallacious (e.g. many people suppose that only solids are metals, but mercury is an exception).[19] The case of language is different – people do have a good many intuitive beliefs about their languages. Given a sequence of English words, any of us will usually be prepared to say whether or not it is a 'good' English sentence (there will be marginal cases where we feel unsure, but Chomsky acknowledges this); and many of us are prepared to issue edicts about particular points of English usage in reply to enquiries by foreign friends anxious to improve their mastery of the language. But this is because everybody is to a greater or lesser extent fascinated by his native language, which is hardly surprising given the central role played by language in all our lives. Every man is to some extent an amateur linguist, and every man encounters plenty of data on which to practise amateur linguistic analysis – when he overhears himself speak, and attends to the speech and writing of others. Chemistry, by contrast, is a minority interest, and the chemical reactions observed in everyday life are few (and largely belong to the most difficult, organic branch of the discipline).

But the fact that we all have 'amateur opinions' on the subject of our native language does not lend these opinions any special status for the linguistic scientist; they may be handy as initial 'working hypotheses', but the scientist's task is to improve on the amateur theories of Everyman, not to take them for granted. (We would not have much respect for a professor of meteorology who saw the aim of his discipline as being to systematize the corpus of old wives' tales about weather forecasting.) People's beliefs about which word-sequences occur in their speech are usually correct, but they are by no means invariably so (for instance, when some particular syntactic trick is regarded as socially *comme il faut* it very often happens that many speakers sincerely believe that they and others in their speech-community invariably use it to the exclusion of the frowned-on alternative – even though, in some cases, *no one* uses the 'preferred' construction other than on the rare occasions when they are consciously thinking about their usage).[20] When we move from particular word-sequences to more general questions, amateur linguistic theories are often quite erroneous. Furthermore, correct beliefs about one's native language often derive ultimately from forgotten parsing lessons at school – this is certainly the case for any statements by laymen about syntactic structure or parts of speech, for instance – so that, if the contemporary linguist regards these statements as data to be explained rather than as hypotheses to be examined critically, then whether he realizes it or not he is presupposing that certain Greeks of the Hellenistic period, on whose ideas the tradition of parsing taught in our schools ultimately rests, had infallible knowledge about the syntax of a language which first came into being more than a millennium after their time.[21]

It is of course possible, as an exercise, to investigate laymen's beliefs about their language and to enquire how far these match the facts of the language – just as it is possible and may be interesting to enquire into the accuracy or otherwise of old wives' tales about weather forecasting. But the very fact that we can ask how well the average speaker's opinions about his language coincide with the facts demonstrates that we must have some way of getting at the facts of a language independently of the speaker's opinions – and plainly we have, we can examine the grammar of a language by observing speakers' unstudied utterances. Chomsky suggests that the data of actual speech behaviour, or 'performance' as he calls it, are affected by so many extraneous factors that there is no serious possibility of recovering the system of grammatical principles, or 'competence', underlying that performance unless we allow speakers' introspections about their competence to count as data; but, although this suggestion has been extremely influential within the discipline, it merely reflects a naïve and crude notion of empiricist scientific method. I have discussed Chomsky's misunderstanding of empiricist methodology elsewhere,[22] and I do not want to spend much time on it here; the issue is primarily of interest to professional linguists. There is no reason why linguistic analysis should not be based on empiricist methodology, and the arguments against rationalist methodology which we have already considered in connexion with introspectionism in psychology apply with full force to linguistics; it seems entirely obvious that linguistics, like any other science, must be empiricist in method if it is to be anything more than a sort of game in which anyone can propose any theory he wants without fear of refutation. Although Chomsky often writes as if his research had *justified* rationalist methodology, this is simply a case of Skinner's fallacy in reverse – a scientific methodology cannot, as a matter of logic, be shown to be right or wrong, it can only be held as an article of faith.[23]

The question of linguistic methodology does, however, have some relevance to the general issues with which this book is concerned.

In the first place, the whole of Chomsky's argument from linguistics to politics would clearly collapse if it were to turn out that Chomsky's 'linguistic universals' were an artefact of his bad methodology, but I believe this will not in fact be so. With one qualification which I believe we may safely ignore,[24] it seems fairly clear that the moderately rationalist *theory* of language and mind which Chomsky derives from his syntactic research will survive perfectly well if we replace rationalist with empiricist *method* in investigating syntax.

From what I have said earlier, it will be obvious that I do not believe any of his or others' semantic theories will survive this change in method. Indeed, I believe that it is only their rationalist methodology which has allowed linguists in recent years to imagine that it is possible to produce semantic descriptions of languages. If one asks a layman a question about his language, whether the question concerns syntax (say, 'How are passive sentences formed from actives?') or semantics (say, 'What does the verb *chase* mean?'), one will in each case get an answer which is informative but incomplete, not wholly accurate in what it does say, and only moderately coherent. Chomskyan linguists are used to explaining this in rationalistic terms by saying that the layman has the correct information within him in the shape of 'tacit knowledge',[25] but that he needs the help of the trained linguist as midwife to draw that knowledge out, to make it systematic and clear. In the syntactic case such an account of the situation contains at least a kernel of truth, in that there *is* a systematic, clear, and accurate answer to the question waiting to be stated, and the layman's answer will be some sort of approximation to the correct answer (but the empiricist sees no reason to suggest that the layman *knows* the correct answer in any useful sense – he will rather assume that what the layman says is likely to be a good guide to what he knows, unless the layman is for some reason determined to be uncooperative). However, if one takes the rationalist line in the syntactic case, then, since the layman's reactions in the semantic case are very similar, one may assume that again there is a systematic, finite answer to the question and that the layman's halting explanation is some kind of approximation to that 'correct answer'; and one may start taking the terms ocurring in the layman's account of *chase* as a working hypothesis about part of the stock of 'semantic primitives' out of which complex concepts are built up. This move will appear particularly attractive to someone who is insensitive to the delicate, endlessly *nuancé* layers of meaning possessed by *chase* or any other word, and such insensitivity is distressingly common among linguists;[26] but of course it does not follow, from the fact that the layman's syntactic statement is an approximation to a correct answer of limited complexity, that there is any such correct answer to which the layman's semantic statement is an approximation – and if the word in question is drawn from the ordinary, everyday vocabulary then there certainly never will be such an answer.

For our purposes the most interesting point about Chomsky's rationalist methodology is the paradox which arises for him (with respect both to language and, as we shall see, to politics) when laymen disagree. If one believes, in the linguistic case, that grammars are based on intuitive knowledge of their languages possessed by ordinary speakers, then one must expect, clearly, that speakers will not normally conflict in their statements about their language. Chomsky does not seem to have considered the question very explicitly in his early days, but from what he did say it seems probable that he took it for granted that no such conflicts would arise. Thus, he suggested in 1957 that a grammar of English will be based on intuitive knowledge that certain word-sequences clearly are grammatical in English and that certain other word-sequences clearly are ungrammatical; there will be intermediate cases in which our intuitions give no clear decision, and we may allow these cases to be decided by seeking the simplest grammar giving correct predictions about the clear cases, but Chomsky does not discuss the possibility that one speaker's 'clearly grammatical' word-sequence might be 'clearly ungrammatical' for another speaker, or for the same speaker on another occasion.[27]

The empiricist, of course, will see no reason to expect agreement between speakers. If laymen's statements about their language are amateur linguistic theories, then it is very likely that they will sometimes contradict each other, just as one man may believe that his rheumatism is a sure sign of rain in the offing while his wife believes that it has much more to do with whether there are jobs needing to be done about the house. Professional scientists constantly disagree with one another and change their minds; it would be odd if the amateurs were, regularly, unanimously correct (which is not to say, of course, than an amateur may not be right and all the professionals wrong on particular individual issues).

After twenty years of research in the Chomskyan paradigm, few linguists would dispute that Chomsky's apparent confidence in the compatibility of speakers' intuitions was misplaced (through few linguists have drawn the empiricist moral). Even with respect to the grammaticality or otherwise of individual word-sequences in their language (let alone with respect to more subtle questions), speakers regularly have conflicting intuitions. As linguists pursue the goal of an adequate grammar of English, for instance, it frequently happens that tentative hypotheses about the rules which this should contain turn crucially on the grammatical status of word-sequences which are moderately unusual, so that even if grammatical they might well be very infrequent in practice, and English-speaking linguists (and their lay English-speaking informants) simply disagree with one another over the status of such word-sequences.[28] (If Chomsky himself has not had much to say on this problem, that is only because his recent professional writings have been much more concerned with general philosophical and psychological issues than with the detailed syntactic analysis of English or other languages.) One might suppose that linguists would be forced to react to this situation by abandoning rationalist methodology. Instead, many linguists have resorted to a device which allows them to say that speakers whose intuitions contradict one another can both be right; the notion of 'dialect' has been extended from its normal use in connexion with clear regional and social differences in speech habits, so that any dispute about grammaticality between speakers from the same region and social background can now be resolved by saying that they speak slightly different dialects.[29]

The methodological debate within linguistics is of interest mainly to linguists. I have discussed it at some length, however, because the errors which are rather clear within the field of linguistics also show up, although they are perhaps less obvious, when Chomsky discusses politics – another area in which everyone has opinions.

Chomsky's perception of the political situation in Vietnam during the years of the war (as reflected in his writings about Vietnam) was one instance of this. As a rationalist, Chomsky supposes that nations 'know' what social arrangements are best for them; and, as a consequence, like other socialists he has to exaggerate the degree of unanimity which existed in South Vietnam as to the desirability of a Communist victory. The truth of the matter was that some South Vietnamese wanted to see the Communists win, others hoped that the Thieu/Ky government would survive, and no doubt many wished principally that the conflict would go away; but Chomsky writes as if, except for a tiny clique of wicked profiteers or the like, South Vietnam as a whole desired a socialist revolution – which is what made it so immoral for the U.S.A. to frustrate this purpose.[30] Since Chomsky confuses what people believe to be right with what is right, it is difficult for him to perceive a situation in which people sincerely differ. For the liberal, on the other hand, there was no paradox in the fact that South Vietnamese disagreed as to what was the better future for their country; people are as likely to make mistakes on political questions as on any others. For that matter, even if the South Vietnamese *had* been unanimous in their opinion about which side should win the war (which they certainly were not), while the liberal would be surprised at such unanimity he would not regard it as evidence for the correctness of the unanimous view. If every Vietnamese man, woman, and child had believed passionately that the best government for Vietnam was the kind of socialist government which now exists there, then certainly a liberal would examine and re-examine his grounds for disagreeing with them to see if he had not overlooked some reason why, in the circumstances obtaining in Vietnam, socialism might not after all be desirable; but, provided that he found no such flaw in his argument, the liberal would reply that every single Vietnamese was wrong, which is a perfectly possible state of affairs. It would be an interesting sociological question why an entire nation should show such bad political judgement; but, *qua* political animals rather than academic sociologists, our task is not to interpret the false political beliefs which exist in the world but to change them.

The paradoxical consequences of Chomsky's methodological rationalism become clearer still, perhaps, if we turn from the specific issue of Vietnam to the more general arena of abstract political philosophy. How can Chomsky reconcile his views with the existence of individuals who disagree with those views?

Notice, in the first place, that Chomsky does not use empirical arguments to any serious extent in his advocacy of socialism.

One might do this, and many socialists do – particularly in the English-speaking world, where even those who advocate socialist policies tend to accept our common inheritance of empiricist presuppositions about human knowledge. One might, for instance, argue that there is some sort of previously overlooked social dynamic which guarantees that an equalitarian distribution of rewards will automatically lead to a faster growth in total production than any other distributive principle. Such an argument, if it were sound, might well be accepted by a liberal as a refutation of his political ideal. I have never encountered an attempt to provide such a radical empirical refutation of liberalism, but many people have argued empirically against particular, limited aspects of liberalism. It is often argued, for instance, that it pays a nation to require all parents to send their children to school for a certain minimum period of years, because otherwise the nation's growth would be hindered by shortage of qualified labour; such a measure is illiberal, but it can be debated empirically and conceivably the liberal side might be defeated.[31] The work of Keynes largely consisted of empirical arguments to the effect that a goal agreed as desirable by liberals and authoritarians alike, namely reduction of unemployment, could best be achieved by illiberal measures. I believe Keynes reached this conclusion only because he regarded the liberal policies needed to achieve the same end as politically impractical in the circumstances of his day (and for present purposes his argument is therefore irrelevant, since I am interested here, as Chomsky is, in the ideal system towards which we ought to be working in the long term, rather than in the practicalities of what reforms are possible in the next year or two); but the question is an open one, and it may be that a technologically advanced society can in principle avoid unemployment *only* by illiberal measures.

But Chomsky is not, at heart, primarily concerned with empirical arguments for equalitarianism, or for the other components of his political ideal. True, the argument from universals of language and psychology to politics, with which this book has been concerned, is an empirical argument. But in Chomsky's own pattern of thought this argument acts only as a confirmation of beliefs held independently; and, from the contemptuous tone of his attacks on the liberal mentality, it is very clear that he regards liberals as guilty of something much less excusable than ignorance of recent developments in academic linguistics and psychology. The main thrust of Chomsky's advocacy is purely rationalistic. If we confront social issues honestly, forsaking the devious sophistries with which we customarily defend the comfortable (for some of us) but indefensible status quo, we *know* that capitalism – economic liberalism – is wrong, Chomsky tells us; we *know* that equalitarian socialism is the only social pattern which decent men ought to be able to consider seriously. One might suggest that Chomsky's scorn for his liberal contemporaries arises from the fact that they ignore earlier empirical arguments against capitalism, which they really ought to know about even if they are excusably ignorant of Chomsky's arguments from language and psychology; but, although (as we have seen) Chomsky does from time to time allude to such arguments, they play a quite subsidiary role in his writings – I do not think that anyone who reads Chomsky could suppose that his contempt for the liberal mind is to be explained in that way. (After all, Chomsky must know that earlier empirical arguments for socialism have all been answered by empirical counter-arguments of at least some prima facie plausibility.) What is wrong with liberals, for Chomsky, is not that they are ignorant, or incapable of working out which of two opposing arguments is fallacious, but that they are dishonest – they pay lip-service to ideas which they *know* to be false because it is convenient for them to pretend that they are true.

But if Chomsky believes that a thinker can know by introspection, more or less independently of subtle empirical argumentation, that liberalism is wrong and socialism right, then it is surely a real paradox for him that there exist other thinkers – myself, for one – who insist with equal passion that Chomsky is quite mistaken, that liberalism is right and socialism a recipe for disaster, and that the poor whose interests Chomsky has so much at heart will lose as much as anyone else by the implementation of the kind of policies of which Chomsky would approve. For the rationalist, thinkers' introspections ought not to conflict.

There are, obviously, various *ad hominem* arguments by which Chomsky might escape from this paradox. He is too decent a man to give public voice to them, but there is no reason why I should not do so on his behalf. Thus, defenders of liberalism such as myself may be simply stupid, or we may be allowing self-interest to cloud our recognition of what to an impartial judge would be an indisputable case for socialism. *Ad hominem* arguments of this kind are by their nature very difficult to rebut, though I may say that it is far from clear to me that liberal reforms in modern Britain *would* favour my own material interests (apart from any other considerations, I draw a more than generous salary from a corporate employer which would have difficulty in surviving if, as they once were and should be today, universities were financed exclusively from fees paid by those who benefit from their services, supplemented by private charitable endowments). But one has finally to reply that such arguments are pointless because they always cut both ways. It is equally reasonable, or unreasonable, to suggest that Chomsky's radical socialism might be motivated by a desire to cut a fine figure amongst the young. I have no doubt that some of the lesser lights of the 'New Left' are motivated by just such an urge for notoriety; at the same time, I have no doubt that Chomsky himself (as well, certainly, as many of his radical colleagues) holds the views he does for worthier reasons, and I can only assume that others will be prepared to admit in the liberal camp the same good faith which I admit in Chomsky, since, without this, debate ceases to be possible.

I conclude, then, that no real solution is available for Chomsky's paradox. If liberalism is wrong at all, we certainly cannot know it to be wrong by mere introspection but must demonstrate it to be wrong by empirical argument; and I have shown Chomsky's empirical argument to be fallacious.

Notice, on the other hand, that there is no paradox for the liberal in ,the fact that many thinkers in the modern world have turned to socialism. The liberal holds that anybody's beliefs may be mistaken, that nobody is infallible. It is perfectly possible for everyone to be mistaken on some particular issue, and in fact such situations are quite normal. There was a time, I believe, when everyone thought the earth stood still and the sun moved round it; no doubt there are many beliefs held by everyone today which are false and which, with luck, we shall eventually discover to be false. Political theory is not a specially privileged domain of enquiry in which the truth is somehow more obvious than in other areas. I take it that, some two and a half millennia ago, before the Greeks began to develop liberal concepts,[32] all inhabitants of this planet took authoritarianism for granted as proper and inevitable; and they were all wrong. The writer is not yet, happily, the last articulate liberal in existence; but if I should eventually find myself in such a situation, I should not see that as any reason to change my opinions. If the socialists come up with better arguments than they have yet advanced, that is another matter; but the mere fact of being alone in one's belief is no reason to change one's mind. 'Any man more right than his neighbours constitutes a majority of one,' to quote Thoreau.

Of course, like others, I am sensitive to the pressure of public opinion, and it may very well be that in such a lonely situation I would lose the courage of my convictions; but that would not mean that the socialists were right all along. Chomsky himself, with his allusion to machine-guns, has pointed out that one cannot demonstrate an assertion to be true by browbeating people into proclaiming it; as an empiricist, I would add that it makes no difference whether the machine-guns win the allegiance of minds as well as tongues (as they often do). What is right and what people believe to be right are two entirely separate issues.

The sceptic will point out that this last remark depends crucially on the ambiguous word 'right'. If 'right' means 'true' (as I in fact intended it), then, except from rationalists of an extremer breed than Chomsky, there will be no argument when the point is put baldly. If 'right' means 'just', it is less obvious that what is just is a question logically independent of what people believe to be just. If Chomsky's argument for socialism appeals largely to the notion of justice, then perhaps it may not be unreasonable of him to argue rationalistically.

But again a paradox arises for Chomsky, since, even among authoritarians, disputes arise as to what constitutes just distribution. One authoritarian will argue that the stakhanovite deserves extra rewards for his extra efforts; another will argue that it is a mere accident of birth that endows some with the will and capacity to become stakhanovites, so that justice demands strictly equal rewards. For the rationalist, paradox. The only solution to the paradox is to allow justice to be determined objectively, rather than by human decision. Provided that we are prepared to accept as a definition of justice the twin principles that each individual's rewards are equal in value to his contribution to society, and that opportunities for him to contribute are as valuable and as diverse as society is able to make them, then it is possible for justice to be determined objectively – by the adoption of a liberal form of government. I find this definition of justice intuitively very satisfying. I am aware of no solution of the rationalist paradox available to one who is not prepared to accept this definition.

At this point, my arguments that rationalistic socialism leads to contradictions may be turned round against me. My opponents may claim that empiricist liberalism is equally fertile in paradoxes.

In the first place, if empiricism prescribes that one should always reckon that any of one's beliefs may be false, why does the liberal not apply this maxim to his liberalism itself? To write, as I did in the last chapter, of liberal imperialism being a desirable state of affairs in certain circumstances, or to claim, as I have just done, that a liberal ought not to change his opinions if he finds that the rest of the world disagrees with them, argues a very firm conviction indeed of intellectual infallibility – which is just what the liberal is not supposed to believe in.

The answer to this is plain enough. Empiricism prescribes that we should always bear an open mind about the possibility of our beliefs being refuted, and for a liberal this certainly does imply that he ought to recognize that his political ideal may be an error. But this does not mean that we should think that any *particular* one of our beliefs – liberalism, or any other – actually *is* wrong, or that we should avoid acting in a way that would be inappropriate if some particular belief is wrong, unless we are given a concrete reason to change our mind about that particular belief. Consider a surgeon faced with a case in which amputation of a limb is indicated. If the surgeon is an empiricist, he will acknowledge if pressed that it is logically possible that he is mistaken to decide on amputation – perhaps the case is not what it seems but some novel condition previously unknown to medicine, which will cure itself if left untreated, or perhaps the surgeon may unknowingly and unexpectedly have been fed a hallucinogenic drug which is playing tricks with his perception of the limb. These are logical possibilities, but even an empiricist surgeon will not act on them (or, rather, will not refrain from acting because of them), and it would be very wrong of him to do so. Responsible men must always act as seems to them best after trying as well as they can to understand the situation; it is right to use fallibility as a ground for inaction only in cases where there are concrete reasons to suspect that the principle on which one might act is a shaky one, and the liberal political ideal seems not to be such a case. The liberal's answer to the socialist is 'Yes, of course logically speaking I *may* be wrong and you right; but unless you can produce better empirical arguments than any socialist has done so far, I see no reason to take the logical possibility seriously.'

But there is another respect in which the empiricist liberal may be felt to court paradox. The liberal justification for setting people free to experiment with novel social and economic arrangements is that social arrangements which increase the happiness of those who participate in them will spread, while less successful social experiments will be abandoned; valuable economic innovations will be adopted widely, inefficient methods of using resources will be given up. However, surely liberalism can itself be regarded as a novel social and economic arrangement in competition with various versions of authoritarianism, and I have admitted that it is losing ground at present to its rivals: is it not convicted by its own standards?

This is a very subtle objection to liberalism, and there are answers to it at several levels.

In the first place, it is premature at present to say that the experiment in liberalism conducted by the English-speaking world over the last three centuries has been decisively abandoned. Liberalism does not suggest that any social or economic innovation which is in fact beneficial is bound to meet with immediate, continuous success, or that alternatives which are in fact inferior are bound to be eliminated immediately. Clearly it is perfectly possible for a firm manufacturing what is in reality a much better mousetrap, say, to go through many vicissitudes for all kinds of reasons, despite the excellence of its product, and for rival firms to stage impressive rallies in the sales of their old-fashioned, resource-wasteful, and inefficient mousetraps, before the new firm eventually succeeds and causes the manufacture of the older mousetraps to be abandoned.[33] Liberalism has been going through a fairly prolonged bad patch, but with luck we may weather it; with hindsight, it may be socialism that appears to be a temporary aberration with which we flirted for a century or so before realizing our error. On the other hand, it is also quite possible that the first new-mousetrap firm might fail before it manages to establish itself, and the potential economic benefits of the invention might perfectly well remain entirely untapped until, perhaps, someone else remembers or reinvents the idea and is more successful in marketing it. Likewise, it may be that liberalism is fated to die out entirely this time round, so that the whole world will relapse into complete authoritarianism until it happens that liberalism reappears in some unpredictable corner of the globe; next time, or the time after, it may be luckier – perhaps there will happen to be no Karl Marx producing specious but plausible arguments for authoritarianism – and it may win the complete victory which it deserves.

But there is an important respect in which the competition between liberalism and various forms of authoritarianism for adoption by the societies of the world is not analogous to the competition between different social or economic arrangements within a liberal society. In a liberal society, one can choose at a given time to offer one's allegiance to some particular one of the options available in a given sphere of life, without losing flexibility for the future; one can keep an eye on developments, and change one's option if the first choice works out less well than alternatives. (Liberal legal systems do not recognize contracts for life-time service, for instance.) It is not to the same extent true that a society which chooses authoritarianism, at least of the socialist variety, retains the option of switching to liberalism if socialism fails to work out. In Russia and Eastern Europe, it is clear that socialism *has* failed to work out; if there is any doubt about the matter it can surely be settled by considering, e.g., the number of Soviet-bloc citizens who risk death to escape to the West, as contrasted with the few citizens of the relatively liberal countries who avail themselves of their complete freedom to leave the West.[34] But we have seen that, under socialism, thought as well as economic and political activity ceases to be free; the average Russian certainly has much less opportunity to learn about the West than we have to learn about Russia, and he has little opportunity to change his nation's political system if he wants to. The only people who could easily move the Soviet bloc in the liberal direction are the philosopher-kings in the Moscow Kremlin, and they have a vested interest in not doing so. The wickedness of the Soviet rulers is not a freakish development but the natural outcome of modern authoritarianism.[35] Socialism is a trap which, if accidentally entered, cannot easily be left.

Paradoxical though it might seem, the past growth of liberalism has made socialism much more dangerous than it would previously have been. In a world of small and technologically primitive nation-states, some progress is possible even though liberal institutions may be unknown. As the nations go their independent ways they will experiment with various economic and social arrangements between them; and only a limited amount of social and economic regimentation can be imposed, even within a small country, when technology is backward. If one small nation happens to think of and adopt socialism, its subsequent poor showing in the pursuit of happiness will be a useful object-lesson to the many others. The growth of liberalism, however, tends to enlarge the units of government, since national boundaries are made irrelevant by a policy of free trade, and the growth of knowledge produces technology that can be turned, by those who are so minded, to the goal of relatively thorough social and economic standardization and control. The fewer independent national units that exist in the world, and the more advanced the technology which is available for such purposes, the greater is the risk that liberalism may die out by accident.

A topical case in point here is the development of the European Economic Community. The impetus to create the E.E.C. in the post-war years was very much one of economic liberalism; the Treaty of Rome, by which the Community was established in 1957, is in most respects an admirably liberal document. Had Britain joined at the outset, when her prestige was relatively great, the Community might well have become a useful device for propagating liberal principles in countries to which they are alien.[36] But the actual evolution of the Community has been in quite the opposite direction. Thanks to its continental legal structure, the Treaty of Rome is in practice interpreted by administrative decree – itself a highly illiberal social form;[37] and the particular interpretation imposed by the E.E.C. Commission is the reverse of liberal. Thus, the Treaty provides for ending of barriers to trade between member states; for a liberal this means that producers should be free to sell any product anywhere and consumers should be free to choose which they prefer, but the Commission interprets it as meaning that producers in one country should not be allowed to gain an 'unfair' advantage by making some general type of product to specifications different and perhaps cheaper than those customary elsewhere, and accordingly it issues an endless flood of decrees standardizing the specifications permissible in various products.[38] The Treaty lays down that inhabitants of the E.E.C. shall be free to seek employment in any of its member nations; for the liberal this means that anyone should be free to practise any trade or profession, and potential employers or clients should be free to decide for themselves what qualifications they require in their doctor, architect, etc. (given legal penalties for misrepresentation); the Commission interprets it as meaning that the contents of university and similar courses leading to professional qualifications should no longer be controlled by the respective teaching institutions but should be standardized throughout the Community by decree.[39] Thus the E.E.C. promotes a kind of 'fair competition' by suppressing just that process of experimentation and innovation which is the main reason for regarding competition as desirable. To quote Ralf Dahrendorf, then a Commissioner (and now Director of the London School of Economics), the E.E.C. Commission has become 'an illiberal and bureaucratic leviathan obsessed with harmonizing things just for the sake of harmonization'.[40] By now it seems fair to describe the E.E.C. as an institution imbued with authoritarianism, even if not, at present, authoritarianism of the socialist variety; it is difficult to see accession to the Community by the dishevelled, uninfluential Britain of the 1970s as anything other than a very serious mistake. Instead of containing a number of independent nations, at least one or two of which kept the torch of liberalism alight, the wealthy part of Europe now consists of a single political and economic unit which as a whole has opted for authoritarianism – leaving the U.S.A. as the only large nation in the world still more or less clearly on the side of the angels.

What if the worst happens, and socialist authoritarianism eventually succeeds in becoming the dominant ideology everywhere in the world?

Over the very long term, it seems unlikely that socialism could be a stable state for the world; in a society in which experimentation is inhibited (and which is not in parasitic contact with a liberal society elsewhere), wealth, technological level, and hence ability to control society would actually decrease as novel problems set by changing natural conditions (such as the exhaustion of particular resources) failed to evoke novel solutions. As the level of civilization declined, a large society would presumably fragment into smaller nations within each of which the possibilities of social and intellectual control would be reduced, so that the chances of liberalism breaking out afresh would increase. It might perhaps be that human society is destined to oscillate upwards and downwards in this way indefinitely; or perhaps we may see the light and take off towards permanent freedom and progress.

Suppose that the last possibility will never in fact occur. The arguments for liberalism are relatively subtle arguments; the arguments for socialism, as we have seen in our time, have great appeal to many people who fail to notice their flaws. It may be that the retreat of liberalism before the onslaught of socialism in the twentieth century is a mere accident of history; but it may not be so. Human beings having the kind of minds they do, perhaps it is inevitable, as Marxists claim, that a liberal society will turn into a socialist society; those who perceive the fallacies of socialism may always be few compared to those who are taken in, and, because of the self-questioning attitude prescribed by liberalism, the few may always be too lacking in self-assurance to take the firm actions needed to preserve society from socialism. I accept that this is possible, although I very much hope that it is false; is acceptance of this possibility incompatible with the axiom that better arrangements will at least *tend* to replace worse ones? – an axiom which is a necessary component in the justification of liberalism, and which seems to imply that if liberalism and socialism are repeatedly pitted against one another then liberalism ought to win, if not invariably, then at least on a majority of occasions when the two theories compete for the allegiance of a society. Is there a further paradox of liberalism here?

Again the paradox can be resolved; but this time we can do so only by taking a very long view indeed. Remember the continuity which exists between the evolution of ideas among men and the biological evolution of species. The development of the human brain was an evolutionary step with enormous advantages for the species which took it, since it enables us to continue the process of evolutionary advance within the species, and indeed within the individual; thus we can improve our lot very much more rapidly than the slow processes of biological mutation will improve it for us, and we can replace the utter disasters of unsuccessful biological mutation with the relatively mild ill-effects of temporary adherence to unsuccessful theories. If the liberal is right in believing that humans have it in them constantly to produce genuinely original innovations (and we have no more reason, but, Chomsky notwithstanding, also no less reason to believe this than we have to infer, from the fact that the sun has risen on every previous day, that it will rise again tomorrow), then nothing in our creative faculty prevents us continuing this process of evolution within the species for ever. I take it as axiomatic that this is desirable, not because the average man is happier than the average blackbird or dandelion – I cannot imagine what that would mean – but because creation, growth, the fulfilment of one's potential, seem to represent an instinct which we all possess – we are all happy when we can follow the instinct, unhappy when it is frustrated. We are creatures for whom it is better to travel hopefully than to arrive. But, if we are so mentally constituted as a species that liberal human societies, whenever they appear, always give way after a time to socialist societies, then there will be a limit to this intra-species evolution: a limit set not, as Chomsky alleges, by restrictions on our faculty of intellectual creativity, but by our inability to choose for ourselves governmental systems which allow us to benefit further from that faculty, once we have progressed far enough to be able to give ourselves governments which successfully frustrate the faculty.

Should this be the case, then the human brain will after all be more closely analogous to other biological innovations than it at present appears to be. If liberalism is here to stay then our brain is an innovation different in kind from any other, since it opens up an entirely new evolutionary process and puts the species possessing it in a position where we, as it were, no longer have an interest in the further progress of the old, biological evolutionary process. But if we are made in such a way that we cannot collectively choose to govern ourselves liberally, then the human brain is merely one more biological advance – a big advance, which puts us a long step ahead of our non-human ancestors, but only a finitely big advance. Should this be the situation, then we may confidently predict that our present unique role among the species on this planet will be a temporary one. After a period that may be longer or shorter on the time-scale of biological evolution (although it will no doubt be very long indeed on the time-scale of human affairs), novel species will emerge with novel organs which serve them better than the brain of *homo sapiens* serves him. Man will perhaps go the way of the dinosaurs, or perhaps will be assigned the tolerated but subordinate role now played by the blackbird and the dandelion.

It seems to me very implausible that this is to be our fate. Evolution has given Man the faculty of intellectual creativity; it has given us the ability to create – among so many other things – a theory as to how to govern ourselves in order to avoid frustrating that faculty; and it has given some of us, at least, the ability to detect the flaws in a plausible, superficially altruistic, but ultimately anti-human alternative theory of government. It would surely be an extraordinary mischance if all these gifts are just not quite enough because there will always be a few too many people who fall for socialism. We are, as far as we know, the only species to have been given a creative intelligence at all;

Providence will surely not have been so cruel as to give the sole participant in the lottery a ticket one number away from the jackpot?

I do not believe that this is so. To infer, from the bad patch that we are going through at present, that replacement of liberalism by socialism is a law of human nature is to fail in shaking off the influence of Marxist historical determinism. Provided we agree that the human intellect is creative, then we know that human history cannot be deterministic, as Marx alleged;[41] and if Marx is wrong about the general issue, then there is little reason to regard our current difficulties as symptomatic of a secular change. We can choose to take the road back to freedom.

It will not be easy. The thought of the difficulties involved in persuading a Briton who is currently a fervent trade unionist, for instance, to support a government which outlaws trade unions is one at which it is easy to lapse into despair. And, unlike one who aims to convert the world to a novel scientific theory, the liberal has only a limited time in which to succeed in his task; the further the world moves in the authoritarian direction, the less opportunity there will be to persuade its inhabitants to reverse the trend – so that if society is not converted soon, it probably will not be. But there is no reason to believe that the rot has already gone too far to cure. We are in a race against time:

but if we fail, then the whole world, including the United States, including all that we have known and cared for, will sink into the abyss of a new Dark Age made more sinister, and perhaps more protracted, by the lights of perverted science.[42]

Endless, patient argument and persuasion are the tools by which we can recover our freedom if we decide to do so. The choice is ours.

7 Conclusion

The preceding pages have covered a large canvas with, necessarily, a very broad brush. I make no apologies for this. Abundant work by others provides the detail missing here; but it is the essential outline of the case for liberalism, not the detailed understanding of how, in modern technological conditions, free markets can produce better results than planning in the various particular spheres of human activity, which is the most serious gap in the current climate of received opinion.[1] The authoritarian's case rests on an impoverished, scientistic idea of Man. Chomsky is an entirely typical socialist in this respect; he differs from his fellows chiefly in making explicit and providing forceful and novel arguments for a view of Man which, in the structure of many socialists' thought, is an inexplicit, unquestioned axiom. Chomsky sees himself as differing from other socialists in treating mind as a fixed given rather than as infinitely malleable. But the issue relevant for the political theorist is whether the actions of mind are foreseeable by the methods of science, or whether, rather, we have the capacity to be truly creative; Chomsky's distinction, though real, is of no importance by comparison.

The central aim of this book has been to show that Chomsky's fine-sounding words about human nature actually mean something close to the opposite of what they appear to say. Chomsky calls us creative, and we applaud him; but if we ask what he means by 'creative', he turns out to mean what many of us would call 'uncreative'. Chomsky is contrasting his view of human mind with something lower still, admittedly – we are, for him, subtle computers rather than, say, speak-your-weight machines; but we are not *creative* organisms. And this verbal confusion spills over from pyschological to political discourse. The proper society for a creative being is a free society, Chomsky says; and again we applaud. But the kind of 'freedom' which Chomsky has in mind for beings who are 'creative' in his sense is a 'freedom' which many of us would rather call unfreedom. Again Chomsky contrasts his society with a society that is even further removed from libertarian ideals. In Skinner's utopia we will be mere automata whose every lightest action is controlled by stimuli arranged by all-wise master planners, while Chomsky's planners will acknowledge that their subjects possess minds capable of formulating and executing rational long-term plans of their own, and they will accordingly take our views into account when they settle the framework of economic and social niches within which we are required to lead our lives. But life which is confined to any such framework constructed by human decisions is not freedom.

I do not believe, and I hope I shall not be taken to suggest, that Chomsky's abuse of the terms 'creativity' and 'freedom' involves the slightest dishonesty on his part. I have no doubt that Chomsky has simply failed utterly – as many people do – to understand the notions properly indicated by those terms. If one's personal stock of concepts does not include those for which 'creativity' and 'freedom', and their synonyms, are the only terms known to me, then it may be reasonable to take those terms to refer to the concepts which Chomsky has in mind. But the sincerity with which Chomsky misuses these crucial words makes his writings all the more dangerous. It is so very easy to agree verbally with Chomsky's central slogans, while failing to notice that the fine print on the contract defines those slogans in such a way that one has committed oneself to the very reverse of what one intended.

Once the alternative concepts of 'creativity' and the alternative concepts of 'freedom' have been made explicit, surely few fellow-men, at least among those whose cultural inheritance is coloured by empiricist and liberal assumptions, will fail to agree that the 'richer' sense is in each case the appropriate one? As soon as we realize that Chomsky appeals to the nature of language to argue for only the impoverished version of 'creativity' and fails to consider the richer version, his linguistic arguments against liberalism melt away like mists before the morning sun. But the situation is worse for Chomsky than that: language gives us some of the most striking positive evidence that Man is creative in the richer sense. We *are* truly creative animals; we *do* merit true freedom. Which of us will be so humble as to deny it?

For those who mark anniversaries, I write at an auspicious time. Two hundred years ago, Adam Smith first described the 'invisible hand' which makes us all wealthiest when we resist the temptation to guide it collectively; and, later in that marvellous year, the Founding Fathers of the United States of America inaugurated that society which, above all others, is dedicated to the ideals of liberalism, and which has so abundantly demonstrated the advantages which flow from adoption of those ideals.

Our tyrants, alas, are not conveniently separated from us by several thousand miles of sea. They live in our streets, drink in our pubs, marry our sisters; and every one of them, Queen and Prime Minister with almost as much justice as the lowliest shop steward or clerk in the Inland Revenue office, can excuse their collaboration in tyranny by saying that they are only following orders. We can recover our freedom not by violent rebellion but only by endless, untiring, patient argument and persuasion. But then, revolutions based on persuasion are likely to be the most successful revolutions in the long run. We can be free again, if we choose; if we choose, we can give our descendants the opportunity to construct a civilization which will make ours seem barbarism by comparison. Will we really choose serfdom? Will we really sentence our posterity to retreat towards the savage state from which we have taken so long to emerge?

Notes

(Works referred to more than once will be cited in abbreviated form; full bibliographical details are given in the list on pp.247ff.)

Chapter 1

1. On the fallacy of scientism, see F. A. Hayek, *The Counter-Revolution of Science*. According to Hayek, both the fallacy itself and, later, the word which describes it originated in France. Hayek associates the rise of scientism with the Ecole Polytechnique, founded in Paris in 1794.

2. This remark is perhaps somewhat unfair to scientists. Those who damage society because of their misguided faith in scientism tend not themselves to be scientists. Great scientific minds are often well aware of the fallacy of scientism.

3. Chomsky's Russell lectures are published in his *Problems of Knowledge and Freedom*. The sentence inscribed on Marx's tomb, 'The philosophers have only *interpreted* the world, in various ways; the point, however, is to *change* it', was Marx's eleventh thesis on Feuerbach, written in 1845 (Marx & Engels, *Selected Works*, vol.ii, p.405).

4. *Language and Mind*, p.114.

5. *Reflections on Language*, pp.123ff.

6. The fact that Chomsky's thought on various individual topics is imbued with the fallacy of scientism will be documented at length in the body of this book. The clearest statement I know of Chomsky's dogmatic adherence to the fallacy in its general form is quoted on pp.211–12 of Ved Mehta, *John is Easy to Please*.

7. In this connexion cf. John Lyons, *Chomsky*, p.117.

8. Some philosophers have attacked Chomsky's political philosophy; see e.g. J. R. Silber, 'Soul politics and political morality', *Ethics*, vol.79, 1968, pp.14–23, and the running debate between Chomsky, Sidney Hook, and Antony Flew, in *The Humanist*, vols.30 and 31, 1970–71.

9. Such a task would be particularly unattractive to a linguist versed in formal logic, who is aware that from not-p one *can* validly infer that p implies q whether q is true or not!

10. Cf. my *Form of Language*.

11. Op. cit., pp.164–5.

Chapter 2

1. This misinterpretation is particularly prevalent among those influenced by the Oxford school of 'linguistic philosophy', which has for some time been preoccupied largely with attempts to tease out features of the usage of philosophically important words in everyday speech; Oxford philosophers have taken the doyen of young American intellectuals to be dealing with issues much closer to their own concerns than he really is.

2. The rule is that a relative pronoun may be omitted whenever it is neither the subject of its clause nor immediately preceded by a preposition; thus the latter sentences should read '... man *who* broke ...' and '... over *which* we have ...' respectively.

3. I present the material as non-technically as possible in my *Form of Language*, ch.5, which contains references to the original literature. The newcomer who wishes to read Chomsky's own presentation of the material might well begin with the first half of his *Problems of Knowledge and Freedom*.

4. There is an (irrelevant) complication in that questions are always derived from 'emphatic' statements where these differ verbally from corresponding unemphatic forms: *John does know* gives *Does John know?*, but we do not in modern English say *Knows John?* (corresponding to *John knows*).

5. I discuss various attempts to 'explain away' Chomsky's linguistic universals in my *Form of Language*, ch.6.

6. *Language and Mind*, p.26.

7. Cf. my *Form of Language*, p. 82.

8. On the connexion between the notion of 'logical form' and Chomsky's hypothesis about linguistic universals, cf. my 'Empirical Hypothesis about Natural Semantics'.

9. τῷ οὐκ εἰδότι ἄρα περὶ ὧν ἂν μὴ εἰδῇ ἔνεισιν ἀληθεῖς δόξαι περὶ τούτων ὧν οὐκ οἶδε (*Meno*, 85c), as translated by Nicholas White in S.P. Stich, ed., *Innate Ideas*, University of California Press, 1975, p.34.

10. *Reflections on Language*, p.7.

11. It should be said that, as history, Chomsky's *Cartesian Linguistics* is very questionable (see e.g. H. Aarsleff, 'The history of linguistics and Professor Chomsky', *Language*, vol.46, 1970, pp.570–85); but this point is scarcely relevant to an evaluation of Chomsky's own philosophy of language and of human nature.

12. Cf. Hume's *Enquiry concerning Human Understanding*, § 4, pt.1.

13. Letter to Mersenne, 22.7.1641 (*Oeuvres*, vol.iii, p.418); *Notes against a Programme*, 1647 (*Oeuvres*, vol.viii/2, pp.358–9).

14. Letter to Mersenne, 16.6.1641 (*Oeuvres*, vol.iii, p.383).

15. Letter to *X*, Aug. 1641 (*Oeuvres*, vol.iii, p.423–4).

16. Cf. e.g. I. M. Crombie, 'The possibility of theological statements', in Basil Mitchell, ed., *Faith and Logic*, Allen & Unwin, 1957. Note that Locke agreed with Descartes in believing that we have certain knowledge of the existence of God; but for Locke this knowledge was something discovered by men rather than inborn in us (*Essay concerning Human Understanding*, bk.iv, ch.10).

17. See e.g. A. H. Rowbotham, *Missionary and Mandarin*, University of California Press, 1942, pp.128ff.

18. *For Reasons of State*, p.184.

19. *Problems of Knowledge and Freedom*, p.46. Here and elsewhere in *Problems* Chomsky attributes quotations to 'Russell', often without giving details of the source. In this case his quotation is from p.266 of Bertand and Dora Russell, *The Prospects of Industrial Civilization*, Allen & Unwin, 1923 (I have corrected two trivial misprints in Chomsky's quotation).

20. *Language and Mind*, p.114; *Reasons*, p.128.

21. *Problems*, p.49; the quotation is from Humboldt's *Limits of State Action*, 1791.

22. 'Science and ideology', p.207.

23. *Problems*, p.51; *American Power and the New Mandarins*, pp.19–20.

24. *Reasons*, pp.180ff.

25. *Problems*, p.49.

26. *Reasons*, p.160.

27. *Problems*, p.55.

28. Quoted e.g. on p.180 of 'Science and ideology'.

29. *Problems*, p.50, my italics. Chomsky attributes the internal quotations to 'Russell' in 1923, which seems to indicate the book by Bertrand and Dora Russell cited in n.19 above; but I have not been able to find the words in that book.

30. *Problems*, pp.54–5.

31. *Reasons*, p.154.

32. *Problems*, p.50.

33. *Problems*, p.51; internal quotations attributed to 'Russell' without precise indication of source (cf. n.19).

34. On anarcho-syndicalism and other versions of anarchist theory, see G. Woodcock, *Anarchism*, 2nd edn., Penguin, 1975. For a critique of syndicalism, see L. von Mises, *Socialism*, pp.270–75. Chomsky's beliefs about the organization of the ideal society seem in fact to owe more to Proudhon than to Bakunin, but he quotes the latter much more frequently.

35. *American Power*, pp.66ff.

36. *American Power*, p.113, n.56.

37. For this analogy see e.g. Chomsky, *American Power*, pp.47–9.

38. *Cartesian Linguistics*, pp. 25–6.

39. *Reflections*, pp. 133–4.

Chapter 3

1. R. N. Carew Hunt, *Theory and Practice of Communism*, p.126.

2. *History of Western Philosophy*, p.481.

3. I do not mean to suggest that there are no respects in which Britain is more liberal than the U.S.A. There are individual points where the reverse is true: e.g., in the U.S. but not in Britain one needs a licence to practise medicine. But on balance it seems to me undeniable that (at least in the economic rather than purely social field) the contemporary U.S.A. is a good deal closer than welfare-state Britain to the liberal ideal.

4. Many Americans nowadays even use the term 'liberal' in the opposite of its original sense, to refer to those who advocate increased intervention by government in the affairs of the governed.

5. Hayek suggests the term 'Old Whig' as historically accurate (*Constitution*, pp.408–10). Rightly or wrongly, I feel that to call oneself a 'Whig' in the 1970s would be to forfeit the opportunity of having one's ideas considered seriously on their merits. For an analysis of the change in meaning of the party labels in Britain over the nineteenth century, see the first essay in Herbert Spencer's *The Man versus the State*. On different national conceptions of liberalism, see Maurice Cranston, *Freedom*, Longmans, 1953.

6. Cf. Roger Soltau, *French Political Thought in the Nineteenth Century*, Ernest Benn, 1931, Introduction and passim. Soltau (p.488) quotes the remark by Emile Faguet, '*Le libéralisme n'est pas français.*'

7. According to J. R. Pennock, 'The political power of British agriculture', *Political Studies*, vol.7, 1959, p.292, the Liberal party compromised the principle of free trade in the early 1950s in order to win more votes. In a discussion of the future of the Liberal party in *The Times*, 2 June 1976, Emlyn Hooson, a candidate for leadership of that party after the resignation of Jeremy Thorpe, wrote among other things, 'No one in his right senses now wishes to dismantle the social services or to reduce the social wage. . . . in the field of industrial relations, only trogl[o]dytes will object to proper security of employment.' Mr. Hooson may feel it appropriate to describe people who hold such views as troglodytes who have taken leave of their senses, but the technical term for them is liberals.

8. This means that my account of liberalism will owe more to Hayek than to Popper, since Popper, despite his great contributions to political theory, is no

economist and fails to grasp the liberal arguments against economic intervention (cf. his *Open Society*, vol.ii, pp.124–5 and 178–9). Thus Popper sees the choice between maintaining a free market in labour and allowing employees the freedom to form trade unions as a paradox for the liberal; he fails to realize that this paradox is solved by the same principle which Popper uses to solve Plato's 'paradox of freedom' (see e.g. op. cit., p.44) – government should protect the free market and forbid monopolistic trade unions, because the latter are conspiracies against freedom, and the one justification for abridgement of freedom is in order to prevent greater abridgement of freedom. Legal moves against trade union monopolies become less unpalatable once it is appreciated that rather than protecting the poor from capitalist exploitation (as their apologists often believe) they in fact serve to impoverish the poor further (cf. Hayek, *Constitution*, ch.18).

9. The earliest philosopher I have identified as a liberal, namely Locke, thought of the proper function of government as being to protect property; the idea that private property derives its value to society and to the individual from its exchangeability, i.e. from the existence of markets, entered the liberal tradition through the work of Adam Smith.

10. Strictly speaking what is impermissible in a liberal society is not trade unionism as such, but monopolistic trade unionism (which has the same adverse consequences for an economy as any other form of monopoly). Historically, trade unions have fulfilled a number of functions other than that of monopolizing particular categories of labour – e.g. they have acted as provident associations, an entirely admirable role. But modern British trade unions have shifted their efforts so completely towards labour-monopoliza-tion (an activity in which they are increasingly being aided by legislation, without the support of which no harmful monopoly can hope to survive long) that it will hardly be misleading to say for short that liberalism requires the outlawing of trade unions.

11. It is not, of course, a logical truism that increase in total wealth of a society must lead to higher living standards on the part of the poorest; it is logically possible that as society as a whole gets richer the poor might get poorer, and Karl Marx, notoriously, claimed that something like this does tend to happen. What I am saying here is that, as a matter of fact rather than as a truth of logic, this will not happen; Marx was wrong. I discuss this on pp.112ff.

12. Except for the word 'cultured' the last remark is based on my own experience, but for the converse situation cf. Chiang Yee, *Chinese Calligraphy* (Methuen, 1938), p.131. E. H. Gombrich's *Art and Illusion* (Phaidon, 1960) is extremely interesting in this connexion, although I would prefer to see the history of art in terms of the divergent process of biological or cultural evolution rather than the (arguably) convergent process of growth of scientific knowledge.

13. It might be argued that creativity is not so centrally characteristic of human life as I suggest, and that there are many people who rarely or never have an original idea. I doubt this; but in any case it would not affect my

argument if I accepted that some people only think of things which, unknown to them, have been thought of before. My claim is that we all have the ability to create things or ideas which are novel with respect to *our own* previous experience, and that a proportion of the creative acts performed by members of a society will be novel with respect to the previous experience of the society, or of mankind, as a whole.

14. Cf. Popper, *The Poverty of Historicism*, pp.v–vii.

15. I have read somewhere recently that 97 per cent of all new products marketed in the U.S.A. turn out to be commercial failures; yet presumably in every case someone thought they were on to a winner.

16. K. Marx and F. Engels, *The Communist Manifesto*, 1848 (Marx & Engels, *Selected Works*, vol.i, pp.38–9).

17. What I called 'authoritarian' government is sometimes called 'totalitarian'; I prefer to avoid that term, first because it seems to refer to an extreme property rather than to a tendency which various governments may possess to a greater or lesser extent, and secondly because the word has such strong negative connotations that to apply it to the style of government against which I am arguing might appear question-begging. A. V. Dicey (*Lectures on the Relation Between Law and Public Opinion in England during the Nineteenth Century*, Macmillan, 1905, pp.64ff.) uses the term 'collectivism' for what is here called 'authoritarianism'; Dicey dates the rise of 'collectivist' thought in England from the late 1860s.

18. Chómsky frequently condemns the disparities in income found in all contemporary societies, from which it may be inferred that he believes distribution should be equalitarian; the most explicit statements of this which I have found in his works are on pp.132ff. of *Reasons*, and in his 'Comment on Herrnstein's response', *Cognition*, vol.i, 1972, e.g. pp.410 and 417. Chomsky is vaguer than one might wish on this crucial aspect of his political ideal (this vagueness is scarcely a point in his favour, of course).

19. In a society with few enough members, individuals have an incentive to maximize production even if distribution is on an equalitarian basis, because the extra production arising from increase in effort by any individual will represent an appreciable benefit to that individual even after it has been divided among the members of the society. This is one of many respects in which liberalism is relevant only to societies having very many members – such as the societies inhabited by Chomsky and by myself.

20. On the impossibility of economic calculation under authoritarianism, cf. Mises, *Socialism*, pp.128ff.

21. Some may object that we may be able to design some new breed of computer that would itself think creatively. I believe that this is a conceptual confusion, but the point is unimportant here; I am quite happy to concede that authoritarianism might possibly be justified in some science-fiction world of the future, provided my opponents concede that liberalism is the appropriate

ideal for the world which we and the next few generations of our descendants will be inhabiting.

22. Compare John Stuart Mill: 'The establishment of the despotism of the Caesars was a great benefit to the entire generation in which it took place. . . . The accumulated riches, and the mental energy and activity, produced by centuries of freedom, remained for the benefit of the first generation of slaves. Yet this was the commencement of a *régime* by whose gradual operation all the civilisation which had been gained insensibly faded away . . .' (*Representative Government*, p.251).

23. Frederic Pryor, *The Communist Foreign Trade System*, Allen & Unwin, 1963, chs.4–5; cf. Mises, *Socialism*, p.136.

24. See e.g. K. Polanyi, *Origins of our Time*, p.245; cf. Chomsky, *Reasons* p.99, and the quotation from Marx's 'Critique of the Gotha Programme' (Marx & Engels, *Selected Works*, vol.ii, p.35) on p.98 of Chomsky, op. cit.

25. Fellow academics will recognize the syndrome. I should stress that I am not complaining about the financial and policy constraints now being imposed on British (and, I believe, also American) universities. Those imposing the constraints are acting as responsible guardians of public money, and if the result is damaging to the interests of scholarship the fault is largely that of academics themselves for having accepted support from an inappropriate source.

26. There is a nice parallel, within the discipline of linguistics, to Chomsky's calling in the name of anarchism for policies which, if implemented, would result in highly coercive government. Chomsky and his followers have often complained about the rigidity of the linguistic world of the 1950s, which was slow to recognize the value of Chomsky's novel ideas; but, as has been re-marked more than once (see e.g. R. Anttila, 'Revelation as linguistic revolution', in A. & V. Makkai, eds., *The First LACUS Forum*, Hornbeam Press, 1975; C. Hagège, *La grammaire générative*, P.U.F., 1976; my *Schools of Linguistics*, ch.6), one of the most striking practical results of the 'Chomskyan revolution' in linguistics has been to replace an ethos which encouraged a wide diversity of scholars to go their independent ways with a highly authoritarian ethos in which individual scholars' reputation, access to channels of publication, even employment prospects are to a quite unprecedented extent determined by a small coterie who succeed in exacting conformity to a particular 'party line'.

27. *Reasons*, pp.153–4.

28. This latter point is one that I might have made more of than I have. It will be obvious to the reader that Chomsky's anarchism and my liberalism are in one way very similar: both of us regard government as an undesirable phenomenon which ideally would not exist. However, some form or other of government does exist everywhere in the world; from the liberal's point of view, the anarchist errs by ignoring this fact, or by treating it as an accident of history, rather than asking why it should be. Since many if not all people are

less than perfectly altruistic, not all conflicts of interests will be resolved amicably; therefore either each conflict will be resolved *ad hoc* by an individual act of coercion, or a society will evolve an institution which exerts a monopoly over the use of coercion – i.e. a government; for various fairly obvious reasons governed societies will have evolutionary advantages over and will replace 'societies' consisting of wars of all against all. If we regard government as bad but inevitable then we must strive to give ourselves a government which practises only just enough coercion to avert greater coercion, i.e. a liberal government. Liberalism, if you like, is practical anarchism.

29. *American Power*, p.74.

30. Bertrand Russell quotes estimates that primitive Man needed at least two square miles of land per individual to feed himself (*Authority and the Individual*, Allen & Unwin, 1949, p.13). At that rate England could support only one in two thousand or so of her present population.

31. *A Theory of Justice*, p.3.

32. This wording suggests that the Eastern European nations came to authoritarianism through a series of gradual institutional changes. Of course that it not so; authoritarianism was imposed on them more or less overnight. We, on the other hand, are moving towards authoritarianism in the step-by-step fashion.

33. Opponents of liberalism sometimes point out that various of the primitive societies studied by anthropologists lack the institution of property. Undoubtedly this is true; for a liberal, the notion of private but alienable property is one of the most important of the intellectual advances that have permitted societies in which they have occurred to better the lives of their members, and there is no reason to want to claim that the notion is in any sense innate.

34. See e.g. J. A. Schumpeter, *Capitalism, Socialism and Democracy*, 4th edn., Allen & Unwin, 1954, p.27.

35. There are two standard arguments tending to show that liberalism is compatible with, or even promotes, involuntary unemployment. One of these is by Marx; Marx's argument depends on issues which are crucial also in Chomsky's novel attack on liberalism, so I defer discussion of it here. The other is by J. M. Keynes, who is sometimes taken to have refuted liberalism by showing that the high unemployment of the inter-war years could be alleviated by government spending on public works, an authoritarian policy. However, the problem which Keynes suggested solving by such means was created by illiquidity stemming from government intervention to maintain an unduly high exchange rate, together with government-tolerated growth of trade unionism which made wage rates 'downwardly rigid'. (See e.g. Axel Leijonhufvud, *Keynes and the Classics*, Institute of Economic Affairs, 1971.) Both of these phenomena would be disallowed by liberalism. In other words, what Keynes showed was that one measure of authoritarianism causes problems that have to be solved by more authoritarianism. This is an important truth, and it explains why the 'mixed economy' is not a stable state for a society;

either we return to liberalism, or we must continue our slide into total authoritarianism.

36. On the high social mobility of relatively liberal Britain as contrasted with relatively authoritarian Continental societies in recent centuries, see e.g. Peter Bauer, 'The irrelevance of class', *Spectator*, 12 November 1977.

37. Even philosophers who have otherwise favoured the liberal economy have often felt that the education of children is a special case, where government intervention is appropriate: see e.g. J. S. Mill, *On Liberty*, ch.5. I do not wish to take up the knotty problem of the morality of government interference as between parents and children (cf. n.41 below); on the practical question there is evidence that British children were better educated, relative to the overall level of prosperity of society at the time, while schooling was purchased for them by their parents in a free market, and that the 1870 Education Act was a retrograde step except from the point of view of the bureaucrats for whom it created new empires to command (E. G. West, *Education and the Industrial Revolution*, Batsford, 1975).

38. *Constitution*, pp.125–6.

39. I will admit that I find the inheritance of wealth one of the less easily justified aspects of liberalism; but I infer from the copyright information in Chomsky's latest book *Reflections on Language* that this is not an issue which Chomsky would dispute with me.

40. Rawls, *A Theory of Justice*, esp. §46.

41. There is a separate issue involved here. Even the liberal of course recognizes that there are certain members of any society – children, the mentally defective, the physically handicapped – who cannot be treated as responsible for their own fate. I am taking it for granted that their own families will be more likely than any higher authority to make good decisions about how to look after such individuals. There is a case, which even a liberal may accept, for using public funds to help them to do so; discussion of this point would take us too far away from our theme. (The obvious counter-argument, strengthened by recent advances in birth-control technology, is that responsibility for providing the resources to maintain those individuals who cannot maintain themselves ought to fall in the same place as responsibility for creating the individuals; few people of any political persuasion, at least in the West, suggest that governments should intervene to control size of families.) The important thing is that one should not slide, from the recognition that certain well-defined categories of people cannot be held responsible for themselves, into thinking that people in general will be best served by having their lives organized by government.

42. P. A. Samuelson, *Economics*, 5th ed., McGraw-Hill, 1961, p.121; cf. R. M. Hartwell, 'The standard of living during the industrial revolution', *Economic History Review*, vol.16, 1963, §6.

43. One of the reasons why J. M. Keynes was happy to tolerate authoritarianism may have been his belief that human needs were exhaustible and

would be satisfied in the not too distant future (cf. the last piece in his *Essays in Persuasion*, Macmillan, 1931). A surprising belief, surely, to be held by one who began his career in the India Office? In the Jawaharlal Nehru Memorial Lecture he gave in New Delhi in 1972, Chomsky referred hopefully to the possibility that 'the assumptions of capitalist ideology may . . . be challenged by people who recognize that there is more to life than consumption of commodities' ('Science and ideology', p.176). His audience's reaction to the remark is not recorded.

44. In particular, I am certainly not naïvely suggesting that the particular legislative arrangements under which British commerce operated at some point in the nineteenth century represent the ultimate liberal ideal. To give one example of an important respect in which they did not, Hayek argued in 1960 that, philosophically, there is no satisfactory justification for shares in an enterprise conferring voting rights when they are owned by entities other than individual people (*Studies in Philosophy, Politics and Economics*, pp.309–10). Notice that if Hayek's principle had been reflected in law it would have rendered impossible the asset-stripping operations which became common in the late 1960s (*after* Hayek wrote) and which have not unreasonably been described (by Edward Heath) as 'the unacceptable face of capitalism'.

45. It would be an error to pick out one particular point in e.g. British history and claim that it represents the zenith of liberalism; it has certainly always been true that society has become less liberal in some individual respects at the same time as it has become more liberal in others (no society has been unanimously liberal in its beliefs, and liberals have been mistaken as to which policies are appropriate to give practical effect to their principles), so that one can speak only of overall comparisons between broad periods. (If pressed, one might identify the high point of liberalism in Britain with Dicey's 'period of Benthamism or Individualism', i.e. 1825–1870, but Bentham's utilitarian philosophy is not identical to liberalism.) I discuss in the next chapter the notion that liberalism has become inappropriate in the conditions of the twentieth century.

46. The empiricism which I am describing and defending in this book is the empiricism of Karl Popper rather than of e.g. John Locke. Popper is, by some, not regarded as an empiricist at all, because he sees concepts and hypotheses as created by men even though only experience winnows the applicable from the inapplicable concepts and the true from the false hypotheses. (Locke, by contrast, believed that our ideas were actually contained in our experiences, so that mind was purely passive and contributed nothing of its own to the growth of knowledge.) The point which distinguishes Locke and Popper on the one hand from Descartes and Chomsky on the other, and which is crucial for the issues discussed in this book, is that both the latter believe in a fixed, limited range of ideas potentially available to a human mind, whereas both the former hold an 'open-ended' view of mind – Locke believed there was no limit to the range of potential ideas because the mind is wholly plastic, Popper because he believes it is limitlessly creative. Like most philosophical 'isms', the words 'empiricism' and 'rationalism' are made to do duty for a gamut of closely

[margin handwritten note:] Locke vs Popper

related but not identical distinctions, and it seems not unreasonable to extend them to this contrast between 'open' and 'closed' views of mind. I must admit that a main reason why I use the term 'empiricism' for the view of mind that I aim to defend is because Chomsky uses that word to describe the views which he attacks, and although he does not explicitly address himself to Popper it is clear that he disagrees with Popper as much as with Locke. Philosophical purists may feel that this is an inadequate defence for my use of the term 'empiricism' – 'which, if anybody dislike, I consent with him to change it for a better'.

47. Cf. D. S. Lehrman, 'Semantic and conceptual issues in the nature–nurture problem', in L. R. Aronson et al., eds., *Development and Evolution of Behavior*, W. H. Freeman, 1970; D. McNeill on 'strong' v. 'weak' universals in 'Explaining linguistic universals', in J. Morton, ed., *Biological and Social Factors in Psycholinguistics*, Logos, 1971; M. Atherton and R. Schwartz, 'Linguistic innateness and its evidence', *Journal of Philosophy*, vol.71, 1974, pp.155–68; Jean Aitchison, *The Articulate Mammal*, Hutchinson, 1976.

48. *Reasons*, pp.155–6; the Bakunin quotation is taken from his essay 'The Paris Commune and the idea of the state', 1871: see S. Dolgoff, ed., *Bakunin on Anarchy*, Allen & Unwin, 1973, pp.261–2.

49. In case readers feel that the example of 'kidney machines' and the like is strained, it is easy to give more 'ordinary' examples. Thus it would be of great benefit in view of the medical emergencies that sometimes arise for there to be a hospital within, say, half an hour's drive of everyone; but, in country districts, resources will not run to it. The creator of the N.H.S., Sir William Beveridge, anticipated that the cost of the scheme would soon reach a ceiling at which all demand for medical services was satisfied; but experience has not borne this prediction out. See Ffrangcon Roberts, *The Cost of Health*, Turnstile Press, 1952.

50. The statement that the societies of France and the other Continental countries are relatively rationalistic, while those of the English-speaking world are relatively empiricist, is true as a generalization but it is of course no more than a generalization. France has produced outstanding individual proponents of liberalism, such as Alexis de Tocqueville, although liberalism did not enter the common currency of political controversy in France in the way that it has in Britain and America.

51. I am grateful to my father for this illustration. Like him, I had thought it obvious that a five-by-two egg box would be too floppy to be practical. Several friends have questioned this; so I am glad to hear from my wife, who has lived in France, that the use of such boxes there leads to a high proportion of broken eggs.

52. It is ironic that the British/American system is being abandoned at just that point in history when the availability of cheap calculating machines, together with the adoption by scientists of exponential notation, have removed its disadvantages relative to the French system. Of course it may be that, even if our system is more practical in itself than the metric system, it is nevertheless

desirable on balance to abandon it in order to facilitate international trade. That the balance of advantage lies in that direction is not as obvious to me as it is to our contemporary Euro-fanatics, however.

53. E. J. King, *Other Schools and Ours*, Holt, Rinehart, and Winston, 3rd edn., 1967, pp.50, 55, and 108–9.

54. In Britain boundary reorganization, together with the contrasting implications of inflation for local rates as opposed to national tax revenues, have recently begun to shift the structure of local government in the French direction. In July 1977, the Taylor Report recommended ending headmasters' control over syllabus.

55. Marx's principle 'From each according to his ability, to each according to his needs' ('Critique of the Gotha Programme', 1875, Marx & Engels, *Selected Works*, vol.ii, p.24; cf. Popper, *Open Society*, vol.ii, p.321, n.8) is doubly rationalist, since a liberal not only would regard the notion of controlling production and distribution by *any* conscious principles as undesirable, but would furthermore deny that *this* principle is even meaningful. What people are able to produce, and what they need, are themselves facts which emerge only from the competitive process. (In the eighteenth century no one was known to be capable of producing a motor-car, and no one was known to need one, yet nowadays many people make cars and many people need them.) Without a price system, the same problem would arise in connexion with Chomsky's version of socialism which advocates equal shares as the distributive principle; unless 'equal' means 'identical', so that everyone gets a toupee whether he needs one or not, how does one decide whether two individuals' aggregate rewards are equivalent in value?

56. Thus the aristocracy of pre-revolutionary France paid no taxes, although their contribution to the wealth-creating process was not great.

57. For the first time in British history the Chancellor of the Exchequer made the income tax rates announced in the budget of Spring 1976 conditional on discussions with the Trade Union Congress, thereby formally acknowledging the principle that the interests of workers represented by the T.U.C. (as perceived by their union leaders) are to carry more weight in determining distribution than the interests of the retired, the self-employed, the unemployed, and other groups not represented by the T.U.C.

58. This last remark would have sounded merely snide in the Britain of a few years ago. So debauched is contemporary public morality, however, that it is now common practice for our governors to exempt themselves from the coercive measures they impose on the rest of us. A partial list of instances occurs in an article by Bernard Levin, *The Times*, 19 May 1976.

59. The liberal holds that in an ideal society the national cake will be unequally divided, but, unlike the versions of authoritarianism cited here, liberalism leaves the question of who is to get the larger slices to be settled by free competition. Liberalism maximizes the possibilities for 'self-made men' to rise up the economic ladder. Therefore the liberal recognizes the notion of

social 'classes' only in the sense of groups of people who happen at a particular time to be playing similar economic roles, not (as Marx seems to have envisaged) permanent castes from which there is no escape in an upward direction.

60. In view of the changed nature of the modern British Conservative party, 'Toryism' might be a less confusing term for the principle discussed here.

61. The liberal reply to love of the familiar and fear of change is that the right not to alter some aspect of one's life is a good, and that one should be free to concentrate one's purchasing power on this good rather than others if one so desires (as when the railwayman sticks to his trade, or the inhabitant of an area of high local unemployment avoids moving, at the cost of a lower material standard of living).

62. *Problems*, p.53.

63. *Problems*, p.51.

64. *Problems*, p.52.

65. *Problems*, pp.47–9; *Reasons*, pp.137 and 142–3.

66. 'Whatever happened to vaudeville? A reply to Professor Chomsky', *Cognition*, vol.1, 1972, p.306. Chomsky quite fails to grasp Herrnstein's point, and persists in misrepresenting his liberal opponents as holding the crude view that individuals' willingness to work is determined exclusively by level of material reward ('Science and ideology', pp.188–9).

67. Quoting Russell, Chomsky suggests that, in an ideal society in which individuals would not be forced to work by economic necessity, the interest of society would be to make work pleasant in order to 'tempt' people to do it (*Problems*, p.48). In a liberal society it is in an employer's interest to make work as pleasant as possible in order to succeed in the competition for labour; in West Germany, where labour is short thanks to a dynamic liberal economy, dustmen arrive in spotless white uniforms and never see the refuse they remove. Society does not as a whole decide the nature of its members' work; and, under authoritarianism, it will not be in any individual planner's interest to experiment with changes in job-specifications.

68. Preface to *A Contribution to the Critique of Political Economy*, 1859 (Marx & Engels, *Selected Works*, vol.1, p.363).

69. Hunt, *Theory and Practice*, pp. 104–6; cf. 'Critique of the Gotha Programme', Marx & Engels, *Selected Works*, vol.ii, p.24.

70. *Reflections*, pp.133–4, already quoted on p.35.

71. *Reflections*, pp.128–9.

72. Ibid.

73. See Engels' letter to Joseph Bloch, 21 Sept. 1890 (Marx & Engels, *Selected Works*, vol.ii, p.488); and cf. D. McLellan, *Marx*, pp.68–9.

74. Despite the fact that its author regards himself as a disciple of Marx,

McLellan's short book on *Marx* very clearly explodes Marx's claim to have provided a scientific theory of economic development; see e.g. the passage on pp.58–9 on the objections to 'treating Marx's views as scientific in the vulgar [sic!] sense of theories that can be shown to be true or false by observation'.

75. *Problems*, p.53.

76. Chomsky quotes with approval (*Problems*, p.48) a claim by the anarchist Petr Kropotkin to the effect that (not in a future communist society, but here and now) work is an enjoyable 'physiological necessity', and only the super-fluous work necessary to 'supply the few with luxury' is 'repulsive to human nature'. No evidence is quoted for this claim, which is grossly implausible. (Indeed, the production of luxury goods for the fortunate few tends to be more enjoyable work than mass-production for the many.) Of course some physical work (though no clerical work) provides enjoyable and healthy exercise when taken in limited doses, but if people did only as much work as they felt like (even if directed in choice of job) I confidently predict that the G.N.P. of Britain or America would be far too low to supply the many with what Chomsky would regard as their minimum needs. If choice of job also were left open, we would have a society of fifth-rate novelists and poets for the short period before starvation set in.

77. We have already seen that, when he discusses anarchist ideals in purely abstract terms, Chomsky refers to a kind of 'freedom' going far beyond anything possible in the real world. The point I am making here, however, is that Chomsky's concrete proposals for the reorganization of society are compatible only with some kind of 'freedom' very much more restricted than the freedom of liberalism; indeed, Chomsky's society could not be 'free' in the usual sense at all. At one point, Chomsky flirts with an admission of this. Quoting a passage in which the anarchosyndicalist Fernand Pelloutier asks, essentially, whether political freedom might not be compatible with socialism, Chomsky comments: 'I do not pretend to know the answer to this question. But it seems clear that unless there is, in some form, a positive answer, the chances for a truly democratic revolution that will achieve the humanistic ideals of the left are not great' (*Reasons*, pp.154–5). But this is disingenuous; the reasons why Pelloutier's question must be answered in the negative are clear.

78. See e.g. Barbara Wootton, *Freedom under Planning*, Allen & Unwin, 1945. Of Miss (now Lady) Wootton's many fallacies perhaps the most serious are her unargued assumption that there are areas of life which can be planned without infringing any freedoms worth having (pp.29ff) and her claim that any aims which are agreed by the major political parties can safely be achieved by planning (p.134). An empiricist, who holds that all men (even politicians) are ignorant, will not accept that any freedom can be known to be worthless, and therefore will deny that any area of life can safely be planned.

Chapter 4

1. Chomsky does not accept that Descartes was refuted by the advance of natural science, and he regards his own work as a vindication of Descartes as

much as a new development. Historians of philosophy have disputed this; but for present purposes it is something of a side issue, since Chomsky's new version of rationalism seems to be by far the most intellectually respectable component in the current trend away from liberal attitudes to society. (Cf. pp.187–9 of Donald Broadbent, *In Defence of Empirical Psychology*, Methuen, 1973.)

2. *Reflections*, p.130.

3. Closer to Chomsky geographically and in point of age is Robert Nozick, although I have not myself found that his *Anarchy, State, and Utopia* (Blackwell, 1974) adds much to the extant body of liberal doctrine (cf. my 'Liberalism and Nozick's "Minimal State"', *Mind*, vol.87, 1978, pp.93–7).

4. Cf. Popper on Hegel's 'philosophy of identity', *Open Society*, vol.ii, pp.40–2.

5. Preface to 1st edn. of *Capital*, 1867 (Marx & Engels, *Selected Works*, vol.i, p.451).

6. Cf. Hunt, *Theory and Practice*, ch.7.

7. The scholarly level of Rocker's book may be judged e.g. from his unqualified statement (p.31) that 'all great culture periods in history have been periods of political weakness'. It would be interesting to know in what sense Rocker would regard T'ang dynasty China, for instance – surely by any reckoning one of the great cultural flowering-times of world history – as a period of 'political weakness'.

8. Polanyi, *Origins*, p.249; cf. Chomsky, *Reflections*, p.134.

9. Marx & Engels, *Selected Works*, vol.i, p.36.

10. I do not, obviously, suggest that the Middle Ages were a totally static period as far as progress in living standards was concerned; but then neither were they by any means totally authoritarian. To quote A. R. Myers:

> The late middle ages, . . . far from remaining static, were characterized by constant change – developments not as rapid as those of our own time, but swift enough to produce in three centuries a new culture. . . . Change was slow, and hard to see, since men still venerated the past, and still looked back, not forward, to an ideal. It was still presumed that innovation and experiment were bad, and were to be tested, not by empirical methods, but by their degree of correspondence with traditional beliefs and authorities. In a changing world this meant an increasing discrepancy between theories and facts.

(*England in the Late Middle Ages*, 2nd edn., Penguin, 1963, p.xiii.) One of the worrying things about the rise of authoritarianism in the modern world is that the progress produced by the liberalism of the recent past has provided tools, such as modern data-processing techniques, which in the hands of a coercive government can be used to impose a degree of social control that looks likely to be more complete than anything known earlier in Europe.

11. *Origins*, ch.5.

12. *Wealth of Nations*, bk. 1, ch. 2: pp. 117–18 of the Penguin edn., 1970.

13. *Origins*, p.245.

14. *Reflections*, pp. 128ff.; cf. 'Science and ideology', pp. 174ff.

15. 'Science and ideology', p.178.

16. The preceding paragraph is the only response I can make here to the critique of liberalism contained in Fred Hirsch's *Social Limits to Growth* (Routledge & Kegan Paul, 1977) – a book which appeared as this one was being prepared for publication, and which deserves much fuller treatment.

17. 'Science and ideology', p.175; *Reasons*, p.13.

18. Cf. 'Science and ideology', pp. 176–7.

19. Though there have recently been disturbing calls for a 'new international economic order' – in connexion with which cf. P. Bauer & J. O'Sullivan, 'How foreign aid makes the world poorer', *Spectator*, 25 June 1977.

20. As we shall see, Chomsky has a particular reason for viewing economies in the contemporary world as zero-sum games; but other anti-liberals seem merely naïve on this point.

21. Of course there can be no alleviation of overall poverty if, while total goods grow rapidly, the number of competitors grows more rapidly still, as Malthus predicted should happen. But, at least in terms of a crude comparison of the growth rates in world production of goods and world population, the reverse is occurring (see N. Keyfitz, 'World resources and the world middle class', for a more sophisticated discussion). One hopeful factor is that, as a cultural universal, family sizes diminish as income increases; cf. pp. 28–9 of the Introduction to N. L. Tranter, ed., *Population and Industrialization*, A. & C. Black, 1973.

22. *Reasons*, pp. 140–41.

23. One of the examples Chomsky gives of distortion in economic activity under a free market economy, namely the large quantity of unproductive labour carried out by accountants helping rich clients to reduce their tax burden, is so extremely ill-chosen from his own point of view that I wonder how seriously it can be intended. The reason why the rich pay tax accountants a lot is that authoritarianism has brought into being extremely high marginal tax rates in the name of distributive 'justice', thus giving the rich a powerful motive for reducing the incidence of tax on themselves; and it has created enormously complex systems of exceptions and exceptions-to-exceptions in order to avoid suppressing business activity altogether while ensuring that personal income does not escape, thus giving accountants plenty of scope for their work. Accountancy will always be a necessary function in a complex economy; but in a liberal society, where tax rates would be low (since minimal government is cheap government), non-progressive (since efficient rationing of labour depends on the income differentials resulting from competition), and simple (since low rates reduce the need for exceptions), it seems unlikely that much would or could be spent by the rich on legal tax avoidance.

24. N. Bennett's *Teaching Styles and Pupil Progress* (Open Books, 1976) suggests that novel teaching methods have not even led to a rise in children's levels of attainment which might offset the extra resources that they consume; in fact children learn less well in 'progressive' than in 'traditional' classes.

25. Chomsky argues (*Reasons*, p.184) that 'predatory capitalism', as he chooses to refer to the liberal economic order, 'is not a fit system for the mid-twentieth century. It is incapable of meeting human needs that can be expressed only in collective terms.' He does not explain what these needs are, and the problem he has in mind may well not be that of large-scale capital investment. But if he seeks to gloss his statement in some other way, one must point out that collectives do not have needs – only individuals have needs. We are familiar enough in the twentieth century with the horrors that arise when the interests of the individual are regarded as subordinate to those of the state.

26. *Topics in the Theory of Generative Grammar*, p.11.

27. 'Linguistic theory', in R. G. Mead, Jr., ed., *Language Teaching: Broader Contexts*, 1966, quoted in J. P. B. Allen and P. van Buren, eds., *Chomsky: Selected Readings*, O.U.P., 1971, pp.153–4.

28. See Jean Aitchison, *The Articulate Mammal*, p.34; Jane Hill, 'Possible continuity theories of language', *Language*, vol.50, 1974, pp.134–50.

29. For a relatively elaborate example of such research, see O. H. Mowrer, 'The psychologist looks at language', *American Psychologist*, vol.9, 1954, pp.660–94.

30. See for instance C. C. Fries, *The Structure of English*.

31. Let me sidestep the issue, which has become topical in view of a number of recent experiments, as to whether non-human species – the experiments have involved chimpanzees – may be able to master human-language-like systems. I have discussed the implications of some of these experiments elsewhere (*Form of Language*, pp.120–29); the important question for present purposes is what human languages are like, not whether we are the only species that can use such systems.

32. The musicologists who wrote the program, on the other hand, *were* creative, since the range of hypotheses available to them concerning the characteristic properties of Mozart concertos was open-ended.

33. See e.g. *Aspects of the Theory of Syntax*, pp.30ff.

34. See e.g. L. J. Cohen, 'Some applications of inductive logic to the theory of language', *American Philosophical Quarterly*, vol.7, 1970, pp.299–310.

35. Cf. Popper, *Open Society*, vol.ii, pp.123–4.

36. *Reasons*, pp.175 and 183.

37. *Reflections*, p.133. The words omitted in the first sentence of the quotation are 'in part'; from the context it is clear that Chomsky means not that creativity is only partly determined but that what determines it is only partly human nature and partly also environment.

38. See e.g. *Reflections*, p.205.

39. J. W. N. Watkins, 'Confirmable and influential metaphysics', *Mind*, vol.67, 1958, pp.344–65.

40. *Reflections*, p.206; and cf. Mehta, *John is Easy to Please*, p.212.

41. Chomsky's scientism here goes beyond Descartes, who stressed the difference, in respect of creativity, between automata and men (although this may well have been only because the kind of automata of which Descartes could conceive were limited to primitive machines which emitted a fixed set of immediate responses to fixed stimuli); cf. *Discours de la Méthode*, 1637, pt.v (*Oeuvres*, vol.vi, pp.56–7). Not that Chomsky is alone in his error; I believe it is fair to say that it is shared by all those working in the modern discipline of 'artificial intelligence'. (Indeed, I have committed the error in the past myself: the passage on pp.193–4 of my *Form of Language* is far too optimistically expressed.) A nice example of Chomsky's pseudo-opposition to scientism occurs in the publisher's advertisements for Joseph Weizenbaum's *Computer Power and Human Reason* (W. H. Freeman, 1976), which is an admirable attack by a professor of computer studies on the scientistic fallacy of regarding non-creative automata as appropriate analogies for creative human minds. Chomsky is quoted in the advertisements as welcoming Weizenbaum's book as a useful corrective to the current climate of opinion – a climate which he has done as much as anyone to bring into being.

42. The idea that the information-generating function of competitive free enterprise had already been fulfilled makes sense of Marx's 'labour theory of value', according to which the value of a good derived exclusively from the value of the work that had gone into producing it – so that profit was by definition theft from employees. The liberal sees profit as the reward to the enterpriser for the production of useful economic knowledge.

43. The incidence of private monopoly in modern Britain is as high as it is largely because of the effects of socialist legislation (see A. Lejeune, 'Killing the geese', in R. Boyson, ed., *Right Turn*, Churchill Press, 1970, and cf. Hayek, *Constitution*, pp.519–20, n.28). A very high incidence of 'monopoly capitalism' in Continental countries arises through direct investment by banks in industry, a practice forbidden in Britain and the U.S.A. It is of course possible to argue that, even if new economic ideas do continue to occur to people, the economies of scale which favour big businesses as against small are so great that monopolies will succeed in maintaining their position; J. K. Galbraith is well known for arguing along these lines. To this the best answer is that it simply does not happen. Galbraith is mistaken; despite the not inconsiderable weight of monopoly-favouring authoritarian legislation, it continues to be true that in the British and American economies 'the top is a slippery place'. (See e.g. J. Jewkes, *Delusions of Dominance*, Institute of Economic Affairs, 1977; and cf. S. Hymer & R. Rowthorn, 'Multinational corporations and international oligopoly', in C. P. Kindleberger, ed., *The International Corporation*, M.I.T. Press, 1970.)

44. Cf. McLellan, *Marx*, pp.55, 56, and 62–4.

45. Engels' letter to C. Schmidt, 5 Aug. 1890 (Marx & Engels, *Selected Works*, vol.ii, p.486).

46. The notion that 'all useful inventions have already been made' is a very ancient fallacy; Benjamin Farrington points out that it was believed by Aristotle (*Greek Science*, Penguin, revised edn. 1961, pp.131–2).

47. *Reflections*, p.124.

48. This is my interpretation of Chomsky's discussion of 'professionalism' (*Reflections*, p.125); it may be incorrect, but I see no other.

49. 'Science and ideology', pp.175–6.

50. In *Cartesian Linguistics*.

51. It seems strange that men who are themselves responsible for important intellectual advances should have difficulty in recognizing the existence of the phenomenon of intellectual creativity in general, but the syndrome is not uncommon. Thus J. M. Keynes, who advocated the 'euthanasia of the rentier', himself set out successfully to make a sizeable fortune on the Stock Exchange in order, as he explained, to provide himself with the leisure he needed to pass on to society the benefit of his novel economic ideas (see Hayek, *Constitution*, p.447, n.7). Apparently it did not occur to Keynes, as it did not occur to Marx and seems not to occur to Chomsky, that he might not be the last of his line.

52. Paul Postal, a follower of Chomsky, explicitly compares linguistic change with changing fashions in dress, *Aspects of Phonological Theory*, Harper & Row, 1968, p.283. I do not mean to suggest that syntactic change may not follow predictable patterns (much recent linguistic research suggests that it does) but rather that it does not extend the range of possibilities open to a speaker (except, in some cases, by giving him two stylistically contrasting ways of saying the same thing).

53. E.g. *Syntactic Structures*, p.15.

54. *Syntactic Structures*, pp.13 and 15.

55. In a world where speakers of different languages exchange ideas there is no reason to predict that boundaries between communities which differ in their stock of word-concepts will necessarily coincide with those between communities of different language. Thus, disagreements among English-speakers as to whether e.g. *gravity wave* or *social wage* are appropriate terms with which to describe the world we inhabit are likely to be paralleled by precisely equivalent disputes about *Schwerkraftwelle* or *Soziallohn, onde gravitationelle* or *salaire social*. The liberal will, however, predict that communities which are not in intellectual contact with one another will develop word-concepts that cannot easily be translated into each other's languages. Consistently with their rationalism, the Cartesians denied this (see e.g. Chomsky, *Cartesian Linguistics*, p.96, n.63); but here the Cartesians were simply wrong, as is readily shown by a study of any non-European language (cf. my discussion of the Chinese translation of 'God', for instance).

56. This is true at least of Chomsky's earlier work (cf. the above quotations from *Syntactic Structures*). Later he blurred the issue; his *Aspects of the Theory of Syntax* contains a chapter (ch.2) which claims to distinguish two classes of nonsensical sentence (cf. examples (13) v. (16), op. cit., pp.75–7), and to provide machinery for distinguishing one of these classes from the set of word-sequences which includes sensical sentences together with the other class of nonsensical sentences. Since from Chomsky's examples I can detect no difference other than a purely quantitative one of length between his two kinds of nonsense, I prefer to ignore this passage.

57. *Reflections*, p.126.

58. See D. H. Hubel and T. N. Wiesel, 'Receptive fields, binocular interaction and functional architecture in the cat's visual cortex', *Journal of Physiology*, vol.160, 1962, pp.106–54. Hubel and Wiesel's work has stimulated a great deal of subsequent research (see e.g. H. B. Barlow, 'Single units and sensation: a neuron doctrine for perceptual psychology?', *Perception*, vol.1, 1972, pp.371–94, and cf. Chomsky, *Reflections*, pp.7–9), while itself springing out of an older tradition (see e.g. E. H. Hess, 'Space perception in the chick', *Scientific American*, vol.195, 1956, reprinted in D. C. Beardslee and M. Wertheimer, eds., *Readings in Perception*, D. van Nostrand Co., 1958, pp.407–14).

59. *Meditations*, 1641, 'Replies to Fifth Objections' (*Oeuvres*, vol.vii, p.382).

60. In this connexion there has recently been carried out an extremely interesting series of psychological tests seeking to establish the perceptual reality of concepts such as 'triangle' and 'square' for members of a New Guinean tribe whose language contains no corresponding vocabulary; see pp.123ff. of Eleanor Rosch, 'On the internal structure of perceptual and semantic categories', in T. E. Moore, ed., *Cognitive Development and the Acquisition of Language*, Academic Press, 1973.

61. Cf. Popper, *Objective Knowledge*, pp.241ff.

62. *Objective Knowledge*, p.261.

63. Cf. Hayek, *Counter-Revolution*, pp.19–21.

64. See e.g. Chomsky, *Cartesian Linguistics*, pp.95–6, n.61.

65. *Open Society*, vol.ii, pp.16ff. The words 'in Britain' are not strictly accurate here: Popper has lived in England since 1945, but this book was written in New Zealand.

66. Cf. his *Philosophical Investigations*.

67. See e.g. 'The status of linguistics as a science', *Language*, vol.5, 1929, pp.207–14, and other articles reprinted in D. G. Mandelbaum, ed., *Selected Writings of Edward Sapir*, University of California Press, 1949; 'Conceptual categories in primitive languages', *Science*, vol.74, 1931, p.578.

68. See articles collected in J. B. Carroll, ed., *Language, Thought and Reality: Selected Writings of Benjamin Lee Whorf*, Wiley, 1956.

69. 'The analytic and the synthetic: an untenable dualism', 1950, reprinted in L. Linsky, ed., *Semantics and the Philosophy of Language*, University of Illinois Press, 1952.

70. 'Two dogmas of empiricism', *Philosophical Review*, vol.60, 1951, pp.20–43.

71. The *terms* 'analytic' and 'synthetic' were coined by Kant, who used them in senses slightly different from those suggested here; my definition of the terms conforms to what is nowadays standard usage.

72. A logician might object that to call a sentence 'nonsensical' is not the same as to say that it contradicts an analytic sentence; nonsensical sentences frequently presuppose rather than asserting contradictions, for instance. But, although a careful statement of my point would entail the observation of some logical distinctions which I have ignored here for brevity's sake, it would involve no difficulties of principle. To one versed in the concepts of formal logic I would express the point I am making here in a more general form by saying that, while the sentences of a human language can be specified by clearcut formation rules, there are no clearcut rules controlling the inferences which users of a human language draw from given sentences as premisses to other sentences as conclusions; we make up and change the rules of inference of our language constantly in using the language (cf. Wittgenstein, *Philosophical Investigations*, §83). The claim that there is no clearcut set of analytic sentences is a special consequence of this claim, since an analytic sentence is one which can be inferred from the null set of premisses.

73. *Philosophical Investigations*, pp. §§66–7.

74. See e.g. Chomsky, *Topics*, pp.13 and 55–6.

75. For instance, Katz leaves the nature of his complex structures to be inferred from examples which, as printed, contain crucial errors connected with unbalanced brackets (see e.g. Katz, *The Philosophy of Language*, p.167); he seems to be in two minds as to whether his semantic primitives are language-specific or universal (cf. the distinction between 'markers' and 'distinguishers' in J. J. Katz and J. A. Fodor, 'The structure of a semantic theory', 1963, reprinted in Fodor and Katz, *The Structure of Language* – Katz abandons this distinction in some of his subsequent work); and he quite arbitrarily treats all his primitives as monadic predicates, in logical terms, which may be satisfactory for the analysis of many nouns and adjectives but is clearly unsatisfactory for the analysis of most verbs together with many other words (cf. Y. Bar-Hillel, 'Universal semantics and philosophy of language', in J. Puhvel, ed., *Substance and Structure of Language*, University of California Press, 1969). Many of the problems in Katz's work stem from the fact that he does not grasp the central role which must be played by the notion of inference in any account of semantics; cf. my 'The concept "semantic representation"', *Semiotica*, vol.7, 1973, pp.97–134.

76. See e.g. Katz, *Semantic Theory*, Harper & Row, 1972, pp.243ff.; for discussion see my *Form of Language*, p.154 and references cited on pp.209–10, and cf. B. Harrison's review of Katz, *Mind*, vol. 83, 1974, pp. 599–606. Katz quotes the

Wittgenstein passage on 'games' *in extenso* (*Philosophy of Language*, pp.71ff.). He comments, first, that Wittgenstein does not explain why there are in general no fixed criteria for the applicability of words, and secondly that there are 'obvious' exceptions to Wittgenstein's claim. The first point is true but irrelevant; Wittgenstein does not discuss human creativity, which is the cause of the 'fluidity' (as we might call it) of word-concepts, but Wittgenstein was concerned not to explain *why* word-concepts are fluid but to show *that* they are (which is enough to make Katz's work futile), and this Wittgenstein did. As for the second point, the existence of a number of exceptions is by no means incompatible with the claim that word-concepts are not *in general* fixed, and there certainly are exceptions, e.g. in technical vocabularies. But Katz's examples are not the clear cases he thinks them. Thus, for Katz, it is 'quite clear' that *brother* has a 'unique defining condition', namely 'that the person be a male sibling of another'. But it is simply untrue that a person's brother is necessarily his sibling; if my parents had adopted the son of a pair of strangers he would be my brother but not my sibling. The concept of 'adoption' is just the sort of cultural development which forces a language to make an unpredictable decision; in another culture, adopted children might not count as 'brothers' of natural children, but in my culture they certainly do.

77. Cf. Chomsky: 'the immediate prospects for universal semantics seem . . . dim, though surely this is no reason for the study to be neglected (quite the opposite conclusion should, obviously, be drawn).' *Topics*, p.13.

78. See e.g. Chomsky, *Aspects*, p.149.

79. For the normality of 'figurative language' in everyday usage, see H. R. Pollio, J. M. Barlow, H. J. Fine and M. R. Pollio, *Psychology and the Poetics of Growth*, Lawrence Erlbaum Associates, 1977.

Chapter 5

1. 'Essence, accident, and race', *Hermathena*, vol.116, 1973, pp.81–96.

2. *Reflections*, pp.130–31.

3. 'Essence', p.83.

4. 'Essence', pp.88–9.

5. 'Empiricism rose to ascendancy . . . in an age of empire, with the concomitant growth (one might almost say "creation") of racist ideology' (*Reflections*, p.130).

6. Bracken might well have strengthened his case by omitting the Marranos, since they were persecuted not for being descended from Jews but for continuing to maintain Jewish religious customs secretly after their enforced baptism.

7. Bracken, 'Essence', p.86.

8. *Aspects*, p.193.

9. Hayek claims that the racial doctrines elaborated by the Nazis stemmed ultimately from France (*Studies*, p.138); he is thinking presumably of the work of Count Arthur de Gobineau and G. Vacher de Lapouge.

10. C.U.P., 1967; cf. pp.39–40, 302–3 and 340–41.

11. Cf. M. Seliger, *The Liberal Politics of John Locke*, Allen & Unwin, 1968, p.116, n.18.

12. It may be worth pointing out that Bracken's statement (p.85) quoted from Laslett (pp.39–40) that Locke 'played a large part in the creation of [the Board of Trade], the architect of the old Colonial System' is highly questionable; see I. K. Steele, *Politics of Colonial Policy*, Clarendon Press, 1968, pp.178–9. But slavery was in any case scarcely a major concern of the Board of Trade.

13. Charles Darwin, *The Descent of Man*, ch.7; cf. Bracken, 'Essence', p.83.

14. The 1956 edition of the *Guinness Book of Records*, under the rubric 'Most primitive language' (p.118), asserts that in the language 'Arunta' (usually called Aranda, a language of Central Australia) 'numbers are only vague expressions of place' and 'words are indeterminate in meaning and form'. It is true that the Aranda stock of word-concepts includes only the first two or three numerals, but syntactically Aranda can scarcely be called primitive; its systems of nominal and verbal inflexion are in some respects more complex than those of Latin. See e.g. T. G. H. Strehlow, 'On Aranda traditions', in Dell Hymes, ed., *Language in Culture and Society*, Harper & Row, 1964, pp.79–85.

15. B. Russell, *History of Western Philosophy*, pp.586 and 609–10.

16. B. Semmel, *The Rise of Free Trade Imperialism*, pp.124ff.; K. E. Knorr, *British Colonial Theories 1570–1850*, University of Toronto Press, 1944, chs.12 and 14.

17. 'The limits of natural selection as applied to Man', in Wallace's *Contributions to the Theory of Natural Selection*, Macmillan, 1870.

18. Cf. Peter Winch, *The Idea of a Social Science and its Relation to Philosophy*, Routledge & Kegan Paul, 1958.

19. Cf. Darwin, *The Descent of Man*, ch.7, on 'monogenists' v. 'polygenists'. The issue has recently been reopened by C. S. Coon in *The Origin of Races*, Cape, 1963.

20. S. H. Roberts, *The History of French Colonial Policy 1870–1925*, first published 1929; see 1963 edn., Frank Cass & Co., pp.27–8.

21. 'The aims of anthropological research', 1932, in F. Boas, *Race, Language and Culture*, Free Press, 1940, pp.254, 258.

22. 'History and science in anthropology: a reply', 1936, in Boas, op. cit., p.311.

23. *The Structure of English*, 1952.

24. *Introductory Linguistics*, Chilton, 1964, p.14.

25. *Topics*, p.12.

26. *Topics*, p.18.

27. Cf. *Aspects*, ch. 1, pp. 4 and 6–7.

28. One might ask here why we must assume that a child *does* ever stop learning and plump for a particular language – why not suppose that we go on slowly deepening our knowledge of our mother tongue all our lives, deciding our own usage in accordance with purely random 'working hypotheses', or paraphrasing to avoid the issue, where we have so far encountered no data to settle some particular question? This strikes me as a more accurate description of my own experience. Chomsky does not discuss this possibility.

29. See e.g. Vennemann's 'Categorial grammar and the order of meaningful elements', in A. Juilland, ed., *A Festschrift for Joseph Greenberg*, forthcoming.

30. C. Spearman, *The Abilities of Man*, Macmillan, 1927; cf. H. J. Eysenck, *The Inequality of Man*, ch.2.

31. Some of my friends clearly feel that the above paragraphs read far more than is justified into Chomsky's words, so I am relieved to find that the philosopher J. R. Searle reaches the same conclusions independently from me (review of Chomsky's *Reflections*, *The Times Literary Supplement*, 10 Sept. 1976, §iii). When racial attitudes akin to those criticized by Bracken were given currency in Britain in the latter half of the nineteenth century by the Anthropological Society of London under the leadership of Dr. James Hunt, they were linked with beliefs similar to Chomsky's about the biological determination of the 'mental and moral' as well as 'physical' aspects of men's natures (see e.g. Hunt, *On the Negro's Place in Nature*, Trübner, 1863). I agree that it might have seemed appropriate not to raise the question of the racial implications of Chomsky's rationalism, had Chomsky not chosen to attack empiricism in these terms.

32. A. R. Jensen, *Educability and Group Differences*, Methuen, 1973; H. J. Eysenck, *Race, Intelligence, and Education*, Temple Smith, 1971.

33. Cf. Peter Urbach, 'Progress and degeneration in the "I.Q. debate"', *British Journal for the Philosophy of Science*, vol.25, 1974, pp.99–135 and 235–59.

34. *Reasons*, pp.146–7.

35. *Reasons*, p.145.

36. 'Science and ideology', p.186.

37. Chomsky blurs the issue by suggesting ('Science and ideology', p.187) that I.Q. is a minor factor in determining success in U.S. society, and that more important factors may be ones such as ruthlessness which we should be happy to see frustrated on moral grounds. But, if ruthlessness is indeed an important factor in the creation of wealth, then society benefits if ruthlessness within the law is encouraged; and, although Chomsky quotes one unpublished paper in support of his contention that I.Q. is unimportant as a factor contributing to success in liberal societies, he ignores a wealth of published literature which demonstrates the converse (cf. Eysenck, *The Inequality of Man*, pp.120ff.).

38. See e.g. Eysenck, *Race, Intelligence, and Education*, pp.56–7; *Inequality of Man*, pp.58–9 and 72.

39. There is a difficulty in equating sensical sentences with propositions, in that non-declarative sentences – questions, commands, and the like – do not express truths (or falsehoods). While this problem is interesting, however, we may safely ignore it here.

40. *Reflections*, pp.24–5; cf. also op. cit., pp.123–4, and *Problems*, p.25.

41. Chomsky's notion that there may be true theories which men are intrinsically incapable of grasping allows him to suggest that Man may be unable fully to understand his own nature, without acknowledging that there are aspects of human nature to which no scientific theory can apply (*Reflections*, p.124). Given only this passage we would not know whether to accuse Chomsky of scientism or not; but in the rest of his writings the notion that human creativity can be described by fixed rules looms very large, while the notion that those rules may be incomprehensible to us occurs nowhere else as far as I know. Chomsky supports his suggestion that Man may be incapable of understanding himself by quoting Gunther Stent ('Limits to the scientific understanding of Man', *Science*, vol.187, 1975, pp.1052–7); this seems somewhat naïve, since Stent's paper is concerned largely to point out that Chomsky's scientistic view of language must founder – is, indeed, already foundering – on the creativity of our semantic behaviour.

42. The British government consistently gave verbal support to U.S. policy in Vietnam as a *quid pro quo* for financial services rendered by the U.S. government, while refraining from committing any men or resources of our own to the fight; after the defeat, Britain reluctantly admitted a trickle of refugees as immigrants.

43. *American Power*, pp.11–12.

44. Though Chomsky is by no means the only man to have drawn the analogy; see H. A. Bedau, 'Genocide in Vietnam?', in Virginia Held et al., eds., *Philosophy, Morality, and International Affairs*, O.U.P., 1974.

45. News that has come out of Vietnam since the above was written makes the current régime seem considerably worse than I had expected (see e.g. Bernard Levin's columns in *The Times*, 17, 18, and 20 January 1978).

46. Chomsky explains very honestly that he only began to oppose American policies concerning Vietnam publicly in 1965, although he came to believe that they ought to have been opposed ten or fifteen years earlier, long before the war began (cf. 'Vietnam, the Cold War, and other matters', *Commentary*, vol.48, 1969, no.4, pp.12–42).

47. *American Power*, p.13.

48. '. . . this quite pervasive pragmatic attitude toward the war in Vietnam is a sign of moral degeneration so severe that talk of using the usual channels of protest and dissent becomes meaningless' ('Philosophers and public policy', *Ethics*, vol.79, 1968, p.2). Cf. also *American Power*, pp.7 and 18.

49. Cf. *American Power*, p.113, n.56.

50. *American Power*, p.13.

51. *American Power*, p.51.

52. *American Power*, p.34.

53. I do not know to what extent this is true of Japan, which is intellectually independent of China in a way that Vietnam has never been.

54. Cf. J. R. Levenson, *Liang Ch'i-ch'ao and the Mind of Modern China*, Thames and Hudson, 1953, pp.92ff.; Philip C. Huang, *Liang Ch'i-ch'ao and Modern Chinese Liberalism*, University of Washington Press, 1972, ch.4; Benjamin Schwartz, *In Search of Wealth and Power*, Belknap Press, 1964. Many factors reinforced the weight of tradition in militating against Chinese acceptance of liberalism: the outbreak of the First World War, which was taken to refute the liberal promise of endless peaceful progress; the fact that the contemporary Western philosophers most influential in China, through their lectures at Peking University, were John Dewey and Bertrand Russell, both of whom could justly be described as pseudo-liberal opponents of liberalism; and the quixotic belief of Sun Yat-sen, leader of the 1911 revolution, that, by comparison with the West, Chinese society had suffered from too much rather than too little liberty (cf. Y. C. Wang, *Chinese Intellectuals and the West 1872–1949*, University of North Carolina Press, 1966, pp.324–5 and 342–3).

55. It might be suggested that the traditional notion that the ideal behaviour for the Emperor was *wu wei*, 'inaction', could be seen as analogous to the liberal notion of *laissez-faire*. But this suggestion would not stand up. The Chinese notion is purely negative: the Emperor should ideally need to do nothing because society will ideally preserve a pre-ordained balance – while for the liberal a government should do nothing in order not to interfere with the innovative actions of subjects (and indeed '*laissez-faire*' is an inadequate, negative description of the liberal ideal of government). Furthermore, the Chinese Emperor was 'inactive' because he was the motionless pivot of a large bureaucracy; the liberal aims to reduce the size of bureaucracy as close as possible to an unattainable zero.

56. This notion is of course commonly made to bear more weight than would be supported even by the foundation that Chomsky provides. Thus, one would need to make some very *ad hoc* assumptions about European genetics in order to use this notion to condone the Soviet enslavement of Eastern Europe.

57. Keyfitz, 'World resources and the world middle class', p.29.

58. H. M. Bracken ('Essence', pp.93–4) claims that it is an error typical of empiricism to fail to distinguish persuasion and coercion, but I fully accept the validity of the distinction. Cf. also remarks by Chomsky (*Reasons*, pp.120–21) on the same mistake as made by the empiricist psychologist B. F. Skinner, to whom we shall return in the next chapter.

59. 'Science and ideology', p.172.

60. See e.g. the blurb to *American Power*.

61. Trade with subjects on open-market terms, of course, is not exploitation, but treatment of colonies as captive markets – 'mercantilism' – certainly is.

62. To quote a liberal philosopher who, unlike Locke, really did play an important part in the growth of British imperial rule, 'leading-strings are only admissible as a means of gradually training the people to walk alone' (J. S. Mill, *Representative Government*, p.199).

63. *American Power*, p.19.

64. Elsewhere (*Reasons*, p.184) Chomsky writes of liberal society being 'incapable of meeting human needs that can be expressed only in collective terms' (he does not explain what these could be). From this remark and the one quoted in the text above one might suppose that Chomsky is a Durkheimian methodological collectivist who sees societies as having a life of their own in some non-metaphorical sense, over and above the lives of the various individuals who make them up. However, in his 'professional' writing Chomsky is rather clearly opposed to methodological collectivism (cf. my *Schools of Linguistics*, ch.2). In the present book I take *methodological* individualism for granted (since I cannot fight on every front at once); the debate between liberalism and authoritarianism as recipes for the substantive organization of society is quite distinct from the theoretical sociological debate between methodological individualism and methodological collectivism, though the two controversies are of course related. On the methodological issue see e.g. S. Lukes, 'Methodological individualism reconsidered', *British Journal of Sociology*, vol.19, 1968, pp.119–29.

65. R. Blake, *A History of Rhodesia*, Eyre Methuen, 1977, p.257; my italics.

66. *American Power*, p.37.

67. W. R. Lewis, *Rome or Brussels. . . ?*, p.49.

68. This assumption about Chomsky's views may be false. In *For Reasons of State*, p.34, he argues that the 'criminal violence' of the U.S. in Indochina was 'in an entirely different category [from any violence perpetrated by Indochinese forces] from a moral as well as legal point of view for the obvious [sic] reason that it is foreign in origin'. If the morality revealed by this comment is not a most objectionable form of racialism, I do not know what is.

69. 'The British rule in India', 1853, (Marx & Engels, *Selected Works*, vol.i, pp. 350–51). Compare the comment of H. Lüthy (who, as a Swiss, may also escape the charge of chauvinism): 'Virtually nowhere did the colonizers come up against . . . peoples who lived in the consciousness of a freedom or independence worth defending, or who cared much if their rulers changed' ('Colonization and the making of mankind').

70. Lucy Sutherland, *The East India Company in Eighteenth-Century Politics*, Clarendon Press, 1952, p.2.

71. See e.g. V.T. Harlow, *The Founding of the Second British Empire 1763–1793*,

particularly vol.ii (Longmans, 1964), ch.2, and cf. the review article by G. C. Bolton, *Economic History Review*, 2nd series, vol.19, 1966, pp.195–200.

72. J. Gallagher and R. Robinson, 'The imperialism of free trade', *Economic History Review*, 2nd series, vol.6, 1953, pp.1–15.

73. On the relationship between late Victorian imperialism and the English Hegelians, see Eric Stokes, *The Political Ideas of English Imperialism*, O.U.P., 1960, e.g. pp. 12–13.

74. This passage is quoted in *American Power*, p.61, from F. Clairmonte, *Economic Liberalism and Underdevelopment*, Asia Publishing House (Bombay), 1960, p.114. Clairmonte does not give his source.

75. D. K. Fieldhouse, *The Colonial Empires*, Weidenfeld & Nicolson, 1966, pp.38off.

76. See *American Power*, pp.111–12, n.46, quoting from Clairmonte, op. cit., p.107.

77. At one point (*Reasons*, p.160) Chomsky actually condemns the division of labour (as did Marx, e.g. in the 'Critique of the Gotha Programme', Marx & Engels, *Selected Works*, vol.ii, p.24). But this cannot be taken seriously. It is only because of the benefits flowing from the division of labour that it is worth belonging to any kind of society at all. Even nowadays, it would not be too difficult for someone who was determined to reject society altogether to find a place to live in complete isolation, but, sensibly, no one does – even the occasional hermit wears cast-off clothes originally made by tailors, and so forth.

78. There was a (long-exploded) economic theory according to which this suggestion would be quite appropriate, namely the eighteenth-century 'physiocratic' school of François Quesnay (cf. B. Semmel, *The Rise of Free Trade Imperialism*, p.24); I take it that Chomsky does not advocate a resurrection of physiocratic economics. Cf. B. J. Cohen, *The Question of Imperialism*, Macmillan, 1974, on Marxist theories of so-called 'neo-colonialism'; though Cohen concedes far too much, to my mind, to the illiberal notion that nations have interests distinct from the several interests of the individuals of which they are composed.

79. B. Semmel, *The Rise of Free Trade Imperialism*, pp.132–3 and 139–40.

80. Eric Stokes, *The English Utilitarians in India*, p.40, n.2.

81. Stokes, *Utilitarians*, pp.40–41.

82. Stokes, *Utilitarians*, p.41.

83. *The Political History of India*, Murray, 1826, vol.ii, p.183.

84. Stokes, *Utilitarians*, p.xvi.

85. Stokes, *Utilitarians*, pp.1–8.

86. *American Power*, p.39.

87. Stokes, *Utilitarians*, p.26.

88. Some of Chomsky's remarks suggest a touchingly innocent belief that certain alien nations led idyllic, coercion-free lives until the wicked European (and other) imperialists appeared on the scene. Consider e.g. the passage (*At War with Asia*, Fontana, 1971, p.205) in which Chomsky faithfully retails his North Vietnamese hosts' version of Vietnamese history as 'an unending series of struggles of resistance against aggression' in which the Vietnamese peasants were 'unified, even in feudal times, in opposition to the aggressor'. Chomsky's hosts evidently did not feel it necessary to explain how the territory we now call South Vietnam became Vietnamese over the five centuries up to about 1900. Anyone familiar with the history of eighteenth-century India must certainly agree that, whatever bad effects may possibly have stemmed from British rule, it greatly reduced the ambient level of violence.

89. A serious attack on the morality of the British Empire would surely be most likely to convince if it concentrated on social issues, which Chomsky ignores, rather than on economic ones. The automatic assumption of social superiority displayed by many Britons towards natives, popularly supposed to have begun when the memsahibs arrived in India in large numbers, must have been extremely humiliating to the governed and was quite inexcusable; it certainly was in no way encouraged by the empiricist frame of mind.

90. Cf. the verdict of Lüthy, 'Colonization'.

91. *American Power*, pp.34–5, 37, and 52.

Chapter 6

1. Review of Skinner's *Verbal Behavior*, 1959.

2. See B. F. Skinner, *Walden Two*, Macmillan, 1948; *Verbal Behavior*, Appleton-Century-Crofts, 1957; *Beyond Freedom and Dignity*, Knopf, 1971.

3. Chomsky's 'Psychology and ideology', in *For Reasons of State*, incorporates a review, which might reasonably be described as savage, of Skinner's *Beyond Freedom and Dignity*.

4. D. E. Broadbent, *Behaviour*, p.18.

5. *Verbal Behavior*, p.425.

6. Review of *Verbal Behavior*, reprinted in Fodor and Katz, *The Structure of Language*, p. 556.

7. *Behaviour*, pp.25–6.

8. L. Bloomfied, *Language*, 1933, British edn. Allen & Unwin, 1935, p. 141.

9. *Beyond Freedom and Dignity*, p.122.

10. One of the points Chomsky makes against Skinner is that Skinner grossly underestimates the complexity of the machinery that is needed merely to decide that two patterns of experience are to count as the 'same' or 'different'

for purposes of learning to react in set ways to set stimuli. This is true; but, since Skinner does underestimate this problem, it remains fair to say that he denies that we have minds in any interesting sense.

11. J. W. Krutch, *The Measure of Man*, 1954, British edn. Alvin Redman, 1956.

12. *Beyond Freedom and Dignity*, pp.161–2.

13. The objection to 'planned diversification' is admirably summed up in a *New Yorker* cartoon depicting a business manager at his desk snapping at a subordinate: 'No, I don't want to hear your idea, Wiggins. What the hell do you think I have a Creative Department for?'

14. Review of *Verbal Behavior*, in Fodor and Katz, *The Structure of Language*, pp.548–9.

15. Quoted on p.158 of A. A. Hill, ed., *Third Texas Conference on Problems of Linguistic Analysis in English*, University of Texas Press, 1962.

16. Cf. Chomsky's 'Some methodological remarks on generative grammar', *Word*, vol. 17, 1961, pp. 219–39, and see references to many later passages in which he and his followers have made substantially the same points in R. P. Botha, *The Function of the Lexicon in Transformational Generative Grammar*, Mouton, 1968, p.70, and in the article 'Methodology' by W. Labov in W. O. Dingwall, ed., *A Survey of Linguistic Science*, University of Maryland Linguistics Programme, 1971.

17. D. T. Langendoen, *The Study of Syntax*, Holt, Rinehart and Winston, 1969, pp.9–10 and 11.

18. It seems reasonable to use the term 'rationalist method' for reliance on data provided by 'intuitive knowledge' even though, insofar as such knowledge concerns the idiosyncratic structure of a particular language, it cannot be Cartesian *innate* knowledge.

19. The intuitions which Chomsky takes to be the data for linguistic analysis are those of the native speaker, who will not be the man constructing the theory except in the special case where a professional linguist describes his own language. Strictly, therefore, the analogue of Chomsky's methodology in chemistry would be for chemists to use as data the intuitions of chemical substances about their own properties – which makes it even clearer why chemists are not tempted to make Chomsky's mistake.

20. For examples of incorrect native-speaker intuitions, see e.g. Labov, 'Empirical foundations'.

21. On the history of traditional grammatical theory see R. H. Robins, *A Short History of Linguistics*, Longmans, 1967, e.g. pp.33–4. One of the reasons why Chomsky and other professional linguists overestimate the 'amateur knowledge' of his language possessed by the average speaker is a very human one. Professional linguists are normally people who were very good at parsing in their schooldays, so that assigning words to parts of speech and determining syntactic structure became second nature to them; after they have forgotten

their schooldays they mistake this ability for 'first nature', overlooking their many less language-minded schoolmates who had greater difficulty with these tasks and perhaps never learned to perform them.

22. *Form of Language*, ch.4.

23. There is of course a sense of 'knowledge' in which we can all agree that the average speaker of a language can be relied on (by definition) to possess accurate knowledge of that language: we sometimes say e.g. 'John knows French' to mean 'John can speak French'. But it does not follow from the fact that an individual can do something (even if the 'something' consists of speaking) that he can also make accurate statements about that ability; thus we cannot infer, simply from the fact that speakers 'know' their languages in this sense, that their answers to linguists' questions about their languages will be reliable (they *may* be, but we could only discover that they *are* by studying the languages via empiricist techniques). Much ink has been spilled in connexion with this ambiguity of 'know' (see e.g. Chomsky's *Reflections*, pp.162ff. and 214ff., and references cited there).

24. *Form of Language*, pp.77ff.

25. C. Graves, J. J. Katz, et al., 'Tacit knowledge', *Journal of Philosophy*, vol. 70, 1973, pp.318–30.

26. I have often wondered whether the crudity of many linguists' discussions of word-meanings may be connected with the fact that so many university students embark on linguistics because they dislike the literary components of traditional language-and-literature courses; I take it that an important aspect of the academic study of literature consists of close attention to the senses of individual words. It is one thing for a linguist to present his semantic theory as an oversimplified first approximation; but many linguists seem blithely unaware that their first approximations are not fairly close to a final truth!

27. *Syntactic Structures*, pp. 13–14.

28. See e.g. C. J. Fillmore, 'On generativity', in S. Peters, ed., *Goals of Linguistic Theory*, Prentice-Hall, 1972.

29. As William Labov ('Empirical foundations', pp.100–102) points out, Chomsky himself often solves the problem of conflicting intuitions in another way: he assumes more or less explicitly that his own intuitions about English are authoritative but those of other English-speakers are fallible.

30. Chomsky summarizes American intervention in Vietnam, quoting Jeffrey Race, as 'the richest and most powerful nation of the late twentieth century us[ing] the resources of modern science to frustrate a social revolution in a poor and distant land'; and he comments, 'This judgement is hardly in doubt' ('Science and ideology', pp.171–2). Chomsky says elsewhere, 'If Americans had the moral courage to do so, they . . . would perceive that the American intervention should be described as a war against the rural society of South Vietnam, not an effort to save it for anyone except collaborationist leaders and such marginal political forces as they could rally' (*Reasons*, p.39 –

note the tendentious use of the word 'collaborationist'). As evidence that Chomsky's portrayal of the situation was not wholly just, consider e.g. that the number of Vietnamese who took advantage of the hundred-day grace period provided by the Geneva Agreements in 1954 to flee the new Communist state and resettle in the South was more than a million, mostly peasants, out of a total population of some 17 million; about 30,000 chose to move from South to North. (D. J. Duncanson, *Government and Revolution in Vietnam*, O.U.P., 1968, pp. 198, 206–7, and 400–401.)

31. Though defeat seems unlikely in view of the evidence referred to in note 37 to Ch.3. The purely economic question is of course closely linked with the moral issue of whether societies ought to assume collective responsibility for the welfare of children whose parents appear to be failing in their duties.

32. On the evolution of the concept of freedom in Greece, see Max Pohlenz, *Freedom in Greek Life and Thought*, D. Reidel, 1966.

33. In this respect the liberal theory of economics preserves the parallel with the Popperian, empiricist theory of the evolution of scientfic knowledge, in view of the modifications made recently by Imre Lakatos to Popper's account of science (cf. 'Falsification and the methodology of scientific research programmes', in I. Lakatos and A. Musgrave, eds., *Criticism and the Growth of Knowledge*, C.U.P., 1970).

34. The sceptic might object that those who have most reason to quit liberal countries are the poor, who are least able to do so. An ideal liberal society might pay the expenses of any of its citizens who wished permanently to emigrate; but while liberal nations have not in practice adopted such a policy, it would surprise me if anyone expected adoption of the policy to be followed by numerous applications for passages to Eastern Europe or China.

35. Cf. Hayek, *The Road to Serfdom*, ch.10.

36. Among the founder members of the E.E.C., the Netherlands, however, are by no means strangers to liberalism.

37. Cf. Hayek, *Constitution*, chs.13 and 14.

38. Decrees which, as an empiricist would predict, turn out to overlook the hosts of special conditions under which particular producers actually operate; as illustrated e.g. when the preference of Continentals for beer made with virgin hops led to a decree against the planting of male hops, which in 1976 caused the extinction of hop-gardens dating back to the Tudors that had relied on fertilization to survive in the relatively damp climate of Kent.

39. Lobbying by representatives of British universities has so far been successful in dissuading the Commission from proceeding with this particular plan.

40. Reported in *The Times*, 2 Aug. 1971. Cf. W. R. Lewis, *Rome or Brussels. . . ?*

41. Cf. Popper, *Poverty*, pp.v–viii.

42. Winston Churchill to House of Commons, 18 June 1940.

Chapter 7

1. For the latter, see e.g. the publications of the Institute of Economic Affairs, London.

Bibliographical References

The following list includes all works which are cited in abbreviated form in the Notes. Where reprinted versions are mentioned, my page-references are to those, but page-references are to the British edition where a separate American edition is listed after a semi-colon.

Aitchison, Jean, *The Articulate Mammal*, Hutchinson, 1976; Universe Books, 1977.

Bracken, H. M., 'Essence, accident, and race', *Hermathena*, vol.116, 1973, pp.81–96.

Broadbent, D. E., *Behaviour*, Eyre & Spottiswoode, 1961.

Chomsky, A. N., *American Power and the New Mandarins*, Penguin, 1969; Pantheon, 1969.

—, *Aspects of the Theory of Syntax*, M.I.T. Press, 1965.

—, *Cartesian Linguistics*, Harper & Row, 1966.

—, *For Reasons of State*, Fontana, 1973; Random House, 1973.

—, *Language and Mind*, enlarged edn., Harcourt Brace Jovanovich, 1972.

—, *Problems of Knowledge and Freedom*, Fontana. 1972; Random House, 1972.

—, *Reflections on Language*, Temple Smith, 1976; Pantheon, 1976.

—, review of B. F. Skinner, *Verbal Behavior*, in *Language*, vol.35, 1959, pp.26–58, reprinted in Fodor and Katz, *The Structure of Language* (see below).

—, 'Science and ideology', in P. M. S. Blackett et. al., *Jawaharlal Nehru Memorial Lectures 1967–72*, published for Jawaharlal Nehru Memorial Fund (New Delhi) by Bharatiya Vidya Bhavan (Bombay), 1973.

—, *Syntactic Structures*, Mouton, 1957.

—, *Topics in the Theory of Generative Grammar*, Mouton, 1966.

Darwin, C., *The Descent of Man and Selection in Relation to Sex*, Murray, 1871; International Publications Service, 1969.

Descartes, René, *Oeuvres*, C. Adam & P. Tannery, eds., 13 vols., Vrin (Paris), 1964–74.

Eysenck, H. J., *The Inequality of Man*, 1973, Fontana edn. 1975; Knapp, 1975.

—, *Race, Intelligence, and Education*, Temple Smith, 1971.

Fodor, J. A., and J. J. Katz, eds., *The Structure of Language*, Prentice-Hall, 1964.

Fries, C. C., *The Structure of English*, 1952, British edn. Longmans, Green, 1957.

Hayek, F. A., *The Constitution of Liberty*, Routledge & Kegan Paul, 1960; University of Chicago Press, 1960.

—, *The Counter-Revolution of Science*, Free Press, 1955.

—, *The Road to Serfdom*, Routledge, 1944; University of Chicago Press, 1944.

—, *Studies in Philosophy Politics and Economics*, Routledge, 1967; Touchstone Books, Simon & Schuster, 1969.

Hunt, R. N. Carew, *The Theory and Practice of Communism*, 1950, Penguin edn. 1963.

Katz, J. J., *The Philosophy of Language*, Harper & Row, 1966.

Keyfitz, N., 'World resources and the world middle class', *Scientific American*, vol.235, no.1, July 1976, pp.28–35.

Kropotkin, P.A., *Mutual Aid*, originally published in instalments in *Nineteenth Century*, 1890–96, Penguin edn. 1939; New York University Press, 1972.

Labov, W., 'Empirical foundations of linguistic theory', in R. Austerlitz, ed., *The Scope of American Linguistics*, Peter de Ridder, 1975; Humanities Press, 1977.

Lewis, W.R., *Rome or Brussels. . . ?*, Institute of Economic Affairs, 1971; Transatlantic Arts, 1972.

Lüthy, Herbert, 'Colonization and the making of mankind', *Journal of Economic History*, Supplement, vol.21, 1961, pp.483–95.

Lyons, John, *Chomsky*, Fontana, 1970; Viking Press, 1970.

McLellan, David, *Marx*, Fontana, 1975; Viking Press, 1975.

Marx, Karl, & F. Engels, *Selected Works,* 2 vols., Lawrence & Wishart, 1958.

Mehta, Ved, *John is Easy to Please*, Secker & Warburg, 1971; Farrar, Strauss & Giroux, 1971.

Mill, J. S., *Considerations on Representative Government*, 1861, Dent edn. (*Utilitarianism, On Liberty*, and *Considerations on Representative Government*) 1972; Bobbs, Merrill, 1958.

von Mises, Ludwig, *Socialism*, 1922, new English edn. Yale University Press, 1951.

Polanyi, Karl, *The Great Transformation*, 1944, published in Britain as *Origins of our Time*, Gollancz, 1945; Beacon Press, 1957.

Popper, K. R., *Objective Knowledge*, O.U.P., 1972.

—, *The Open Society and its Enemies*, 2 vols., Routledge & Kegan Paul, 1945; Princeton University Press, 5th imp., 1966.

—, *The Poverty of Historicism*, Routledge & Kegan Paul, 1957; Harper & Row, 1977.

Rawls, John, *A Theory of Justice*, O.U.P., 1972; Harvard University Press, 1971.

Rocker, Rudolf, *Anarcho-Syndicalism*, Secker & Warburg, 1938.

Russell, Bertrand, *History of Western Philosophy*, 1946, new edn. Allen & Unwin, 1961; Simon & Schuster, 1945.

Sampson, G. R., 'An empirical hypothesis about natural semantics', *Journal of Philosophical Logic*, vol.5, 1976, pp.209–36.

—, *The Form of Language*, Weidenfeld & Nicolson, 1975.

—, *Schools of Linguistics*, forthcoming.

Semmel, Bernard, *The Rise of Free Trade Imperialism*, C.U.P., 1970.

Skinner, B. F., *Beyond Freedom and Dignity*, Knopf, 1971.

—, *Verbal Behavior*, Appleton-Century-Crofts, 1957.

—, *Walden Two*, Macmillan, 1948.

Spencer, Herbert, *The Man versus the State*, 1884, Penguin edn. 1969.

Stokes, Eric, *The English Utilitarians and India*, O.U.P., 1959.

Tawney, R. H., *Religion and the Rise of Capitalism*, 1926, Penguin edn. 1938.

Wittgenstein, Ludwig, *Philosophical Investigations*, 1953, 2nd edn. Blackwell, 1958; 3rd edn. Macmillan Co., New York, 1973.

Index of Names

Aarsleff, H. 215 n.11
Aitchison, J. 224 n.47, 230 n.28
Anttila, R. 220 n.26
Aristotle 130, 232 n.46
Atherton, M. 224 n.47

Bach, J. S. 106
Bakunin, M. A. 32, 33, 37, 75, 224 n.48
Bar-Hillel, Y. 234 n.75
Barlow, H. B. 233 n.58
Barlow, J. M. 235 n.79
Bauer, P. 222 n.36, 229 n.19
Bedau, H. A. 238 n.44
Beethoven, L. van 116
Bennett, N. 230 n.24
Bentham, J. 223 n.45
Berkeley, G. 21
Beveridge, W. H. 224 n.49
Blake, R. 167–8
Bloomfield, L. 183
Boas, F, 139–40
Bolton, G. C. 241 n.71
Botha, R. P. 243, n.16
Bracken, H. M. 130–36, 237 n.31, 239 n.58
Broadbent, D. E. 179, 183, 228 n.1

Carlyle, T. 93
Carroll, L. 44
Cézanne, P. 43, 45, 116
Chaucer, G. 117, 120
Chiang Yee 218 n.12
Chomsky, A. N. 4 and passim
Churchill, W. S. 209, 245 n.42
Clairmonte, F. 241 n.74
Clive, R. 170
Cohen, B. J. 241 n.78
Cohen, L. J. 230 n.34
Coon, C. S. 236 n.19

Cornwallis, C. 174
Cranston, M. 217 n.5
Crombie, I. M. 216, n.16
Crosland, A. 83

Dahrendorf, R. 205
Darwin, C. 91, 135, 138, 236 n.19
Descartes, R. 25–6, 28–9, 77, 90, 120, 122, 130–32, 146, 216 n.16, 223 n.46, 227 n.1, 231 n.41, 232 n.55, 243 n.18
Dewey, J. 239 n.54
Dicey, A. V. 219 n.17, 223 n.45
Duncanson, D. J. 245 n.30
Durkheim, E. 165, 240 n.64

Einstein, A. 4, 27, 43–5, 110
Engels, F. 48, 88, 93, 113, 219 n.16, 226 n.73, 232 n.45
Euclid 27
Eysenck, H. J. 237 nn.30, 32 and 37, 238 n.38

Faguet, E. 217 n.6
Farrington, B. 232, n.46
Fieldhouse, D. K. 241 n.75
Fillmore, C. J. 244 n.28
Fine, H. J. 235 n.79
Flew, A. 214 n.8
Fodor, J. A. 234, n.75
Freud, S. 4
Fries, C. C. 140, 230 n.30

Galbraith, J. K. 231 n.43
Gallagher, J. 241 n.72
Gobineau, A. de 236 n.9
Goebbels, P. J. 148
van Gogh, V. 43
Gombrich, E. H. 218 n.12
Gramsci, A. 87–8
Graves, C. 244 n.25

Hagège, C. 220 n.26
Hall, R. A. 141
Harlow, V. T., 240–41 n.71
Harrison, B. 234 n.76
Hartwell, R. M. 222 n.42
Hayek, F. A. 37–8, 70, 91, 93, 214
  n.1, 217 n.5, 217–18 n.8, 223
  n.44, 231 n.43, 232 n.51, 233
  n.63, 236 n.9, 245 nn.35 and 37
Heath, E. 223 n.44
Hegel, G. W. F. 92, 228 n.4, 241
  n.73
Henry II 41
Herrnstein, R. J. 85, 226 n.66
Hess, E. H. 233 n.58
Hill, J. 230 n.28
Hirsch, F. 229 n.16
Hitler, A. 173
Hook, S. 214 n.8
Hooson, E. 217 n.7
Hubel, D. 122, 124
Huang, P. C. 239 n.54
Humboldt, K. W. von 31–2, 216
  n.21
Hume, D. 21, 131, 215 n.12
Hunt, J. 237 n.31
Hunt, R. N. C. 217 n.1, 226 n.69,
  228 n.6
Hymer, S. 231 n.43

Jensen, A. R. 146–51, 237 n.32
Jewkes, J. 231 n.43
Joseph, K. 39

Kant, I. 120, 234 n.71
Katz, J. J. 128, 234 n.75, 234–5
  n.76, 244 n.25
Keyfitz, N. 229 n.21, 239 n.57
Keynes, J. M. 196, 221 n.35,
  222–3 n.43, 232 n.51
King, E. J. 225 n.53
Knorr, K. E. 236 n.16
Köhler, W. 19
Kropotkin, P. 227 n.76
Krutch, J. W. 185
Ng. cao Ky 35, 156–8

Labov, W. 243 nn.16 and 20, 244
  n.29
Lakatos, I, 245 n.33
Langendoen, D. T. 187
Laslett, P. 134, 236 n.12
Lapouge, G. V. de 236 n.9
Lehrman, D. S. 224 n.47
Leijonhufvud, A. 221 n.35
Lejeune, A. 231 n.43
Lenin, V. I. 4
Levenson, J. R. 239 n.54
Lévi-Strauss, C. 4
Levin, B. 225 n.58, 238 n.45
Lewis, W. R. 240 n.67, 245 n.40
Locke, J. 21, 25, 26, 37, 91, 131,
  134–6, 144, 216 n.16, 218 n.9,
  223–4 n.46, 236 n.12
Lüthy, H. 240 n.69, 242 n.90
Lukes, S. 240 n.64
Lyons, J. 4, 214 n.7

Magee, B. 39
McLellan, D. 226 n.73, 226–7
  n.74, 231 n.44
McNeill, D. 224 n.47
Malaviya, H. D. 171–2
Malcolm, J. 173
Malson, L. 87
Malthus, T. R. 229 n.21
Marx, K. 5, 48, 67, 86–8, 92, 93,
  112–15, 170–71, 203, 206, 209, 214
  n.3, 218 n.11, 219 n.16, 220
  n.24, 221 n.35, 225 n.55, 226
  nn.59 and 69, 226–7 n.74, 231
  n.42, 232 n.51, 241 nn.77 and
  78
Mehta, V. 214 n.6, 231 n.40
Mill, J. S. 220 n.22, 222 n.37,
  240 n.62
Mises, L. von 216 n.34, 219 n.20,
  220 n.23
Mowrer, O. H. 230 n.29
Mozart, W. A. 106
Myers, A. R. 228 n.10

Nozick, R. 228 n.3

O'Sullivan, J. 229 n.19

Pelloutier, F. 33, 59, 227 n.77
Pennock, J. R. 217 n.7
Plato 24–7, 77, 80, 90, 218 n.8
Pohlenz, M. 245 n.32
Polanyi, K. 91, 93–4, 220 n.24
Pollio, H. R. & M. R. 235 n.79
Popper, K. R. 37, 39, 91, 123,
    125, 145–6, 217–18 n.8, 219 n.14,
    223–4 n.46, 225 n.55, 228 n.4,
    230 n.35, 233 nn. 61 and 65,
    244 nn.33 and 41
Postal, P. M. 232 n.52
Powell, J. E. 39
Proudhon, P. J. 33, 37
Pryor, F. 220 n.23

Quesnay, F. 241 n.78
Quine, W. van O. 125–6, 128

Race, J. 244 n.30
Rawls, J. 60, 70, 222 n.40
Roberts, F. 224 n.49
Roberts, S. H. 236 n.20
Robins, R. H. 243 n.21
Robinson, R. 241 n.72
Rocker, R. 91, 93, 166, 228 n.7
Rosch, E. 233 n.60
Rosenberg, A. 148
Rowbotham, A. H. 216 n.17
Rowthorn, R. 231 n.43
Russell, B. A. W. 5, 31–2, 33, 37,
    216 nn.19, and 33, 221 n.30
    226 n.67, 236 n.15, 239 n.54
Russell, D. 216 nn.19 and 29

Samuelson, P. A. 82, 222 n.42
Santillan, D. A. de 56
Sapir, E. 125
Schumpeter, J. A. 221 n.34
Schwartz, B. 239 n.54
Schwartz, R. 224 n.47
Searle, J. R. 237 n.31
Seliger, M. 236 n.11
Semmel, B. 236 n.16, 241 nn.78
    and 79

Silber, J. R. 214 n.8
Skinner, B. F. 178–86, 211, 239
    n.58
Smith, A. 91, 94, 212, 218 n.9
Soltau, R. 217 n.6
Spearman, C. 237 n.30
Spencer, H. 217 n.5
Steele, I. K. 236 n.12
Stent, G. 238, n.41
Stokes, E. 241 nn.73 and 80–86
    242 n.87
Strehlow, T. G. H. 236 n.14
Sun Yat-sen 239 n.54
Sutherland, L. 240 n.70

Tawney, R. H. 93
Thatcher, M. 39
Ng. van Thieu 35, 156–8
Thoreau, H. D. 199
Thorpe, J. 217 n.7
Tocqueville, A de 224 n.50
Tranter, N. L. 229 n.21

Urbach, P. 237 n.33

Vennemann, T. 142–3

Wallace, A. R. 138
Wang, Y. C. 239 n.54
Watkins, J. W. N. 231 n.39
Watson, J. B. 179
Weizenbaum, J. 231 n.41
Wellesley, R. 174
West, E. G. 222 n.37
White, M. G. 125
Whorf, B. L. 125
Wiesel, T. 122, 124
Wilde, O. 9
Winch, P. 236 n.18
Wittgenstein, L. 125–8, 234 n.72,
    235 n.76
Woodcock, G. 216 n.34
Wootton, B. 227 n.78